A COMPARISON BETWEEN A KING AND A MONK/ AGAINST THE OPPONENTS OF THE MONASTIC LIFE

Two Treatises by John Chrysostom

Translated with an Introduction

by

David G. Hunter

Studies in the Bible and Early Christianity
Volume 13

The Edwin Mellen Press
Lewiston/Queenston
Lampeter

Library of Congress Cataloging-in-Publication Data

John Chrysostom, Saint, d. 407.
　　[Dokimion synkrisis Basileos pros monachon. English]
　　A comparison between a king and a monk and Against the
opponents of the monastic life / John Chrysostom ; translated with an
introduction by David G. Hunter.
　　　　p. cm. -- (Studies in the Bible and early Christianity ; v.
13)
　　Bibliography: p.
　　Includes index.
　　ISBN 0-88946-613-0
　　1. Monastic and religious life--Early works to 1800. I. Hunter,
David G. II. John Chrysostom, Saint, d. 407. Pros tous polemious
tou monachikou biou. English. 1988. III. Title. IV. Series.
BR65.C45D6513　1988
255-dc19　　　　　　　　　　　　　　　　　　　　　　88-24463
　　　　　　　　　　　　　　　　　　　　　　　　　　　CIP

This is volume 13 in the continuing series
Studies in Bible & Early Christianity
Volume 13 ISBN 0-88946-613-0
SBEC Series ISBN 0-88946-913-X

The Edwin Mellen Press

Box 450　　　　　　　　　　　　　　　　　　　　　Box 67
Lewiston, New York　　　　　　　　　　　　Queenston, Ontario
USA 14092　　　　　　　　　　　　　　　　　L0S 1L0 CANADA
　　　　　　　　　　Mellen House
　　　　　　　　Lampeter, Dyfed, Wales
　　　　　　UNITED KINGDOM SA48 7DY

Printed in the United States of America

For Lynn

... dulci coniugi et benemerenti

Table of Contents

ACKNOWLEDGEMENTS

This study of Chrysostom's monastic works began several years ago as part of a doctoral dissertation completed at the University of Notre Dame in 1986. I am deeply indebted to Robert L. Wilken, now William R. Kenan Professor at the University of Virginia, for suggesting that Chrysostom's treatises might be worth paying attention to. To Wilken also I owe the insight that contemporary pagans were Chrysostom's partners in dialogue. The readers of my original dissertation, Professors Charles Kannengiesser, Jean Laporte, and Harold Attridge, also offered helpful comments along the way.

A special thanks is due to Professor Elizabeth A. Clark of Duke University who proposed this book to the Edwin Mellen Press. Her consistent encouragement and critique of my work has been greatly appreciated. The College of St. Thomas in St. Paul, Minnesota generously provided summer stipends in 1985 and 1987 which enabled me to prepare the translations and to revise my earlier studies. Mrs. Sue Carlson Moro of the Word Processing Department at the College of St. Thomas must be acknowledged for her expert typesetting of a sometimes difficult manuscript.

Finally, to my wife Lynn Joyce Hunter, who has provided not only her patience and support but also her keen editorial skills, this work is gratefully dedicated.

CHAPTER ONE

THE YOUNG JOHN CHRYSOSTOM AND MONASTICISM

1. Introduction

John of Antioch, surnamed the "Golden-mouthed" (*Chrysostom*), is perhaps better known as a preacher than as an ascetical or monastic writer.[1] The sheer volume of his sermons, together with the dramatic story of his rise and fall as patriarch of Constantinople, have assured his reputation as a reformer of church and society in the Greek East. But Chrysostom's early interest in the ascetical life also has recently attracted the notice of scholars.[2] A large number of treatises survive which were composed before his ordination to the priesthood in 386. These documents reveal Chrysostom's enthusiasm for asceticism as well as the diverse impact of this movement on Antiochene society.[3]

---

[1] On the origins of the epithet "Chrysostom," see E.A. Clark, "Introduction," in *John Chrysostom. On Virginity. Against Remarriage.* Studies in Women and Religion, 9 (New York and Toronto: Edwin Mellen Press, 1983) xxix, n. 1. The title first was recorded by Pope Vigilius in 553: *Constitutum Vigilii papae de tribus capitulis* (PL 69.101).

[2] Earlier studies of Chrysostom's ascetical views exist, but these have been concerned less with the historical context and development of his thought than with presenting a synthetic portrait of his teaching. See the works of A. Moulard (1923) and L. Meyer (1934) cited in the bibliography below. The same is true of the two articles by J.M. Leroux on Chrysostom and monasticism (1961; 1975).

[3] The treatises *On Virginity* and *Against Remarriage* have been translated by Sally Rieger Shore. See the volume cited in note 1 above. E.A. Clark has translated Chrysostom's two treatises on the *virgines subintroductae*, unmarried women who cohabited with male ascetics. See her *Jerome, Chrysostom, and Friends. Essays and Translations.* Studies in Women and Religion, 2 (New York and Toronto: Edwin Mellen Press, 1979). Chrysostom's other ascetical works include *Ad Theodorum lapsum* 1-2 (SC 117; ed. Dumortier); *De compunctione* 1-2 (PG 47.393-422); *Ad Stagirium a daemone vexatum* 1-3 (PG 47.423-94); *Ad viduam iuniorem* (SC 138; ed. Grillet and Ettlinger).

The two treatises, which are presented here for the first time in English translation, *A Comparison Between a King and a Monk* and *Against the Opponents of the Monastic Life*, are found among these early literary works.[4] As I hope to show in the remainder of this introduction, these two monastic treatises deserve much closer scrutiny than they previously have received. Both works articulate not only Chrysostom's profound sympathy for the monastic life, but also his engagement with a pressing problem of his time: the relation between Christianity and classical culture.

In chapter one of this introduction I will review Chrysostom's early life and discuss the factors which shaped him in the years preceding his ordination to the priesthood. Foremost among these formative influences were his rhetorical education under the sophist Libanius and his early experience as a monk. Libanius' own attitude towards education and its moral benefits will be treated in some detail. For, as I will argue subsequently, Libanius' views on the matter were the target of Chrysostom's attack in his monastic works.

Chapter two will examine questions concerning the authenticity, purpose, and dating of the two treatises. In this chapter I will demonstrate that these two texts reflect Chrysostom's efforts not only to reform Christian life, but also to refute the contemporary claims of Libanius regarding the moral and religious value of Greek culture.

The third chapter will place these monastic treatises in a larger context. I will show that the moral and apologetic interests which Chrysostom displays in his monastic works were part of a broader apologetic initiative apparent in his other ascetical works, as well as in his explicitly apologetic treatises. The pagan argument also will be examined further, particularly as it relates to the pagan revival of the apostate emperor Julian.

When read in this context, these two monastic treatises take on a significance which has not previously been recognized by scholars. Both works are concerned with the tensions between monasticism and the life of urban Christians; but they also show evidence of a struggle between an ascetically-minded Christian like John Chrysostom and the contemporary advocates of Greek culture. These treatises, therefore, should be of interest both to students of monasticism and John

---

[4] The date of these works is discussed below, pp. 36-41. In the remainder of this introduction the *Comparison Between a King and a Monk (Comparatio)* will be cited according to the edition of this work in the *Patrologia graeca* 47. 387-392. *Against the Opponents of the Monastic Life (Oppugnatores)* will be cited according to the edition of F. Dübner, *Sancti Joannis Chrysostomi opera selecta*. vol. 1 (Paris: Didot, 1861) 1-75.

Chrysostom, as well as to historians of the culture of late antiquity more generally. The fourth and final chapter will discuss briefly the previous editions and translations of these works.

2. The Pupil of Libanius

John Chrysostom was born at Antioch probably around the year 349.[5] His parents, Secundus and Anthusa, were of moderate means, and his father held a position in the service of the Syrian military commander, the *magister militum per Orientem*.[6] In his treatise *On the Priesthood* Chrysostom himself tells us that his mother, while not possessing great wealth, spared no expense to provide him with a "liberal education" (ἐλευθερίως...Θρέψαι). Out of her own dowry she provided everything "which would be beneficial for a good reputation" (εὐδοκίμησις).[7] Anthusa's motherly vigilance ensured not only that young John's career prospects would be bright, but also that the Christian church would receive its finest preacher. For the master to whom John was entrusted was none other than Libanius, the distinguished sophist of Antioch.[8]

The identification of Libanius as Chrysostom's teacher of rhetoric occasionally has been questioned by modern scholars.[9] Indeed, the case for such an identification is not airtight. For example, neither the sophist nor the preacher ever mentions the other by name. The first writer to claim that Chrysostom was taught by Libanius is the

---

[5] I have followed the dating of R.E. Carter, "The Chronology of Saint John Chrysostom's Early Life," *Traditio* 18 (1962) 357- 64. But see J. Dumortier, "La valeur historique du Dialogue de Palladius et la chronologie de saint Jean Chrysostome," *Mélanges de science religieuse 8* (1951) 51-56.

[6] A.H.M. Jones, "St. John Chrysostom's Parentage and Education," *Harvard Theological Review* 46 (1953) 171-73. The names of John's parents are provided by Socrates in his *Ecclesiastical History* 6.3. The claims of Socrates and Sozomen (*H.E.* 8.2) regarding Chrysostom's "noble birth" are somewhat exaggerated.

[7] *De sacerdotio* 1.2 (SC 272.68).

[8] On Libanius as an educator, see P. Wolf, *Vom Schulwesen der Spätantike. Studien zu Libanius* (Baden, 1952); also B. Schouler, *La tradition hellénique chez Libanios* (Paris: Les Belles Lettres, 1984).

[9] A brief account of the discussion can be found in C. Baur, *John Chrysostom and his Time*. vol. 1. Translated by M. Gonzaga (Westminster, MD: Newman Press, 1959) 22-23. Baur favors the view that Libanius taught Chrysostom. A.J. Festugière also has examined the evidence and suspended judgment: *Antioche païenne et chrétienne. Libanius, Chrysostome, et les moines de Syrie* (Paris: Éditions de Boccard, 1959) 409-10.

historian Socrates who is not always reliable.[10] Nothing is said about
Libanius by Palladius, Chrysostom's earliest biographer, except that
John was "carefully schooled in letters" and that at the age of eighteen
he "revolted against the sophists of word-mongering, for he had
arrived at man's estate and thirsted for living knowledge."[11]

The case in favor of Libanius as Chrysostom's teacher, however, can
be made with the highest degree of probability.[12] In his letter to a
young widow Chrysostom refers to his teacher (although not by name)
as "my sophist, who was of all men the most attached to pagan
superstition" (δεισιδαιμονέστερος).[13] In another early work, the
Discourse on Blessed Babylas, Chrysostom refers to "the sophist of the
city" and proceeds to quote at length and to ridicule Libanius' *Monody*
(or. 60) on the temple of Apollo at Daphne.[14] While neither of these
references conclusively proves that Chrysostom was Libanius'
student, together they make such a supposition very likely.

Furthermore, several studies of Chrysostom's style and literary
allusions have found numerous affinities between the works of
Chrysostom, especially the early works, and those of Libanius.[15]
Others have seen evidence of an ongoing polemic between Chrysostom
and Libanius, particularly in their respective discourses after the
famous Riot of the Statues in 387.[16] Finally, the research of Caius

---

[10] *Ecclesiastical History* 6.3. In the same paragraph Socrates erroneously identifies
Chrysostom's friend Basil, whom Chrysostom mentions in *De sacerdotio*, with the
famous Cappadocian bishop, Basil of Caesarea.

[11] Palladius, *Dialogue on the Life of St. John Chrysostom* 5. Translated by R.T.
Meyer. Ancient Christian Writers, 45 (New York: Newman Press, 1985) 35.

[12] The argument in favor of this identification was made very forcefully by A.
Nägele, "Chrysostomos und Libanios," in *XPYCOCTOMIKA. Studi e richerche intorno
a. S. Giovanni Crisostomo* (Rome: Pustet, 1908) 81-142. P. Petit, *Les étudiants de
Libanius* (Paris, 1956) 40-41, also thinks such an identification is possible, though not
conclusively demonstrable.

[13] *Ad viduam iuniorem* 2 (SC 138.120).

[14] *De sancto Babyla contra Julianum et gentiles* 98-113. I have adopted the
numbering of this treatise devised by M. Schatkin in her recent translation: *St. John
Chrysostom. Apologist.* Fathers of the Church, 73 (Washington, DC: Catholic
University of America Press, 1983). This enumeration will be followed in the
forthcoming *Sources chrétiennes* edition of this text.

[15] See T.E. Ameringer, *The Stylistic Influence of the Second Sophistic on the
Panegyrical Sermons of St. John Chrysostom* (Washington, DC: Catholic University of
America Press, 1920); J. Dumortier, "La culture profane de saint Jean Chrysostome,"
Mélanges de science religieuse 10 (1953) 53-62.

[16] R. Göbel, *De Ioanni Chrysostomi et Libanii orationibus quae sunt de seditione
Antiochensium* (Göttingen, 1910). Cf. the review of J. Misson in *Analecta Bollandiana*
33 (1914) 223-24.

Caius Fabricius into Chrysostom's "classicism" has uncovered several quotations from works of Libanius in Chrysostom's *Comparison Between a King and a Monk*, as well as numerous echoes in other early works.[17] That such borrowings should appear in what is probably Chrysostom's earliest work again points in favor of the view that Libanius was indeed Chrysostom's teacher of rhetoric.

In the school of Libanius Chrysostom would have received a thorough grounding in the Greek classics: "Homer, Hesiod and other poets, Demosthenes, Lysias and other orators, Herodotus, Thucydides and other historians" is Libanius' own description of the course of study he provided.[18] Nor was philosophy absent, as is evident from Chrysostom's own quotations from Plato and echoes of Xenophon in the present treatises.[19] The primary aim of such an education was to prepare a young man for a career in rhetoric, as a teacher, advocate, or city councillor. Chrysostom himself speaks of his early enthusiasm for a legal career in his treatise *On the Priesthood*, and this is confirmed by later biographers.[20]

But from Libanius Chrysostom also would have learned that an education in rhetoric had ethical as well as practical aims. "All Libanius' educational ideals derived from his passionate faith in 'logoi', in the power of the classical literature of Greece to inculcate in its reader both the practical and moral qualities required for life."[21] Assertions of the moral value of Greek *paideia*, and of rhetorical education in particular, can be found throughout Libanius' voluminous writings.[22] In his mind the power of rhetoric was linked both to the well-being of the city and civic life and to traditional Greek religion. For example, in his encomium on Antioch Libanius enthu-

[17] C. Fabricius, "Vier Libaniusstellen bei Johannes Chrysostomos," *Symbolae Osloenses* 33 (1957) 135-36; see also his *Zu den Jugendschriften des Johannes Chrysostomos. Untersuchungen zum Klassizismus des vierten Jahrhunderts* (Lund: Gleerup, 1962) 118-21.

[18] Ep. 1036, cited in A.F. Norman, "The Library of Libanius," *Rheinisches Museum für Philologie* 107 (1964) 159.

[19] Norman, "Library," 159; see also P.R. Coleman-Norton, "St. John Chrysostom and the Greek Philosophers," *Classical Philology* 25 (1930) 305-17.

[20] *De sacerdotio* 1.2. Socrates, *Ecclesiastical History* 6.3, says that John was on the verge of a career in civil law when he turned to "a more tranquil mode of life."

[21] J.H.W.G. Liebeschuetz, *Antioch. City and Imperial Administration in the Later Roman Empire* (Oxford: Clarendon Press, 1972) 11.

[22] A valuable dossier of texts can be found in Festugière, *Antioche païenne et chrétienne* 101-19 and 215-25.

siastically describes the role of rhetoric (λόγοι) in forming the
members of the city council (βουλή):[23]

> Among us the power of eloquence (δεινότης) preserves the
> freedom of the senate in clear-cut fashion, compelling the
> administrators to appear in their tasks what they are
> supposed to be, inciting sensible men to the discovery of
> what is best, resisting the lawlessness of insolent men
> through the compelling power of wisdom, and through the
> charm of rhetoric, so to speak, turning their hearts to
> gentleness.

As this passage shows, Libanius believed that rhetoric served an
essential civic function: to preserve the freedom of the city before
governors and imperial officials. Rhetoric is the "mind of the city" (ὁ
νοῦς πόλεως), Libanius argues, and Antioch is the center of rhetoric in
the Greek East.[24]

But rhetoric in Libanius' eyes did more than simply enable a person
to perform a civic function; it possessed a religious value as well. And
yet this is already to import into the discussion a modern dichotomy
which is foreign to Libanius' mind. For it is precisely the union of
culture, traditional piety, and civic life that Libanius wished to affirm
and which he believed was severely threatened in his own day,
particularly by the rise of Christianity.

In two places in his works Libanius explicitly affirms this
connection. The first occurs in his funeral oration over the emperor
Julian. Unlike his predecessor Constantius, Libanius notes, who had
filled his court with eunuchs and monks and had appointed
stenographers and secretaries to be provincial governors, the emperor

---

[23] Or. 11.141. Translated by G. Downey, "Libanius' *Oration in Praise of Antioch
(Oration XI)*," *Proceedings of the American Philosophical Society* 103 (1959) 668,
slightly altered. On the nature and purpose of this very interesting treatise, see A.D.
Nock, "The Praises of Antioch," *Journal of Egyptian Archaeology* 40 (1954) 76-82. P.
Petit has called the treatise "a manifesto of the pagan party, provoked by the arrival of
Julian to power." See *Libanius et la vie municipale à Antioche au IVe siècle après J.-C.*
(Paris: P. Geuthner, 1955) 206.

[24] Or. 11.181. Like Athens of old, Libanius says, Antioch is distinguished by its
love of wisdom; students who come there for education return home bearing their
rhetorical skills as "salvation (σωτηρία) for their native cities." Cf. or. 11. 182- 86.

Julian had selected persons skilled in rhetoric to rule cities and provinces:[25]

> Also considering learning (λόγους) and religion (θεῶν ἱερά) to be akin, and seeing the one nearly ruined, the other totally so, he directed his actions to the complete restoration of learning to its position and its renewal in men's regard, first by honoring its exponents, and again, by personally composing discourses.

The same expression occurs in his sixty-second oration, *Against Those Who Criticize His Teaching System*, where Libanius addresses the criticism that his school failed to train young people for profitable careers. Again Libanius blames Constantius, "who received from his father [Constantine] a spark of evils," for rejecting pagan religion and for excluding philosophers and orators from his court. Constantius stripped the gods of wealth, overthrew the temples, and extended the dishonor to λόγοι, Libanius argues. "And with good reason! For to my way of thinking these two are related: religion and rhetoric."[26]

By linking rhetoric (λόγοι) and religion (ἱερά) in this way, and by connecting both with the life of the city, Libanius reveals his commitment to what Liebeschuetz has called "the religion of the Muses."[27] His religion was both a cultural and a social conservatism; the city, its gods, and its culture were one indissoluble unity.[28] Libanius had articulated a religious vision of the Greek city as a bulwark of Hellenic civilization, the dwelling-place of the gods, whose continued prosperity depended on her continued devotion to the gods.[29] Essential to the proper functioning of the city was the continued education of young men in λόγοι. What Libanius saw at work in the rise of Christianity was the displacement of rhetoric from

---

[25] Or. 18.157. Translated by A.F. Norman, *Libanius. Selected Works.* vol. 1. Loeb Classical Library (Cambridge, MA: Harvard University Press, 1969) 383.

[26] Or. 62.8 (Förster 4.360). Libanius goes on to ridicule Constantius for taking "barbarians and pestilent eunuchs" as his advisors, for seeking out monks, "those pale men, the enemies of the gods, who frequent the tombs." See or. 62.9-10.

[27] *Antioch* 16.

[28] Cf. P. Petit, *Libanius et la vie municipale à Antioche* 192: "...sa religion est avant tout civique et antiochéene."

[29] Hence Libanius' encomium on Antioch can be seen as a "manifesto of the pagan party." See particularly or. 11.125 and note 23 above.

its place of supremacy; what he feared was the social rise of persons outside of the rhetorical tradition.[30]

The relationship between Libanius and Julian's pagan revival will be considered in greater detail below.[31] Here it is sufficient to note that the culture which Chrysostom imbibed in the school of Libanius was not ideologically neutral. Rather, Libanius' *paideia* represented the sophist's commitment to the social, religious, and moral value of Greek literature. Chrysostom did not forget the lessons learned from his teacher. Libanius' claims on behalf of Greek culture exercised a formative and, I will argue, an enduring influence on the young John Chrysostom. Long after he had left the master's school, Chrysostom continued to attack that amalgam of rhetoric, religion, and civic life espoused by Libanius.

3. The Lure of Syrian Asceticism

Around the year 367, when he was eighteen years old, Chrysostom completed his rhetorical studies under Libanius. At this point, the historian Socrates tells us, Chrysostom was on the verge of entering a legal career. But "after reflecting on the restless and unjust course of those who devote themselves to the forensic courts," John decided to pursue a "tranquil life" and to put his mind to the study of scripture.[32] He soon was baptized by bishop Meletius and, after a period of three years, was appointed lector (c. 371).[33]

These years at Antioch mark the beginning of Chrysostom's religious formation. Socrates writes that Chrysostom, along with his friends Maximus and Theodore who had been fellow students under Libanius, entered an ascetic community (ἀσκητηρίον) under the guidance of Carterius and Diodore, the future bishop of Tarsus.[34] Little is known about the precise nature of this *askētērion*. It seems

---

[30] See the comments of B. Schouler, *Libanios. Discours moraux* (Paris, 1973) 120-21; Liebeschuetz, *Antioch* 15-16. In or. 48.31 Libanius bemoans the attempt to improve one's social status outside of the schools of rhetoric by means of the study of Latin, law or--much worse--stenography: "This is simply to undo the social order (πολιτεία) in which we live."

[31] See pp. 60-62.

[32] *Ecclesiastical History* 6.3 (PG 67.665). Socrates' comment may well be correct. Libanius also criticized the conduct of lawyers, especially those who had not received the moral benefit of a rhetorical education. See or. 62.41-45.

[33] Palladius, *Dialogue* 5; Carter, "Chronology," 162.

[34] *Ecclesiastical History* 6.3 (PG 67.665).

that its members did not live in a monastery, for in his treatise *On the Priesthood* when referring to these years, Chrysostom says that he remained at home out of deference to his widowed mother.[35] The close relations which existed between Diodore, bishop Meletius, and Flavian, Meletius' successor at Antioch, also support the surmise that Diodore's school may have provided the equivalent of seminary training to those destined for the clergy.[36] In an encomium on Diodore, preached perhaps in 392, Chrysostom refers to Diodore as his "teacher" (διδάσκαλος) which may indicate a more academic relationship. Further, Diodore's reputation as an exegete committed to the literal interpretation of scripture likewise suggests that training in the *askētērion* may have emphasized the study of the bible more than ascetic practices.[37]

In any case, during this period Chrysostom appears to have been pursuing a career in the clergy. Such a choice of life did not necessarily entail any dramatic break with the lifestyle or values of most citizens of Antioch. As Robert Wilken recently has noted, members of the clergy, especially urban bishops, usually were drawn from the higher social classes.[38] Their salaries often surpassed those of other professionals, such as public doctors or professors of rhetoric. Further, a career in the clergy would have provided Chrysostom (as it eventually did) with suitable opportunities to display his remarkable oratorical gifts cultivated in the school of Libanius.

But John's pursuit of the clerical vocation was interrupted for six years by an experience that was permanently to shape his perception of the Christian life. In the year 372 he withdrew from the city and, we must believe, from his ecclesiastical ambitions to live the life of a monk in the hills near Antioch. Chrysostom's motivation is described by his biographer Palladius:[39]

---

[35] *De sacerdotio* 1.2 (SC 272.68). See Festugière, *Antioche païenne et chrétienne* 183.

[36] Festugière, *Antioche païenne et chrétienne* 183; cf. Theodoret, *Religious History* 2.16 and 8.6-7, and *Ecclesiastical History* 4.22.

[37] Cf. Carter, "Chronology," 363: "*The asketerion*, then, would not have been a monastery or boarding school, but a center for spiritual conferences, lectures on Scripture and theology, and perhaps common worship, such as the antiphonal singing of the Psalms, which Theodoret [PG 82.1060C] mentions." On Diodore as Chrysostom's teacher, see the latter's *Laus Diodori episcopi* (PG 50.761).

[38] R.L. Wilken, *John Chrysostom and the Jews: Rhetoric and Reality in the Late 4th Century* (Berkeley: University of California Press, 1983) 6-7.

[39] Palladius, *Dialogue* 5 (PG 47.18). Translated in Meyer, 35.

> Being well aware of the fact that he could not be satisfied
> working in the city as his youthful nature was bursting
> within him though his mind was perfectly sound, he betook
> himself to the nearby mountains.

Four years were spent in the company of an old Syrian monk; then
Chrysostom withdrew to a cave where he lived in complete solitude for
two more years.

To appreciate adequately Chrysostom's state of mind at this time,
we should look more closely at the phenomenon of Syrian asceticism.
Palladius' claim that Chrysostom's own passionate nature could not
be properly bridled in the city may well be true; it does not completely
explain, however, the significance of Chrysostom's choice or the
special place that monasticism will hold in his mind from this point
on. A closer look at the impact of the ascetic and monastic movement
in Syria, and especially on the citizens of Antioch, is in order.

It is well known that a strongly ascetic strain of Christianity
existed in Syria and Mesopotamia from the very beginnings of the
church.[40] From the encratite tendencies of a Tatian to the apocryphal
Acts of Thomas to the hymn cycles of the poet Ephrem, we have a
constant tradition of devotion to the life of celibacy and poverty.[41]
Likewise, the persistence of Marcionite and Manichean communities
in these regions also testifies to the rigorist inclinations of Syrian
Christians.

But the middle and later years of the fourth century witnessed a
blossoming of enthusiasm for the more extravagant, even theatrical,
forms of asceticism characteristic of Syrian monks. The bearing of
chains and iron collars, life in the open air, sleeping on the ground,
wearing little or no clothing, the eating of roots, grass or wild
fruits—all these formed the regimen of many ascetic devotees.[42]
Rather than focus on the more exotic aspects of their *askēsis*, however,
it will be more relevant to examine the relations between the monks
and the citizens of Antioch. Chrysostom's attraction to the ascetic
ideal can be comprehended best in this context.

---

[40] The classic study is that of A. Vööbus, *A History of Asceticism in the Syrian
Orient.* vol. 1. CSCO, Subsidia 14 (Louvain, 1958). See also S. Brock, "Early Syrian
Asceticism," *Numen* 20 (1973) 1-19.

[41] Brock, "Early Syrian Asceticism," 6-10.

[42] See Theodoret, *Religious History. passim.* Also Festugière, *Antioche païenne et
chrétienne,* ch. IX "Traits charactéristiques de l'anachorétisme syrien," 291-310.

It is the proximity of the Syrian monks to the city of Antioch that first strikes the modern observer.[43] Major monastic centers were easily accessible to the populace, some close enough for an afternoon's stroll. First and nearest was Mount Sylpios, which dominated the skyline of ancient Antioch at about 1660 feet, immediately northeast of the city.[44] In Chrysostom's day its slopes were "decked like a meadow" with the huts and caves of the monks, some of whose names are known: "Peter the Galatian, his namesake the Egyptian, Romanus Severus, Zeno, Moses, and Malchus, and many others of whom the world is ignorant, but whose names are known to God."[45] Also nearby was Mount Amanus, north of the city and home to the hermit Symeon the Elder (died c. 390). This Symeon (not to be confused with his famous Syrian namesake Symeon the Stylite) was active in the conversion of the local populace to Christianity and the object of constant visits from the citizens of Antioch.[46]

Further away lay the monastery of Gindarus, forty-seven kilometers northeast of Antioch, along the desert route leading to Edessa through Cyrrhus.[47] Probably the oldest monastery in the region, it was founded c. 330 by Asterius, a disciple of the famous Julian Saba of Osrhoene.[48] Not only was Gindarus a large village and important stopping-place on the road to Mesopotamia, but it also stood in a client relationship to Antioch.[49] Close ties existed between the

---

[43] In a now classic study of the social role of the Syrian holy man, Peter Brown pointed out that in contrast to Egypt, the "desert of Syria was never true desert.... To go to the 'ἔρημος in Syria was to wander into the ever present fringe of the οἰκουμένη." See "The Rise and Function of the Holy Man in Late Antiquity," *Journal of Roman Studies* 60 (1971) 83.

[44] G. Downey, *A History of Antioch in Syria from Seleucus to the Arab Conquest* (Princeton: Princeton University Press, 1961) 15.

[45] Theodoret, *Ecclesiastical History* 6.25. Theodoret's *Religious History* has preserved the lives of several of these monks. See P. Canivet, *Le monachisme syrien selon Théodoret de Cyr*. Théologie Historique, 42 (Paris: Beauchesne, 1977) 157-63. Mt. Sylpios also was probably the place of Chrysostom's own monastic experiment.

[46] Theodoret, *Religious History* 6.4-6. On the role of the monks in the conversion of rural Syria, see W. Liebeschuetz, "Problems Arising from the Conversion of Syria," in *The Church in Town and Country*. Edited by D. Baker (Oxford: B. Blackwell, 1979) 17-24.

[47] Canivet, *Le monachisme syrien* 163.

[48] Theodoret, *Religious History* 2.9. A series of Syriac hymns on Julian exist, attributed to Ephrem (CSCO 322 and 323). John Chrysostom also speaks about this Julian: Homily 21.3 on Ephesians (PG 62.153).

[49] Theodoret, *Religious History* 2.9.

churches of Antioch and Gindarus, and the clergy of Antioch maintained contact with the monks of Gindarus.[50]

But by far the most outstanding center of monastic life in the region was the foundation at Teleda. Located on the periphery of the fertile plain of Dana, east of Antioch near Gindarus, Teleda became the focus of a dramatic monastic expansion in the fifth and sixth centuries.[51] Already in Chrysostom's day, however, Teleda was attracting monks: at the death of Julian Saba (c. 367), several of his followers came to Teleda and submitted themselves to the guidance of the monk Eusebius.[52] Arabs, Greeks, and Latins all found themselves among Eusebius' clientele.[53]

The nearness of these monastic sites led to constant interaction between the citizens of Antioch and the monks. *The Religious History* of Theodoret of Cyrrhus narrates many stories of those who came to the monks for healing, exorcism, or spiritual exhortation.[54] The hermit Aphraat, who lived just outside of the city during Chrysostom's youth, did not disdain to heal a horse of a bladder infection or to restore a philandering husband's affection for his abandoned wife.[55] Nor was it unheard of for the monks to enter the city and to interfere in civic or ecclesiastical affairs.[56] The exercise of such influence infuriated pagans such as Libanius who preferred more traditional forms of social power.[57]

But the abundance of monastic sites and their easy access, however, take us only a short way towards understanding the enormous appeal of the Syrian ascetics. In a study which has greatly influenced recent scholars, Peter Brown has offered a combination of social and anthropological explanations to account for this phenomenon. Brown argues that the Syrian holy man rose to prominence at a time of

---

[50] For example, when bishop Meletius was exiled by the Arian emperor Valens (365-367) and the priests Diodore and Flavian wished to investigate the alleged Arian sympathies of Julian Saba, they chose two monks from Gindarus, Asterius and Acacius, to escort the holy man to the city.

[51] Canivet, *Le monachisme syrien* 165-72; G. Tchalenko, *Villages antiques de la Syrie du Nord.* vol. 1 (Paris: P. Geuthner, 1953) 145-55.

[52] Theodoret, *Religious History* 4.8.

[53] Theodoret, *Religious History* 4.10-12.

[54] Theodoret, *Religious History* 3.9-11,22; 6.6; 8.2-6; 9.4-10,13-14; 11.3; etc.

[55] Theodoret, *Religious History* 8.11 and 15.

[56] For example, the intervention of the monk Macedonius after the Riot of the Statues in 387: Theodoret, *Religious History* 13.7; cf. Chrysostom, homily 17 *On the Statues.* See also Aphraat's refutation of the Arians: Theodoret, *Religious History* 8.2.

[57] Libanius, or. 45.26. Cf. Eunapius, *Vitae sophistarum* 472.

unusual prosperity in the Syrian countryside.[58] The proliferation of small farms, together with a lack of sense of community, created a need for arbitrators and mediators in rural life. The monk embodied all that the populace looked for in an ideal rural patron.[59] His asceticism constituted an elaborate ritual of "dissociation" which, paradoxically, gained for the monk the "objectivity" necessary to provide leadership in village life.[60] The miracles, and especially the exorcisms, of the holy man were simply one minor expression of a more general tendency in late antiquity towards "charging the person of the holy man himself with utterly objective, inalienable power."[61]

Brown's account is one with which Chrysostom could readily agree. At several places in *Against the Opponents of the Monastic Life* Chrysostom refers to the "patronage" (προστασία) exercised by the Syrian monk.[62] The monk, who is free of all worldly attachments, "will address kings with exceedingly great power (ἐξουσία)"; thus he serves as a more powerful patron than those engaged in worldly affairs. The social power of the monk, therefore, is acknowledged by Chrysostom and used for his apologetic purposes. Similarly, Chrysostom argues, it is the detachment of the monk from the pursuits and values of the general populace that gains him the trust of his clients.[63]

But these explanations, illuminating as they are, do not take us to the heart of the matter. What stands out most in Chrysostom's descriptions of the monastic life, however, is the idea that the monk lived on earth the life of heaven.[64] "Go to the dwellings of the holy ones. To go to the monastery of a holy man is to pass, as it were, from earth to heaven."[65] Throughout the two works translated below, and well into his later years, Chrysostom continually harks back to this theme: the monks live on earth the life of angels and, as such, represent living patterns of Christian perfection.[66] Even the

---

[58] Brown, "Rise and Function," 85.

[59] Brown, "Rise and Function," 85-87.

[60] Brown, "Rise and Function," 91-92.

[61] Brown, "Rise and Function," 96-97.

[62] *Oppugnatores* 2.7; translated below, pp. 112-13.

[63] *Oppugnatores* 2.8; translated below, p. 115.

[64] P. Brown also has discussed this dimension of monastic "power" in *The Making of Late Antiquity* (Cambridge: Harvard University Press, 1978) 70-71. See also R.M. Price's introduction to *A History of the Monks of Syria* (Kalamazoo, MI: Cistercian Publications, 1985) xxix-xxxii.

[65] Chrysostom, Homily 14 in 1 Timothy (PG 62.575).

[66] See *Oppugnatores* 3.11, below p. 147; *Comparatio* 3, below p. 72.

illiterate, who are unable to read and to benefit from the scripture, Chrysostom writes, can go to the hills and see for themselves examples of supreme virtue:[67]

> Although you do not know by the Scriptures those who have died, these living men you ought to see.... Come to me, and I will show you the places of refuge of these holy men; come and learn from them something beneficial. Shining lamps are they in every part of the world; as walls they are set about the cities. For this reason they have occupied the deserts, that they may instruct you to despise the tumults in the midst of the world.

Two aspects of Chrysostom's enthusiasm for the ascetic life must be noted. First, Chrysostom clearly was captivated by a display of behavior that seemed to defy human nature. Like many of his contemporaries he believed that the monk had breached the boundary between the human and the divine) The extreme ascetic behavior characteristic of Syrian monks was simultaneously a denial and a transcendence of human limitations. The monk thus had achieved a unique status as advocate in the heavenly court, a freedom of access (παρρησία) before the divine King.[68]

But the monk was also a model, an example of the ethical and spiritual possibilities available, in principle, to all human beings. He was not only an ideal patron, but also an ideal Christian. Even in later years, when Chrysostom had long since abandoned his monastic aspirations and had turned his attention to reforming the lives of Christians in the city, he continually holds up the monks as living images of Christian perfection. "Go there often," Chrysostom exhorts his flock, "so that, having purged away the abiding stain by their prayers and admonitions, you may both pass in the best manner the present life, and attain the good things to come."[69]

---

[67] Homily 72.3 on Matthew (PG 58.673). Cf. Theodoret, *Religious History* 11.3, who writes of the Antiochene monk Romanus: "Many he made lovers of the things of God simply by being seen" (Price, 95).

[68] Brown, "Rise and Function," 94 and 97-98.

[69] Homily 73.2 on Matthew (PG 58.673).

4. Return to the City

Living the angelic life, however, is not easy. Chrysostom's attempt at the rigorous asceticism of a Syrian monk proved to be too much for someone reared in the comfort of the city.[70] His life as a hermit ended in a severe stomach injury that was to plague Chrysostom for the rest of his life:[71]

> He never relaxed for that two-year period, not in the day nor at night, and his gastric organs became lifeless and the proper functions of the kidneys were impaired by cold. Since he could no longer take care of himself alone, he went back once more to the haven of the Church.

This departure from monastic life occured in 378.[72] After several more years of service under bishop Meletius, Chrysostom was ordained a deacon in 381. It is at this time that Chrysostom's literary activity seems to have begun in earnest.

Chrysostom's abandonment of the monastic life may have been due largely to his physical ailments, as Palladius states. But there is evidence which suggests that other factors may have motivated him as well. In one of the works dating from this period, the double treatise *On Compunction* addressed to the monks Demetrius and Stelechius, Chrysostom indicates that his enthusiasm for monasticism may have diminished somewhat.[73] In the first book Chrysostom criticizes certain monks for exhibiting excessive concern for their own leisure (ἀνάπαυσις) and for refusing to accept a ministry (οἰκονομία) in the church.[74] He cites his own experience as a young monk, when he found himself preoccupied with thoughts of what sort of food, drink,

---

[70] See his treatise *De compunctione* 1.6 where Chrysostom describes the difficulties he experienced at the lack of luxury in his new monastic habitat. Cf. B. Grillet, "Introduction Generale," *Jean Chrysostome. La Virginité*. SC 125 (Paris, 1966) 18.

[71] Palladius, *Dialogue* 5 (Meyer 35). Later as patriarch of Constantinople, Chrysostom was criticized for his frugality in offering hospitality. Palladius, *Dialogue* 12, attributes this to his stomach ailment.

[72] Carter, "Chronology," 362.

[73] On the dating of the two books *De compunctione*, see Festugière, *Antioche païenne et chrétienne* 14-15, n. 2.

[74] *De compunctione* 1.6 (PG 47.403-404). Theodoret tells several stories about monks who refused to be ordained or to exercise the functions of the priesthood. See his *Religious History* 3.11, 13.4, 15.4, and 19.2.

and work he would have to endure: "In short, I was in great turmoil about having a tranquil life."

In the second book of the same treatise, Chrysostom extolls the apostle Paul as someone who managed to be "crucified to the world," while still living in the midst of cities:[75]

> So do not talk to me about the mountain-tops, or the ravines, or the valleys, or the inaccessible solitudes. For these things alone are insufficient to ease a tumultuous spirit. Rather, there is need of that flame which Christ enkindled in the soul of Paul.

Later in the same treatise he presents the king David as an example of someone who remained in the city and yet conceived a love for God even greater than that of the monks. He concludes that it is solitude of "purpose" (προαίρεσις) not of place, which leads to love of God: "For with that sort of disposition the blessed David dwelt in the city and administered his kingdom, and, although he was surrounded by infinite cares, he maintained the desire for God more ardently than those who live in solitude."[76]

Chrysostom's experience of the monastic life seems to have freed him of any illusion that monasticism represented the only true path towards Christian perfection.[77] He is quite conscious of the foibles of the monks and aware that self-preoccupation might lead a monk to neglect his responsibility to the larger body of Christ. In fact, Chrysostom's concern for the well-being of the church leads him eventually to declare that a life of service in the clergy surpasses the virtue displayed by the monk. The monk is like a man in the harbor whose ship is calm because it is not at sea, he will write in his treatise *On the Priesthood*; the bishop, by contrast, is one whose virtue is tested on the stormy sea and who guides the ship safely.[78]

> We need not, then, give lavish or excessive admiration to the monk because, by keeping himself to himself, he avoids

---

[75] *De compunctione* 2.2 (PG 47.413).

[76] *De compunctione* 2.3 (PG 47.414).

[77] See J.M. Leroux, "Monachisme et communauté chrétienne d'après saint Jean Chrysostome," in *Théologie de la vie monastique* (Paris: Aubier, 1961) 152, for a similar interpretation of John's development.

[78] *De sacerdotio* 6.5 (SC 272.321-23). Malingrey tentatively dates this treatise to the year 390. See her discussion in SC 272.10-13.

> agitation and does not commit many serious sins; for he has nothing to goad and excite his soul. But if a man has devoted himself to the whole community and has been forced to endure the sins of all, and still remains firm and unwavering...he is the one who deserves everyone's applause and admiration, for he has given proof enough of his prowess.[79]

Clearly, after his return to the city and his ordination to the diaconate, Chrysostom's perception of monasticism was neither naive nor uncritical. He was aware of the limitations of monastic life, particularly the failure of monks to undertake an active ministry in the church.[80] Nonetheless, despite these criticisms, Chrysostom did not cease to regard the life of the monks as a vivid ideal of spiritual achievement. He apparently believed that the monastic life, while deficient to some degree in its value for the entire Christian community, still represented a viable, and indeed exemplary, path towards virtue. In this state of mind, then, Chrysostom began his clerical and literary careers. As we will see in the next chapter, the two monastic treatises translated here probably date from this period. As such, they will reflect Chrysostom's enthusiasm for the ascetic ideal, tempered by his experience of the monastic reality.

---

[79] *De sacerdotio* 6.5. Translated by G. Neville, *St. John Chrysostom. Six Books on the Priesthood* (Crestwood, NY: St. Vladimir's Seminary Press, 1984) 144.

[80] Later, as patriarch of Constantinople, Chrysostom will instigate a pioneering attempt to use Christian monks for missionary purposes. On this subject see I. auf der Maur, *Mönchtum und Glaubensverkündigung in den Schriften des hl. Johannes Chrysostomus*. Paradosis, 14 (Freiburg: Universitätsverlag, 1959). Auf der Maur, 158, argues that already in his earliest works (e.g. *Oppugnatores* 1.8) Chrysostom links the monastic vocation to service in the church.

CHAPTER TWO

THE TWO TREATISES: AUTHENTICITY, PURPOSE, DATING

1. Authenticity

No doubts have ever been raised about the authenticity of Chrysostom's *Against the Opponents of the Monastic Life*. The work is found within the earliest collections of Chrysostom's *ascetica*, and numerous parallels of thought and language can be drawn between this treatise and other undisputed works.[1] The same cannot be said, however, about the *Comparison Between a King and a Monk*; there is not universal agreement that it is a genuine work of Chrysostom. On the one hand, the work has been listed among the *dubia* by J.A. Aldama in the standard handbook of inauthentic works.[2] Aldama's classification has been followed by M. Geerard and by H.J. Sieben.[3] On the other hand, most Chrysostom scholars, past and present, have not been dissuaded from belief in Chrysostom's authorship and have treated the work as authentic.[4] Therefore, a fuller discussion of the question of authenticity is in order.

---

[1] See J. Dumortier, "L'auteur présumé du *Corpus asceticum* de s. Jean Chrysostome," *Journal of Theological Studies* n.s. 6 (1955) 99-102, for a discussion of the ninth century collection. Many parallels between the *Oppugnatores* and Chrysostom's other treatises have been cited in the notes to the translation below.

[2] *Repertorium Pseudochrysostomicum* (Paris: Centre Nationale de la Recherche Scientifique, 1965) 120, no. 327.

[3] M. Geerard, *Clavis Patrum Graecorum.* vol. 2 (Turnhout: Brepols, 1974) no. 4500; H.J. Sieben, "Jean Chrysostome (Pseudo-)," in *Dictionaire de Spiritualité* 8 (1974) 355.

[4] Among them are C. Baur, *John Chrysostom and His Time* 115-17; J. Quasten, *Patrology.* vol. 3. *The Golden Age of Greek Patristic Literature* (Westminster, MD: Newman Press, 1960) 463; E.A. Clark, *Jerome, Chrysostom and Friends* 17; M. Schatkin, "The Authenticity of St. John Chrysotom's *De sancto Babyla, contra Julianum et Gentiles*," in *Kyriakon. Festschrift Johannes Quasten.* vol. 1. Edited by P. Granfield and J. Jungmann (Münster: Aschendorff, 1970) 487.

Doubts about the authenticity of the work were raised as early as the seventeenth century by H. Savile in the Eton edition of Chrysostom's works.[5] Savile first edited the work among the *spuria*; later he changed his mind and judged it to be merely *dubia*.[6] Saville's doubts were based primarily on the question of style; he thought that the treatise was unworthy of Chrysostom's eloquence. Exactly the opposite view was taken by Bernard de Montfaucon, who edited the text again in the eighteenth century and whose version is reprinted in the *Patrologia graeca*. Montfaucon considers the text to be among Chrysostom's "more elegant" works.[7]

The more recent doubts of Aldama and the others appear to be based solely on the unpublished dissertation of J. Weyer.[8] Weyer argued that the language of the treatise is foreign to that of Chrysostom's authentic works and that it contains certain metrical clausulae that vary from Chrysostom's usual arrangement.[9] Certain flaws, however, have been pointed out in Weyer's study. R.E. Carter has noted that Weyer drew his criteria of authenticity from a relatively limited body of Chrysostom's works: the *Homilies on the Statues*, the *Homilies on John*, and a few other homilies.[10] "Little reference, however, was made to the *corpus asceticum*; yet the early ascetical works are more relevant than the later homilies for establishing the authenticity or spuriousness of the *Comparatio regis et monachi*, which has been thought by many to be the earliest of Chrysostom's writings."[11]

Carter's comments are especially relevant in light of the fact that Chrysostom's later writings do differ in language from the earlier works, a point recognized as early as the ninth century by Photius, patriarch of Constantinople.[12] The later homilies were composed with less care than the early works.[13] I intend to argue that the treatise in

---

[5] H. Savile, *S. Johannis Chrysostomi opera omnia.* vol. 8 (Eton, 1612) 861. A brief account of the discussion can be found in Aldama, *Repertorium* 120.

[6] According to Bernard de Montfaucon (PG 47.387), "Savilius, qui inter spuria hoc opusculum incaute posuerat, in notis postea suis id incogitanter ac temere factum esse declaravit, vereque Chrysostomo dignum opus esse fassus est."

[7] PG 47.387-88: "Certe non modo Chrysostomi fetum, sed etiam inter elegantiores numerandum esse censemus."

[8] *De homiliis quae Joanni Chrysostomi falso attribuuntur* (Bonn, 1952). This work has not been available to me. I have relied upon the summaries given in Aldama and in R.E. Carter, "The Future of Chrysostom Studies," *Studia Patristica* 10 (1970) 18.

[9] Aldama, *Repertorium* 120.

[10] Carter, "Future of Chrysostom Studies," 18.

[11] Carter, "Future of Chrysostom Studies," 18.

[12] PG 103.504-505, cited in Fabricius, *Zu den Jugendschriften* 19.

[13] Fabricius, *Zu den Jugendschriften* 19-20.

question is an authentic work of Chrysostom. I first will base my case, as Carter has suggested, on the relations between this work and the indisputably authentic monastic treatise, *Against the Opponents of the Monastic Life*. Then, I will present evidence of quotations from Libanius which appear in the *Comparison Between a King and a Monk*. These borrowings, which first were noted by Caius Fabricius, will support the argument on behalf of this work's authenticity.

The *Comparatio* can be considered a more detailed discussion of a theme which is treated briefly in *Against the Opponents of the Monastic Life*, book two, chapter six: the superiority of the wealth, power, and virtue of the monk to that of an earthly king.[14] Not only in this chapter, however, but also throughout the body of the *Oppugnatores*, many similarities of thought and word choice can be discerned. The parallels between the two works fall into three categories: common biblical references, similar treatment of themes, and verbal reminiscences.

First, unlike the longer treatise, the *Comparatio* quotes scripture only sparingly. There are only two direct quotations: Luke 17:21 and Matthew 7:7.[15] There are, however, numerous biblical allusions which are relevant to the question of authenticity. In the *Comparatio* Chrysostom shows a special interest in 1 and 2 Kings. These are the only books of the Old Testament to which he refers. He cites the king Achab's reliance on the prayers of Elijah, described in 1 Kings 17-18.[16] He also mentions the king Hezekiah's deathbed discussion with the prophet Isaiah in 2 Kings 20.[17] A story about the intervention of the prophet Elisha during wartime is mentioned, which is probably an allusion to 2 Kings 3. Finally, there are clear references to 2 Kings 19, a passage which narrates the dependence of king Hezekiah on the prayers of Isaiah.[18]

A similar interest in these books is displayed in *Against the Opponents of the Monastic Life*. The first book of the treatise contains an echo of 1 Kings 19:4.[19] As in the *Comparatio* 2, the prophet Isaiah is mentioned in passing.[20] A story involving the prophet Elisha is

---

[14] Quasten, *Patrology* 3.463.

[15] There are, however, four quotations from the seventh chapter of Matthew in book one of *Oppugnatores*, but no citation of Matthew 7:7.

[16] *Comparatio* 4; translated below p. 74.

[17] *Comparatio* 4; translated below p. 74.

[18] *Comparatio* 4; translated below p. 74.

[19] *Oppugnatores* 1.2; translated below p. 80.

[20] *Oppugnatores* 1.1; translated below p. 78.

alluded to in the third book of *Oppugnatores*.[21]   And, as in the
Comparatio, the nineteenth chapter of the second book of Kings is
cited as evidence of the reliance of king Hezekiah on the prophet
Isaiah.[22] It is significant that some of the same chapters from 1 and 2
Kings should appear in both monastic treatises, especially since these
are the only Old Testament books cited in the *Comparatio*. In both
works Chrysostom's attention is drawn to these chapters when he
reflects on the contrast between the prayer of the monk and the power
of the king.

A second argument for the common authorship of the two treatises
rests upon the numerous treatments of the same themes. Both works
intend to prove that the monk possesses "goods" (ἀγαθά) superior to
those of the wealthy and powerful. The *Comparatio* offers "to compare
the goods (ἀγαθά) of philosophy and the apparent benefits of power
and glory in this life."[23]   The *Oppugnatores* likewise wishes to
demonstrate that the monk "suffers no evil, but enjoys great goods
(ἀγαθῶν), than which none greater can be found."[24]   Both works
contrast the true goods of the monastic life with the merely apparent
benefits of wealth and power in this life.   The author of the
Comparatio writes that "most people love and admire things which
seem to be good, rather than things which are by nature beneficial and
truly good."[25] In *Oppugnatores* Chrysostom writes that the young
monk has exchanged "transient goods, or rather things which are not
true goods, for those which are true and lasting goods."[26]

The similar treatment of themes extends also to details regarding
the conduct of the monks. Both treatises speak of the activity of the
monks as exorcists.[27]   Both also refer to the "angelic" life of the
monks.[28] In both treatises the monk is described as a "savior" of those
on earth. In the *Comparatio* Chrysostom writes that "God taught the
kings to regard those who serve him as the common saviors (κοινοὺς...
σωτῆρας) of the earth."[29] Likewise, in *Oppugnatores* the monks are

---

[21] *Oppugnatores* 3.17; translated below p. 165. The reference is to 2 Kings 2:23-25.

[22] 2 Kings 19:34, cited in *Oppugnatores* 3.20; translated below p. 172.

[23] *Comparatio* 1 (PG 47.387-88).

[24] *Oppugnatores* 2.3 (Dübner 18).

[25] *Comparatio* 1 (PG 47.387).

[26] *Oppugnatores* 2.10 (Dübner 31).

[27] *Comparatio* 2 and 4; translated below p. 71 and pp. 73-74. *Oppugnatores* 1.7;
translated below p. 91.

[28] *Comparatio* 3; translated below p. 22. *Oppugnatores* 3.11 and 18; translated
below p. 147 and p. 169.

[29] *Comparatio* 4 (PG 47.391).

hailed as the "common benefactors, patrons, and saviors" (εὐεργέται κοινοὶ καί προστάται καί σωτῆρες).30 The use of the adjective "common" (κοινός) is frequent in Chrysostom and is found applied to the monks in several expressions in both treatises. In *Comparatio* 3 the monk is the "common healer (κοινός...ἰατρὸς) of rich and poor alike." *Comparatio* 3 also speaks of tax-collectors as the "common enemy (κοινοὶ...πολέμιοι) of the countryside."31 *Oppugnatores* 3.10 refers to the wealthy as the "common enemies" (κοινοὺς...ἐχθρούς), and *Oppugnatores* 3.11 speaks hypothetically of the monks as the "common enemies of society" (κοινοὺς τῆς πολιτείας ἐχθρούς).32 These many parallel expressions, applied both to the monks and to their opponents, support the view that Chrysostom authored both treatises.

Besides referring to the monks as the "common saviors," both works speak of the monk's ability to ask for money from the wealthy and to distribute it to the poor.33 The monk's fearlessness in the face of death is asserted in both treatises.34 Also in both works one finds the view that the king is weaker and more vulnerable to attack than the monks.35 The easy accessibility of the monastic life, in contrast to a life spent in pursuit of worldly wealth and success, is maintained in both treatises.36 Finally, both works argue that the monk's destiny lies in his own power; the person who pursues worldly success, by contrast, is dependent on the help and goodwill of others.37 These numerous examples of the treatment of parallel themes, together with the common interest in 1 and 2 Kings, support the view that Chrysostom composed the *Comparison Between a King and a Monk*.

To conclude this examination of parallels between the *Comparatio* and the *Oppugnatores*, I will offer two final examples of passages which display both thematic and verbal similarities. First, in the *Comparatio* Chrysostom refers to the king (βασιλεύς) as "one who wears a shining, purple robe and crown and sits upon a golden throne."38 Later, he describes the king as one who "wears a crown of

---

30 *Oppugnatores* 3.18 (Dübner 68).

31 *Comparatio* 3 (PG 47.390).

32 *Oppugnatores* 3.10 (Dübner 52) and 3.11 (Dübner 53).

33 *Comparatio* 3; translated below p. 73. *Oppugnatores* 2.4; translated below pp. 102-3.

34 *Comparatio* 4; translated below p. 75. *Oppugnatores* 2.7; translated below p. 112.

35 *Comparatio* 4; translated below p. 75. *Oppugnatores* 2.6 and 7; translated below pp. 110-11 and pp. 111-13.

36 *Comparatio* 1; translated below pp. 67-70. *Oppugnatores* 3.13; translated below pp. 155-156.

37 *Comparatio* 4; translated below p. 75. *Oppugnatores* 3.13; translated below p. 155.

38 *Comparatio* 1 (PG 47.388): τὸν ἁλουργίδι καὶ στεφάνῳ λαμπόμενον, καὶ καθήμενον ἐπὶ θρόνου χρυσοῦ.

gems and gold" and whose "whole body shines with a purple robe."[39]
Several verbal parallels can be found in the following passage from
the *Oppugnatores*: "If he were dressed in gold, or even in purple with
the king's crown upon his head...he would not amaze everyone as
much as he does now."[40] In both works the description of the king is
strikingly similar.

Chrysostom's picture of the monk in both works also presents us
with a set of parallel passages. In the *Comparatio* the author portrays
the monk "using one cloak (ἱματίῳ μὲν ἑνὶ) the whole year long,
drinking water with greater pleasure than others drink marvellous
wine."[41] As we will see below, this passage has been borrowed from a
description of Socrates in Libanius' first declamation, the *Apologia
Socratis*. But the significance of this text for the present discussion is
that the *Oppugnatores* contains a similar description, but one which is
applied to Socrates: "[Socrates] had only one cloak (ἑνὸς ἱματίου) and
in this he was clothed winter and summer and throughout the year."[42]
The fact that the author of the *Comparatio* has borrowed his portrait
of the monks from a work of Libanius itself suggests that this author
was Chrysostom. But that the same description, borrowed from
Libanius' description of Socrates, is then applied to Socrates in the
Oppugnatores makes it extremely likely that Chrysostom authored
both treatises.

The final evidence for Chrysostom's authorship of the *Comparatio*
lies in the several borrowings from Libanius which appear in the
treatise. In 1957 the Swedish classicist Caius Fabricius published a
brief article which identified four passages from works of Libanius in
the *Comparatio*.[43] Several years later Fabricius published a more
comprehensive study in which he added two further examples of such
borrowings.[44] In the earlier article Fabricius showed that
Chrysostom had drawn from Libanius' twelfth oration and from the
first declamation, the *Apologia Socratis*. The two passages
subsequently identified are from Libanius' thirteenth and sixty-fourth

---

[39] *Comparatio* 2 (PG 47.389): στέφανον μὲν φορεῖ λιθοκόλλητον καὶ χρυσοῦν...
'αλουργίδι μὲν 'ὅλον τὸ σῶμα λάμπεται.

[40] *Oppugnatores* 2.6 (Dübner, 23-24): Οὐ γὰρ 'άν οὕτους 'άπαντας ἐξέπλητε
χρυσοφορῶν, μᾶλλον δὲ καὶ ἁλουργίδα, καὶ αὐτὸν τὸν στέφανον περικείμενος ἐπὶ τῆς
κεφαλῆς. A few lines further down Chrysostom refers to the king "wearing a golden
stole"(στολὴν περιβέβληται χρυσῆν).

[41] *Comparatio* 3 (PG 47.390).

[42] *Oppugnatores* 2.5 (Dübner 22-23).

[43] "Vier Libaniusstellen bei Johannes Chrysostomos." See above, p. 4, n. 17.

[44] *Zu den Jugendschriften des Johannes Chrysostomos*. See above, p. 4, n. 17.

orations. The precise character and significance of these quotations from Libanius will be treated in the next section of this chapter. Here it is enough to note that the presence in the *Comparison Between a King and a Monk* of these quotations from Libanius, when considered along with the other evidence which has been cited here, provides reasonable assurance that the work is genuinely from the hand of Chrysostom.

2. Content and Purpose

The *Comparison Between a King and a Monk* is composed in the form of a well-known rhetorical genre, the "comparison" (σύγκρισις).[45] Such works were common textbook exercises (προγυμνάσματα) practiced in the school of Libanius.[46] In theme the treatise employs an old philosophical commonplace: the contrast between the philosopher-king and the tyrant.[47] In Chrysostom's hands, however, the hackneyed topic is put to a new purpose: the Christian monk is portrayed as the true "philosopher," and his way of life is extolled as encompassing greater power, glory, wealth, and freedom than is possessed by those in secular authority. The work, then, functions as a discourse of exhortation (λόγος προτρεπτικός), urging Christians to pursue the monastic life and to despise worldly values.[48]

To see the *Comparatio* merely as a tract on behalf of monasticism, however, is to miss an important, and indeed essential, aspect of Chrysostom's intention. The quotations from Libanius reveal another dimension to the treatise. Not only do they point towards the authenticity of the text, but they also provide a key to understanding

---

[45] Cf. Fabricius, *Zu den Jugendschriften* 19.

[46] Five συγκρίσεις are included in Libanius' προγυμνάσματα: Förster, v. 8, pp. 334-60.

[47] See R.E. Carter, "St. John Chrysostom's Rhetorical Use of the Socratic Distinction between Kingship and Tyranny," *Traditio* 14 (1958) 368-69. Carter discusses the use of this commonplace in several works of Chrysostom, including the *Comparatio*. C. Baur, *John Chrysostom and his Time*, vol. 1, 115, suggests that the work was composed as a Christian counterpart to Plato's comparison between a philosopher and a tyrant in book nine of the *Republic*.

[48] Carter, "Chrysostom's Rhetorical Use of the Socratic Distinction," 368. As Chrysostom notes in the concluding lines of the treatise, the wealthy ought not to be considered blessed: "For wealth is transitory, and what seems to be good perishes along with this life. But when you see the monk walking alone, meek and humble and tranquil and gentle, emulate the man, show yourself to be an imitator of his philosophy, pray to become like the just man" (PG 47.392).

the purpose of the work. While Fabricius noted the presence of these quotations, he did not discuss their purpose or significance.[49] As I will show, each of the works of Libanius from which Chrysostom has borrowed is concerned in some way with the emperor Julian and with his pagan revival. The presence of these quotations will reveal that Chrysostom's early monastic treatise is engaged in an apologetic endeavor against his former teacher, Libanius, and, beyond him, against the emperor Julian.[50]

Three of the passages in question are taken from orations of Libanius. Both of these works (or. 12 and or. 13) are panegyrics addressed to the emperor Julian and probably were actually delivered before him.[51] Both orations also take the opportunity to praise Julian's accession to the throne and to reveal their author, Libanius, as an ally of Julian's pagan restoration. Chrysostom's interest in these texts, therefore, will not be merely a literary one; like Libanius himself, his concerns are also religious and apologetic.

Let us examine the borrowings. In oration 12 Libanius had extolled the freedom brought by Julian's reign and claimed that the fortunes of the empire had been "changed by a man who has of himself laid the foundations of freedom and who has forbidden the tyranny of pleasure to dominate his soul."[52] The parallel passage in Chrysostom describes the Christian monk as an ideal king in these words: "For he truly is a king...who keeps his mind free and does not allow the power of the pleasures to dominate his soul."[53] Also in the twelfth oration Libanius had praised Julian's literary abilities and said that Julian's ascetic habits, particularly his inclination to arise early in the morning, accounted for his prolific accomplishments: "While the night

---

[49] See my discussion of these passages and their significance in "Borrowings from Libanius in the *Comparatio regis et monachi* of St. John Chrysostom," *Journal of Theological Studies* n.s. 39 (1988) 525-31.

[50] I will discuss only the excerpts from orations 12 and 13 and from the *Apologia Socratis*. The passage from oration 64 seems to be merely an echo of a typical phrase of Libanius' rather than an actual quotation.

[51] On this question see P. Petit, "Recherches sur le publication et la diffusion des discours de Libanius," *Historia* 5 (1956) 479-86. The thirteenth oration is dated to July 362 and was written at Julian's request upon his entry into Antioch. See or. 1.101, where Libanius describes the meeting. The twelfth oration also was commissioned by Julian and was dedicated to him at the start of his fourth consulship on Jan. 1, 363.

[52] Or. 12.101 (Förster, v. 2, p. 45): οὐκ ἐάσας ἐνδυναστεῦσαι τῇ ψυχῇ τὴν δεσποτείαν τῶν ἡδονῶν.

[53] *Comparatio* 1 (PG 47.388): οὐκ ἐῶν ἐνδυναστεῦσαι τῇ ψυχῇ τὴν δεσποτείαν τῶν ἡδονῶν.

is still young, you sing much earlier than do the birds."⁵⁴ Similarly, Chrysostom writes, "we will see the monk singing much earlier than do the birds."⁵⁵ Finally, in oration 13 Libanius had addressed Julian in these words: "Your table is a modest one, and your companions pupils of Plato."⁵⁶ With only a slight change of words, Chrysostom describes the monk as one who keeps "a modest table, and whose companions are athletes of virtue."⁵⁷

In each of these three examples we see that Chrysostom has taken Libanius' praise of the emperor Julian's ascetic character and applied these descriptions to the Christian monks. It is impossible that Chrysostom could have been unaware of the tendentious nature of his source. Libanius' pagan sympathies were well-known, and elsewhere Chrysostom explicitly attacks Libanius and the sophist's support of the emperor Julian.⁵⁸ These borrowings from Libanius, therefore, serve as Chrysostom's subtle rejoinder to his teacher. The *Comparison Between a King and a Monk* implicitly argues against Libanius that the Christian monk, and not the pagan emperor, authentically embodies the ideal of the true philosopher.

This impression is confirmed by an examination of the remaining quotations from Libanius found in the *Comparatio*. Fabricius also discovered two passages from Libanius' first declamation, the *Apologia Socratis*, in Chrysostom's monastic treatise. In one place Libanius writes that Socrates "used only one threadbare cloak throughout the year, drinking water with greater pleasure than others drink Thasian wine."⁵⁹ Quoting most of the same words, Chrysostom writes that the monk "uses one cloak throughout the year, drinking water with greater pleasure than others drink marvellous wine."⁶⁰ As was noted above, this is the passage which is

---

⁵⁴ Or. 12.94 (Förster, v. 2, p. 42): σὺ δὲ ᾄδεις πολὺ πρότερος τῶν ὀρνίθων.

⁵⁵ *Comparatio* 3 (PG 47.389): τὸν μοναχὸν...ὀψόμεθα...πολὺ πρότερον ᾄδοντα τῶν ὀρνίθων.

⁵⁶ Or. 13.44 (Förster, v. 2, pp. 78-79): τράπεζα δέ σοι μετρία καὶ σύσσιτοι Πλάτωνος ὁμιληταί.

⁵⁷ *Comparatio* 3 (PG 47.389): τράπεζα μετρία καὶ σύσσιτοι τῆς αὐτῆς ἀρετῆς ἀθληταί.

⁵⁸ See the treatise *De sancto Babyla, contra Julianum et gentiles*, discussed below pp. 50-54.

⁵⁹ Decl. 1.18 (Förster, v. 5, p. 24): τρίβωνι μὲν ἑνὶ δι' ἔτους χρώμενος, ὕδωρ δὲ πίνων ἥδιον ἢ θάσιον οἶνον ἕτεροι.

⁶⁰ *Comparatio* 3 (PG 47.390): ἱματίῳ μὲν ἑνὶ δι' ἔτους χρώμενος, ὕδωρ δὲ πίνων ἥδιον ἢ θαυμάστον οἶνον ἕτεροι.

echoed again in *Against the Opponents of the Monastic Life,* when Chrysostom describes the ascetic life of Socrates.

A second passage from the *Apologia Socratis* also is used by Chrysostom to portray the Christian monks. Libanius claims that "the person who has conquered the pleasures, for the sake of which the multitude desires to live, will necessarily bear more easily a change from that state."[61] Chrysostom writes that the monk "who shows contempt for wealth and pleasure and luxury, for the sake of which the multitude desires to live, will necessarily bear more easily a change from that state."[62] It is clear that Chrysostom has borrowed from Libanius' description of a pagan hero and applied the praise to the Christian monks.

Here again, however, Chrysostom has relied on a work of Libanius that is related to Julian's pagan revival. The *Apologia Socratis* was Libanius' earliest attack on Christianity. It was composed early in 362, when Julian had only recently come to power.[63] The declamation takes the form of a speech placed on the lips of an anonymous friend of Socrates, who has appeared to defend the philosopher against the charges brought by Anytus. Socrates is portrayed as one who embodies the highest virtues of a teacher, a *pater familias,* and a citizen. Libanius' declamation has been recognized as a thinly veiled apology for the Hellenic tradition and for Julian's pagan revival: "He wished to show that holier and more venerable men arose among his contemporaries in Greek philosophy than among the Galileans."[64]

The figure of Socrates, therefore, as he appears in Libanius' work, is not ideologically neutral. Rather, he represents the intellectual tradition of Hellenism, specifically in opposition to Christianity.[65] Whether he is describing the virtuous life of Socrates or the ascetic inclinations of the emperor Julian, Libanius' point is the same: he

---

61 Decl. 1.3 (Förster, v. 5, p. 15): τόν τε κεκρατηκότατῶν ἡδονῶν, ὧν 'ἕνεκα ζῆν ἐπιθυμοῦσιν οἱ πολλοί, καὶ τὴν ἐνθένδε μετανάστασιν ἀνάγκη ῥᾳδίως φέρειν.

62 *Comparatio* 4 (PG 47.392): τὸν γὰρ ὑπερορῶντα πλούτου καὶ ἡδονῆς καὶ τρυφῆς, ὧν 'ἕνεκα ζῆν ἐπιθυμοῦσιν οἱ πολλοί, καὶ τὴν ἐνθένδε μετάστασιν ἀνάγκη ῥᾳδίως φέρειν.

63 J. Misson, "Libanius et christianisme," *Musée Belge* 24 (1920) 74.

64 H. Markowski, *De Libanio Socratis defensore* (Breslau, 1910; reprint New York/Hildesheim: G. Olms Verlag, 1970) 168-69. A similar argument has been made regarding Libanius' second declamation, *De silentio Socratis.* See M. Crosby and W.M. Calder, "Libanius, *On the Silence of Socrates.* A First Translation and an Introduction," *Greek, Roman, and Byzantine Studies* 3 (1960) 199-200.

65 See P. de Labriolle, *La réaction païenne. Étude sur la polémique antichrétienne du Ier au VIe siècle* (Paris, 1934) 431, for a similar comment.

wishes to assert the moral benefits of Hellenic culture and to endorse Julian's incipient restoration.

When the aggressively pagan character of Libanius' orations and of the declamation is acknowledged, Chrysostom's *Comparison Between a King and a Monk* takes on a significance which has not been recognized previously. The work is not simply a paean to the monastic life *per se*. It is, rather, John Chrysostom's response to the polemics of Libanius against Christianity. By borrowing Libanius' descriptions of the ascetic lives of Socrates and Julian and by applying these to the monks, Chrysostom has subtly inverted the pagan argument. Against Libanius, who presents the virtue of his pagan heroes as an argument on behalf of Greek *paideia*, Chrysostom claims these virtues for the Christian monks, the "true philosophers."[66]

When the apologetic character of Chrysostom's *Comparison Between a King and a Monk* is recognized, it becomes plausible to view the larger monastic treatise, *Against the Opponents of the Monastic Life*, in a similar context. Like the *Comparatio* this work can be read on two levels. First, it intends to endorse the monastic life as an example of the virtue required of all Christians, but it also articulates specifically apologetic arguments. An examination of the structure and content of the work will make this plain.

The *Oppugnatores* consists of three distinct books or discourses (λόγοι). The first book is an introduction to the treatise as a whole. It begins by describing a popular persecution against the monks who have recruited young Antiochenes into the monastic life. The citizens of Antioch, Chrysostom writes, "drive away those who lead others to philosophy and with many threats they forbid them to speak at all or to teach anyone anything like it."[67] While the book begins as a defense of monks against their abusers, its chief topic, as a recent commentator has noted, "is not mistreatment of the monks but the clash of their ascetic lifestyles and the lifestyles of the upper-classes, both Christian and pagan."[68] Most of the treatise is spent arguing that the values and aspirations of the well-to-do, educated citizens are

---

[66] "Philosophy" is Chrysostom's usual term in the *Comparatio* and *Oppugnatores* for the monastic life. See A.M. Malingrey, *"Philosophia": Étude d'un groupe de mots dans la littérature grecque, des Présocratiques au IVe siècle apres J.-C.* (Paris: Klincksieck, 1961) 272. As Malingrey notes (270-71), Chrysostom often speaks of "Christian philosophy" in opposition to "Hellenic philosophy" and, therefore, seems to be writing in an atmosphere animated by the struggle with paganism.

[67] *Oppugnatores* 1.2; translated below p. 79.

[68] R.L. Wilken, *John Chrysostom and the Jews* 26.

opposed to Christian ideals and that the monks represent the authentically Christian way of life.

This treatise, therefore, like the *Comparison Between a King and a Monk*, was intended to be a discourse of exhortation, a λόγος προτρεπτικός, inciting Christians, as well as pagans, to disdain the pursuit of worldly wealth and success and to pursue the "philosophy" of the monks.[69] But there also are indications throughout the work that Chrysostom's anti-pagan apologetics, and his interest in Libanius in particular, were not forgotten. Like the *Comparatio*, the *Oppugnatores* can be read on another level as a response to pagan claims about the Hellenic tradition; in this work, Chrysostom presents the monastic life as an alternative mode of moral education and, therefore, as a rival to traditional Greek *paideia*.

The first argument for this interpretation of the *Oppugnatores* is the nature of its second book. This discourse is addressed specifically to pagan parents and proposes to offer arguments on behalf of the monastic life based entirely on grounds that the pagan can accept. As he did in the *Comparatio* Chrysostom treats a series of "goods" (αγαθά) which the pagan parent values: money, health, glory, power and pleasure. He proceeds throughout book two to demonstrate that the monk possesses these goods in a manner far superior to that of those engaged in worldly activities. As in the *Comparatio*, Chrysostom portrays the monk as a "philosopher" and employs commonplace descriptions of philosophical virtue derived especially from the Stoic and Cynic traditions.[70] The similarity of theme between the *Comparatio* and the *Oppugnatores* at this point suggests a similarity of purpose in the two works.

Chrysostom further supports these allusions to the philosophical tradition with explicit references to the philosophers Socrates, Plato, and Diogenes the Cynic. First, he likens the opponents of the monks

---

[69] Q. Cataudella has argued that the *Oppugnatores* was consciously modelled after the λόγοι προτρεπτικοί of Greek philosophy. He has drawn numerous parallels between this treatise and the protreptic works of Aristotle, Galen, and Iamblichus. See his "Di un ignorato protreptico cristiano alla filosofia," *Rendiconti della Classe di Scienze morali, storiche e filologiche dell' Accademia dei Lincei* 29 (1974) 39-60.

[70] Cataudella, "Di un ignorato protreptico," 52-53 *et passim*. Numerous parallels between Chrysostom's descriptions of the monks and those in the philosophical tradition have been drawn in the notes to the translation below.

to those who tried to silence Socrates.[71] Then he quotes Plato's *Crito* (45bc) to demonstrate that the monk, like the philosopher Socrates, has a limitless supply of money at his disposal.[72] Similarly, the Cynic Diogenes is adduced as one whose "wealth of virtue," like that of the Christian monks, is envied even by the great Alexander.[73] Later in book two Chrysostom appeals to the glory of the philosophers Plato, Socrates, and Diogenes, a glory far surpassing that of the kings Dionysius, Archelaus, or Alexander.[74] Again, Chrysostom's point is to claim that the glory achieved by the Christian monks far exceeds that which can be gained in secular life.

It was shown above that Chrysostom knew Libanius' arguments on behalf of Julian and particularly Libanius' use of the figure of Socrates. The *Comparatio*, as I suggested, was a (Christian inversion of the pagan argument.) Chrysostom's willingness to address pagans directly in book two of the *Oppugnatores*, and especially his free use of the Hellenic examples of virtue, may indicate a similar encounter with Libanius. (The monks are portrayed as embodying the way of life espoused by the noblest pagan philosophers. Therefore, the monks represent a living argument for the virtue present in the Christian tradition.

Furthermore, it should be noted that Chrysostom's appeal to the Greek philosophers in the *Oppugnatores* is highly uncharacteristic of him. His more usual approach is to criticize the philosophers; he customarily either accuses them of moral turpitude or claims that their moral virtue was vitiated by their vainglory.[75] His positive treatment of the philosophers is virtually limited to these passages in the *Oppugnatores*. Why did Chrysostom choose only in this work to adopt such a positive stance towards these classical figures in the philosophical tradition? The answer lies in his (apologetic purpose.) The second book, aimed towards a non-Christian audience, bases its

---

[71] *Oppugnatores* 2.1; translated below p. 96. According to M. Crosby and W.M. Calder, Libanius took the silencing of Socrates as a symbol of paganism and Christianity in conflict. See their "Libanius' *On the Silence of Socrates*," cited above, p. 28, n. 64.

[72] *Oppugnatores* 2.4; translated below pp. 103-4.

[73] *Oppugnatores* 2.4; translated below p. 104.

[74] *Oppugnatores* 2.5; translated below pp. 107-8.

[75] A.M. Malingrey, "*Philosophia*" 267; see her "Le personnage de Socrate chez quelques auteurs chrétiens du IVe siècle," in *Forma futuri. Studi in onore de M. Pellegrino* (Turin, 1975) 170-74. See also P.R. Coleman-Norton, "St. John Chrysostom and the Greek Philosophers," *Classical Philology* 25 (1930) 305-17.

case exclusively on pagan grounds.   The parallel between
Chrysostom's appeal to the philosophers and that of Libanius is not
likely to have been unintentional, especially in light of the argument
of Chrysostom's *Comparatio*.

Before proceeding to the third book of the treatise, I would like to
present one further argument from book two for the apologetic nature
of the work. At the beginning of the second book, after stating that his
aim will be to address pagans, Chrysostom acknowledges that an
argument made entirely on pagan grounds will be more difficult than
one addressed to Christians. Nonetheless, he maintains, if the pagan
parent is willing to listen to his arguments with reason, "we will
quickly convert him (μεταστήσομεν) not only to a love of that way of
life, but also to the same enthusiasm for the doctrines which are the
foundation of that way of life."[76] Chrysostom explicitly states that the
purpose of his discourse to the pagan is not simply to endorse the
monastic life. He envisioned the work also as an argument on behalf
of the Christian tradition itself, designed specifically to convert the
pagan to Christianity.

The third book of the *Oppugnatores* addresses the Christian parent.
After a brief introduction in which Chrysostom argues that the
Christian bears responsibility not only for his own salvation, but also
for that of his fellows (sec. 2), he turns to the topic of child-rearing.
Citing several biblical examples, he argues at length that God has
placed the highest value on the moral education of young people
(sec. 3-4). He then launches an attack on the values which he believes
are characteristic of Christians at Antioch: "the love of money
and—what is even more wicked—the love of vain and empty glory."[77]
Chrysostom proceeds to argue that behavior which the Christian
typically considers civic virtue is actually vice (sec. 7); conversely, the
virtue displayed by the monks is true "philanthropy," as opposed to
the misanthropic luxury of the wealthy citizens (sec. 9-10).

In book three Chrysostom makes it clear that the lifestyles and
ambitions of the Christians at Antioch differ in no way from those of
their pagan counterparts. To attack the values of his fellow
Christians, therefore, is clearly one of Chrysostom's aims. But
Chrysostom seems to have another opponent in mind as well: the
Hellenic system of education. Here, perhaps, one may see another
encounter with his teacher Libanius. For imbedded in his polemic

---

[76] *Oppugnatores* 2.2 (Dübner 16).
[77] *Oppugnatores* 3.6; translated below p. 135.

against the love of money and of vainglory is a critique of the cult of
rhetoric or λόγοι.[78]

When he first speaks of λόγοι, Chrysostom links rhetorical
education with the vain pursuit of wealth, power, and worldly success:

> When parents urge their children to study rhetoric (ὑπὲρ τῆς
> τῶν λόγων σπουδῆς), all they say are words like these: "A
> certain man, of low estate, born of lowly parents, after
> achieving the power that comes from rhetoric, obtained the
> highest positions, gained great wealth, married a rich
> woman, built a splendid house, and is feared and respected
> by all."[79]

Later in the middle of speaking about the vicious character of the lust
for money and glory, Chrysostom also develops a lengthy attack on
pederasty, a vice he naturally associates with Hellenic education.[80]
While Chrysostom does not directly blame rhetorical education for
moral failure, he does argue that an education in λόγοι exposes young
people to moral dangers without contributing anything beneficial to
their moral formation.

Finally, Chrysostom addresses the issue of rhetorical education
directly in the light of its moral value. Responding to the objection of
his anonymous opponent, "Shall we completely eliminate education?"
he replies:

> I do not say this, but let us not destroy the edifice of virtue,
> nor bury the soul alive. When the soul is self-controlled, no
> harm will come from a lack of knowledge of rhetoric (λόγων);
> but when the soul is corrupted, the greatest damage will
> result, even if the tongue is quite sharp; indeed, the damage
> will be greater the more skilled in rhetoric he becomes. For
> when wickedness gains experience in speaking, it does far
> worse deeds than ignorance.[81]

---

[78] It has been argued that even Chrysostom's attack on the vice of vainglory is
directed against the contemporary exaltation of "glory" (δόξα) as a motive for human
action by Libanius and the emperor Julian. See F. Leduc, "La thème de la vaine gloire
chez saint Jean Chrysostome," *Proche-orient chrétienne* 29 (1969) 3-32, especially 21-32.

[79] *Oppugnatores* 3.5 (Dübner 42).

[80] *Oppugnatores* 3.8; translated below pp. 139-42.

[81] *Oppugnatores* 3.11 (Dübner 53).

Chrysostom goes on to argue that, while an education in rhetoric is not forbidden, rhetoric should be considered merely an external ornament, like plaster on a house which may be applied only after the walls are standing firm.[82]

It is difficult to believe that Chrysostom's attack on the pursuit of rhetorical education could have been written without Libanius in mind.[83] As was noted above, Libanius was devoted to the cult of λόγοι, particularly because of his belief in the moral value of Greek literature.[84] Furthermore, his literary and moral interests were inseparable from his view of the place of rhetoric in city life and its connection with traditional piety towards the gods.[85] Chrysostom's tack in the *Oppugnatores* is not to forbid altogether the learning or practice of rhetoric. No doubt he realized that such a position would be utterly impractical and, indeed, self-contradictory given his own ample use of sophistic devices in this very treatise.[86] But Chrysostom does radically devalue rhetoric. He strips λόγοι of any moral value and suggests that the pursuit of rhetoric exposes young people to the dangers of city life without offering them adequate moral benefit or protection. Chrysostom's point would not have been lost on Libanius. He attacks precisely that characteristic of *paideia* which, for Libanius, was its glory: the ability to form virtue.

To conclude this discussion, I would like to offer one further piece of evidence to support my argument. In section eleven of book three, Chrysostom again appeals to the Greek philosophical tradition to support his polemic against rhetoric. He mentions the Cynics Anacharsis, Crates, and Diogenes as examples of philosophers who cared little for rhetoric and who spent their lives in "the more ethical

---

[82] *Oppugnatores* 3.12; translated below p. 151.

[83] For a similar argument, see M. Soffray, "S. Jean Chrysostome et la littérature païenne," *Phoenix* 2 (1947) 82-85. Soffray notes John's hostility to rhetoric and links it to Libanius' defense of pagan religion.

[84] See above, pp. 5-8. On this dimension of Libanius' work, see the important study of B. Schouler, *La tradition hellénique chez Libanios*, 941-87. Schouler demonstates that the sophists of the fourth century, particularly Libanius and Themistius, were more preoccupied with the issue of moral formation than their second century counterparts.

[85] As I will suggest below, these various strands of Libanius' thought are woven together in his defence of the emperor Julian. See below, pp. 60-62.

[86] In his treatise *On the Priesthood* Chrysostom deals explicitly with the question of the use of rhetoric in Christian preaching. See the interesting commentary on this dimension of Chrysostom's work in R.L. Wilken, *John Chrysostom and the Jews*, ch. 4, "Fourth Century Preaching and the Rhetoric of Abuse," 95-127.

part of philosophy." Then Chrysostom refers to Socrates, citing a passage from Plato's *Apology* (17bc), where Socrates tells the court that he will forego elaborate oratory and speak plainly and simply.[87] Socrates refused to learn rhetoric, Chrysostom argues, not because he was lazy, but "because he did not think that it was very important."[88] Eloquence, Chrysostom writes, is not appropriate for philosophers, nor even for grown men; rather, it is an "ostentatious display (φιλοτιμία) of adolescents at play."[89]

Given the role that Socrates played in Libanius' own defense of Julian and the Hellenic tradition, and in light of the way in which Chrysostom used Libanius' argument in the *Comparison Between a King and a Monk*, it is plausible to see in the treatise *Against the Opponents of the Monastic Life* at least an indirect response to Libanius' own exaltation of rhetoric. Chrysostom's reply to the sophist's claims on behalf of pagan culture is that the monastic life contains the true, character-forming *paideia*. Again the Greek philosophers are invoked: this time to claim that even the finest representatives of Greek culture showed disdain for rhetoric and saw no intrinsic value in it. By denigrating rhetorical culture in this way, Chrysostom did not intend simply to urge the Christian parents to reform their lives; he wished also to demonstrate that pagan claims on behalf of the moral value of λόγοι were false.

Throughout the remainder of the third book, the monks are portrayed as pedagogues and teachers, the bible is depicted as an alternative to Hellenic literature, and the monastery is proposed as the appropriate place for a young person's moral formation.[90] Chrysostom even suggests that after ten or twenty years in the cloister the young man will be ready to return to city life and to serve as a "benefactor, patron, and savior."[91] Nowhere does the rhetorical character of Chrysostom's argument become clearer than in these final chapters of the *Oppugnatores*. There is no evidence that the

---

[87] *Oppugnatores* 3.11; translated below p. 150.

[88] *Oppugnatores* 3.11 (Dübner 54): διὰ τὸ μὴ μέγα τὸ πρᾶγμα ἡγεῖσθαι.

[89] There is a curious parallel between this passage and Chrysostom's apologetic work *De sancto Babyla*. In the latter treatise, after quoting at length from Libanius' *Monody* (or. 60) and ridiculing Libanius' defense of Julian, Chrysostom refers to the puerility of his teacher, citing a dictum of Plato's *Timaeus* (22b): "Greeks are always children; there is no old man among them."

[90] See, for example, *Oppugnatores* 3.12, where Chrysostom tells a story about the young man who remained in the city and studied rhetoric, but who had a monk as his pedagogue.

[91] *Oppugnatores* 3.18; translated below p. 168.

monasteries in the region of Antioch served as temporary schools for
the moral formation of young men, nor is it likely that Chrysostom
intended to be taken seriously.[92] His concern is to reform the lives of
Christians in the city, but to do so puts him at odds with the
educational system that shaped their values and aspirations.
Chrysostom's efforts at reform, therefore, necessarily involved him in
a debate over the moral values inherent in Greek culture. If my
argument in this chapter is correct, Chrysostom met the pagan claims
head on. The moral value of rhetoric is denied, and the monastic life is
portrayed as usurping the Hellenic task: the monk is philosopher and
teacher, the monastery is a school of virtue.

In the next chapter I will examine several other works of
Chrysostom which date from the same period as these monastic
writings. The purpose of that discussion will be to place these
monastic works within a larger context. We will see that
Chrysostom's blending of ethical and apologetic concerns was not
limited to the monastic treatises, but is found in other early works as
well. I also will suggest that Julian's pagan revival, and Libanius'
defense of it, had sharpened the issue for Christians, and for John
Chrysostom in particular. Before that task can be assumed, however,
an attempt must be made to date the treatises as accurately as
possible.

3. Dating

Neither the *Comparison Between a King and a Monk* nor *Against
the Opponents of the Monastic Life* can be dated with absolute
certainty to a precise year. There are indications in both works,
however, which enable one to make reasonably safe conjectures about
a general time period. The quotations from Libanius in the
Comparatio provide a firm *terminus a quo* of 363 for the composition of
this work. This was the year in which Libanius' twelfth oration was
composed. In the year 363, however, Chrysostom was still in the
middle of his rhetorical studies, and, although he could easily have
had access to Libanius' orations, it is unlikely that he would have

---

[92] See the comments of H. Marrou, "Antioche et Hellenisme chrétien. À propos d'un
livre recent," *Revue des études grecques* 76 (1963) 430-36. Marrou criticizes Festugière's
Antioche païenne et chrétienne for taking Chrysostom's recommendations too literally.
Cf. Marrou, *A History of Education in Antiquity*. Translated by G. Lamb (New York:
Sheed and Ward, 1956) 332.

undertaken such a polemic, even a veiled one, while still a student of Libanius.

Most Chrysostom scholars have been content to consider the *Comparatio* Chrysostom's earliest work and to place it in his monastic period, that is, between the years 372-378.[93] The theme of the work seems to imply a certain naive enthusiasm for monasticism, the argument goes, which is best explained if Chrysostom himself was still a monk when he wrote it. Further, it has been suggested that the theme of the superiority of the monk to the king (i.e., emperor) may have had a particular political aim: the emperor Valens, who occasionally resided at Antioch during these years, was hostile to monasticism. Therefore, Chrysostom had in mind a particular tyrant, Valens, to whom he contrasted the Christian monks.[94]

There seems to be no reason to doubt that the treatise is a very early work, probably Chrysostom's first literary effort. The artificiality of its structure, theme, and style suggests as much. My discussion above, however, demonstrated that Chrysostom's work also had an apologetic dimension: it was a response to Libanius' defense of the emperor Julian. A polemic against Valens, therefore, while not definitely ruled out, becomes less likely in this view.

The period during which Chrysostom studied under Diodore of Tarsus (367-371) may have witnessed the composition of the *Comparatio*. Indeed, Diodore himself had engaged in apologetic activity, and he was explicitly attacked by the emperor Julian for doing so.[95] Chrysostom's own apologetic interests may have been formed in Diodore's school. Further, a very early date for the *Comparatio* would explain why its style and language sometimes have been thought to be different from that of the other authentic works.

I would like to suggest, however, that a later dating of the treatise has several reasons to recommend itself. First, as we saw above, Chrysostom's enthusiasm for the monastic life did not develop

---

[93] For example, C. Baur, *John Chrysostom and His Time* 115; R.E. Carter, "Chrysostom's Rhetorical Use of the Socratic Distinction," 368.

[94] Carter, "Chrysostom's Rhetorical Use of the Socratic Distinction," 368-69.

[95] Julian, ep. 90 (Bidez): "For the fellow [Diodore] sailed to Athens to the injury of the general welfare, then rashly took to philosophy and engaged in the study of literature, and by the devices of rhetoric armed his hateful tongue against the heavenly gods, and being utterly ignorant of the Mysteries of the pagans he so to speak imbibed most deplorably the whole mistaken folly of the base and ignorant creed-making fisherman." Translated in W.C. Wright, *The Works of the Emperor Julian.* vol. 3 Loeb Classical Library (Cambridge, MA: Harvard University Press, 1954) 189. Nothing remains of Diodore's apologetic work.

immediately upon leaving the school of Libanius, nor did it cease upon
his departure from the monastic life in 378.[96] On *prima facie* grounds,
therefore, it seems more plausible to place the work either during or
immediately after his monastic sojourn. Moreover, given
Chrysostom's polemic against Libanius in this work, it may be
possible to connect the *Comparison Between a King and a Monk* with
the literary activity of Libanius.[97]

After the death of the emperor Valens, shortly after the accession of
Theodosius I to the Eastern throne (early 379), Libanius composed a
discourse, "Upon Avenging Julian" (or. 24).[98] In this oration Libanius
addressed the new emperor urging him to restore the memory of
Julian and to reverse the anti-Hellenic policies of Valens. For the first
time Libanius clearly accuses the Christians of assassinating Julian,
something he had only implied in earlier orations.[99] The recent defeat
of Valens by the Goths and other Roman disasters at the hands of the
Goths are attributed to divine wrath at the failure of the emperors to
avenge Julian's untimely death. Libanius urges Theodosius to
investigate Julian's death and to bring the culprits to justice. Julian's
concern for restoring temples and sacrifices, Libanius argues, merited
for him the special concern of the gods.[100]

Libanius had been virtually silent on religious matters since 365,
the date of his funeral oration over Julian. The death of Valens and
the revival of Libanius' defense of Julian may have been the occasion
which sparked Chrysostom's *Comparatio*. Libanius himself, a year or
two after composing the twenty-fourth oration, reveals that his views
on Julian had not been well received among the Christians.[101]
Further, there are several places in the *Comparatio* where
Chrysostom refers to the transitory and vulnerable nature of imperial
power which could be references to recent events. In one place he
writes that "the possession of rule is utterly destroyed with this life, or

---

[96] See above, pp. 9-17.

[97] I have advanced these suggestions in my article, "Borrowings from Libanius in
the *Comparatio regis et monachi*," cited above, p. 26, n. 49.

[98] This oration is dated by Förster to sometime before November 17, 379. See
Libanii opera, vol. 2, pp. 508-9.

[99] Or. 24.6-8, and especially 17-21. Cf. the comments of A.F. Norman in *Libanius.
Selected Works*. vol. 1 Loeb Classical Library (Cambridge, MA: Harvard University
Press, 1969) xxxvii- xxxviii.

[100] Or. 24.28, 35-37.

[101] See or. 2.58-61. This work is dated to 380/381. In or. 2.60 Libanius states that
his constant harking back to Julian's reign has earned him the epithet "tiresome"
(βαρύς).

rather it abandons those who desire it even while they live, and already (ἤδη) it has led some even into the greatest danger or disgrace."[102] Later he notes that, unlike the monk, the emperor "combats barbarians for the sake of seizing places or mountains or money, since avarice and desire for unjust power call him to battle. In such wars many kings, lusting for greater things, often have lost even what was present."[103] While such comments are commonplace in a rhetorical treatise of this type, it also is possible that Chrysostom is referring to the recent defeat of Valens at Adrianople.

If these suggestions are valid, the *Comparison Between a King and a Monk* would have been composed not long after 379. This would still place the work among Chrysostom's earliest writings. If so, it would have been written shortly after his return to Antioch from the monastic life in 378. While these arguments for a *terminus a quo* of 379 are not conclusive, they do provide a plausible *Sitz im Leben* for the composition of the *Comparatio*.

The same difficulty with dating also confronts us in the case of the treatise *Against the Opponents of the Monastic Life*. There are no clear and explicit indications which would provide an exact date of composition. Again, as with the *Comparatio*, most scholars have located the treatise among Chrysostom's first literary works, written while he still was living the monastic life near Antioch, that is, between 372-378.[104] It has been suggested that the abuse of monks to which Chrysostom refers at the beginning of his treatise is connected with an edict of the emperor Valens regarding the restoration of the city councils.[105] This decree, issued in Beirut, reads as follows:

> Certain adherents of inaction, by having deserted their communities' public services, strive to seize solitudes and secret places and under religion's pretext associate with bands of monks. Therefore, we have commanded by a considered precept that these and others of their ilk, when

---

[102] *Comparatio* 1 (PG 47.387).

[103] *Comparatio* 2 (PG 47.389).

[104] C. Baur, *John Chrysostom and His Time* 117. Roughly the same date is given by the following: B. de Montfaucon, PG 47.317- 318; L. Meyer, *Saint Jean Chrysostome. Maître de perfection chrétienne* (Paris: Beauchesne, 1933) xv; J. Dumortier, *Saint Jean Chrysostome. Les cohabitations suspectes* (Paris: Les Belles Lettres, 1955) 15; B. Grillet, *Saint Jean Chrysostome. À une jeune veuve.* Sources Chrétiennes, 138 (Paris, 1968) 12.

[105] See, for example, P. Legrand, *Saint Jean Chrysostome. Contre les détracteurs de la vie monastique* (Paris, 1933) 5-6.

caught within Egypt by the Count of the East, should be
plucked from their hiding places and should be recalled to
undergo their native municipalities' public services; or
pursuant to our sanction's tenor should be deprived of the
allurements of their familial properties, which we have
decided must be claimed by those persons who would be
about to undergo the public services of public duties.[106]

This decree, however, appears to be directed specifically to the
situation in Egypt; there is no mention of Antioch or Syria.
Furthermore, in the *Oppugnatores* Chrysostom does not refer to the
removal of monks from their solitudes to the city by the imperial
forces. He does not speak of any official persecution, but only of a local
and apparently spontaneous abuse of monks by the parents of
Christian children. In fact, in Chrysostom's work the monks are being
driven from the city, rather than taken to it. There does not appear to
be any convincing reason to connect Chrysostom's treatise with the
edict of Valens.

A.J. Festugière, on the other hand, places the work slightly later,
between Chrysostom's entrance into the diaconate (381) and his
ordination to the priesthood (386).[107] The issue revolves around a few
words which are the only possible indication of a date. In the first
book of the treatise Chrysostom expresses horror that the abuse of
monks takes place "in the middle of the cities while the emperors live
in piety" (ἐν εὐσεβείᾳ ζώντων).[108] Festugière claims that the
expression "to live in piety" can refer only to an orthodox emperor (i.e.,
Theodosius), and that the plural indicates the reign of Theodosius
with his son Arcadius, who was declared Augustus in January 383.
Therefore, he dates the treatise to the years 383-386.

Festugière's argument, however, is not airtight. Montfaucon had
already pointed out that orthodox Christians sometimes referred to
Arian emperors as "pious" (εὐσεβεῖς) meaning "Christian" as opposed
to "pagan," even though they were Arians. He refers to Gregory
Nazianzen's first oration against Julian, in which Gregory refers to

---

[106] *Codex Theodosianus* 12.1.63. Translated in P.R. Coleman-Norton, *Roman State
and Christian Church.* vol. 1 (London: SPCK, 1966) 322-23. The date of the edict is
January 1, 370; it was reissued in 373. See C. Pharr, *The Theodosian Code and Novels
and the Sirmondian Constitutions* (Princeton University Press, 1952) 351.

[107] *Antioche païenne et chrétienne* 192.

[108] *Oppugnatores* 1.2 (Dübner 3). Cf. 2.9 (Dübner 28): βασιλέων ὄντων εὐσεβῶν.

the Arians Constantius and Valens as "pious" emperors.[109] The context in which Chrysostom refers to the "piety" of the emperors likewise seems to indicate that he is referring to Christian, as opposed to pagan, emperors.

While Festugière's precise dates may not be entirely well founded, they are probably roughly correct. The style and greater sophistication of the *Oppugnatores* suggest that it was written after the *Comparison Between a King and a Monk*. The abundance of classical allusions and the lengthy citations of Plato and Josephus which appear in the treatise make it unlikely that it was composed while Chrysostom was living the ascetic life in his mountain cave. Chrysostom's concern with the pastoral problem of how Christians should live in the city and his willingness to engage in a literary defense of the monks are best explained if the treatise is dated to sometime after his return to the city in 378 and before his ordination to the priesthood in 386.

---

[109] PG 47.317-18. Montfaucon thinks that Chrysostom could be referring the persecution of monks under Valens and thus dates the treatise to Chrysostom's monastic period.

CHAPTER THREE

PAGAN AND CHRISTIAN AT ANTIOCH

1. Introduction

In the preceding chapter I suggested that the two monastic treatises translated here were composed with an apologetic aim: to respond to Libanius' defense of the Hellenic tradition, particularly the sophist's claims on behalf of the moral value of a Greek literary education. The purpose of the present chapter is to view these concerns of Chrysostom's within a larger context. In the first section I will show that in several other works composed during this period (c. 378-386) Chrysostom displays a similar blending of ethical and apologetic interests. Especially in his apologetic treatise *De sancto Babyla, contra Julianum et gentiles*, directed specifically against Libanius and the emperor Julian, Chrysostom is intent on demonstrating the superior moral resources which he believes are present in Christianity. Chrysostom's argument in the monastic treatises, therefore, can be seen as part of a broader apologetic effort against contemporary paganism.

The second part of this chapter will examine more closely the pagan apologetics of Libanius and Julian. I will show that Julian and Libanius defended the Hellenic tradition partly on moral grounds. Both men claimed that Greek *paideia* could make a person morally better and that this education surpassed what Christians could provide. I will suggest that it was precisely their identification of Hellenic culture's moral benefits and its specifically pagan character that shaped Chrysostom's early polemics against these pagans.

The third section of this chapter will relate Chrysostom's thinking on monasticism to the work of these pagan critics. Libanius and the emperor Julian included a critique of monastic life within their more general repudiation of Christianity. The monks are portrayed as rejecting all civic and cultural values; they are guilty of "misanthropy," the pagans will argue. Chrysostom's defense of the monks, on the other hand, can be seen as a response to the pagan view of the monks as misanthropic; the monks, he will argue, embody true "philanthropy." While the arguments of Chrysostom and his pagan opponents are cast almost exclusively in moral terms, the underlying issues are not ethical in a narrow sense. The opposition between monasticism and Greek culture, I will suggest, was rooted in a more fundamental conflict between an Hellenic ideal of civic piety and Chrysostom's conception of the Christian life.

2. John Chrysostom the Apologist

The years between Chrysostom's return from monastic life and his ordination to the priesthood witnessed the composition of several treatises. Some of these works dealt explicitly with ascetical matters, such as the two books *On Compunction*, addressed to the monks Demetrios and Stelechios, the two treatises on the *subintroductae*, the works *On Virginity* and *Against Remarriage*, the treatise and letter to the lapsed monk Theodore, and a letter *To a Young Widow*.[1] These years also saw the composition of two apologetic treatises, the *Discourse on Blessed Babylas and Against the Greeks* and the *Demonstration Against the Pagans that Christ is God*.[2] The two monastic treatises translated here, as I suggested above, probably date from this same period. Although ascetic and apologetic concerns might seem to be poles apart, I will argue that the two were closely linked in Chrysostom's mind at this time. The linkage can be found in the apologetic works and also in the ascetic works.

First, Chrysostom's early ascetical treatises present ample evidence of their author's concern for the moral life of Christians, especially as it was perceived by pagan critics. He frequently expresses concern that Christian misbehavior causes scandal among the pagans. For example, in his treatise against the *virgines subintroductae*, unmarried women who cohabited with male ascetics, Chrysostom noted that such illicit liaisons prompt "many accusations about the church community, giving unbelievers the opportunity to gossip, and

---

[1] See above, p. 1, n. 3.

[2] These two works have been translated by Margaret A. Schatkin and Paul Harkins in *Saint John Chrysostom. Apologist*. Fathers of the Church, 73 (Washington, DC: The Catholic University of America Press, 1983).

bringing everyone into bad repute."[3]   When an ascetic, allegedly devoted to the chaste life, displays such lust, Chrysostom writes, he "dishonors himself, harms those who are weaker, provides great opportunities to both Greeks and Jews, trips up both our own people and outsiders,...inflicts an unsavory reputation on the church community and provides many excuses for those inclined to licentiousness."[4]

The suspicious behavior of Christian virgins, however, was not all that was subject to the scrutiny of pagans. The lives of most Christians, Chrysostom tells us, have been examined and found wanting by those outside of the Church. In the treatise *On Compunction* Chrysostom notes that the great discrepancy between the way most Christians live and the words of Jesus causes scandal among the pagans:

> If someone should come to us from the outside ('ἔξωθεν) and should carefully examine both the injunctions of Christ and the confusion of our way of life, I do not know if he would find greater enemies of Christ than we. For we travel this road as if we earnestly wished to go entirely contrary to his commands.[5]

The entire treatise *On Compunction* is structured around a series of contrasts between the commands of Christ and actual Christian behavior.[6] Chrysostom's point is that Christ's words are a sufficient guide for action, but that Christians rarely follow them. "This is the life I now seek, which I see lying only in the scriptures, but nowhere in reality."[7] The result is a scandal to the pagans.

This same concern with pagan perceptions of Christian morality is evident in *Against the Opponents of the Monastic Life*. Early in the first book, after describing the persecution of monks by Christians at

---

[3] *Adversus eos qui apud se habent subintroductas virgines* 4. Translated in E.A. Clark, *Jerome, Chrysostom, and Friends* 75.

[4] *De subintroductis* 13 (Clark 203, slightly altered). Similar sentiments are voiced in another work against the *subintroductae: Quod regulares feminae viris cohabitare non debeant* 1.

[5] *De compunctione* 1.1 (PG 47.395).

[6] John treats in succession the verses of Matthew 5:21-22, 23-24, 39-42, Luke 6:28-32, Matthew 6:34, 7:1-2, 11:29, 7:6, and 7:12. Many of these are the same verses cited in the *Oppugnatores*.

[7] *De compunctione* 1.4 (PG 47.399).

Antioch, Chrysostom notes that such behavior causes pagans to believe that all Christians are "hostile to virtue and philosophy." If the Greeks should realize that Christians drive the monks away from the city, he writes, "they will think that we Christians are not human, but beasts and wild animals in human form, some wretched demons, and enemies of the common nature, and they will make this judgement not only about those who are responsible, but about our entire people."[8] It is clear that Chrysostom was concerned about how Christian morality was perceived by pagans; lax Christian morality caused pagans to deprecate Christianity.

The obverse side of Chrysostom's argument is that exemplary virtue could be used as evidence of the value of a religious tradition. This theme also is found in the early ascetical works, and in one case Chrysostom links it specifically with Libanius. In his letter *To a Young Widow*, in which he urges an anonymous young woman to remain unmarried, Chrysostom notes that Christian women who remained widows were admired and honored "not only among us who believe, but also among unbelievers."[9] He then recalls that his former teacher of rhetoric, "my sophist, who was of all men the most attached to pagan superstition," publicly praised Chrysostom's widowed mother Anthusa. When the pagan rhetor learned that Anthusa had remained a widow for twenty years, he is said to have exclaimed, "Bless me! What women there are among the Christians!" Such is the praise and honor which virginity enjoys, Chrysostom writes, "not only among us, but among outsiders (οἱ 'ἐξωθεν) as well."

Clearly, Chrysostom approached the issue of moral reformation with one eye on the pagan world. His exhortations to Christians on behalf of virginity, poverty, almsgiving, or other laudatory behavior are often accompanied by a reminder that pagans are judging their performance. The example of a virtuous life had apologetic value; it was an argument for the "goods" present in the Christian religion.[10] Conversely, Christian immorality told against the truth-claims of

---

[8] *Oppugnatores* 1.2 (Dübner 4).

[9] *Ad viduam iuniorem* 2 (SC 138.120).

[10] See, for example, Chrysostom's homily 43 on Matthew (PG 57.463-64): "Let us show forth a new kind of life. Let us make earth heaven. Let us show the Greeks how great are the goods of which they are deprived."

Christianity; it was evidence against the moral value of the Christian tradition.[11]

It is significant that in the letter *To a Young Widow* Chrysostom attributes to the pagan sophist the praise of Christian virtue. Although Chrysostom does not mention Libanius by name, it is virtually certain that Libanius is the former teacher he had in mind.[12] While the anecdote may not accurately reflect Libanius' own views, it certainly reveals that Chrysostom's enthusiasm for the ascetic life took shape in an apologetic context and that Libanius was not far from his mind. When the young John Chrysostom speaks about the apologetic value of Christian behavior, he instinctively thinks back to his former teacher.

I would like now to examine the two works of Chrysostom which are explicitly apologetic in nature. In both treatises the same ethical concerns are present. The two works also show evidence of a polemic against Libanius and Julian. In one treatise, the *Demonstration Against the Pagans that Christ is God*, the attack is implicit; in the other, the *Discourse on Blessed Babylas*, it is quite explicit. Both works, however, reveal that Chrysostom's apologetic arguments against the Hellenic tradition involved a rejection of the moral value of Greek literature and an assertion of the moral benefits of Christianity.

Chrysostom's significance as an apologist has been recognized only recently.[13] Questions of authenticity surrounded the two works which are clearly apologetic. Thanks to a pair of recent studies, both the authenticity and the apologetic nature of these two treatises have been brought to light.[14] An examination of these works reveals that Chrysostom has incorporated an ethical argument into his apologetics

---

[11] See, for example, Chrysostom's homily 10 on 1 Timothy (PG 62.551): "For those who are taught look to the virtue of their teachers. And when they see us manifesting the same desires, pursuing the same objects--power and honor--how can they admire Christianity? They see our lives open to reproach, our souls worldly.... How, then, can they believe?"

[12] See A. Nägele, "Chrysostomos und Libanios," and the arguments presented above, pp. 3-5.

[13] Cf. the comments of R.L. Wilken, *John Chrysostom and the Jews* 130-32.

[14] On the *Demonstratio* see P. Harkins, "Chrysostom the Apologist on the Divinity of Christ," in *Kyriakon. Festschrift Johannes Quasten* 440-51. On *De sancto Babyla* see M. Schatkin, "The Authenticity of St. John Chrysostom's *De sancto Babyla, contra Julianum et gentiles*," *Kyriakon* 474-89. Schatkin's discussion of Chrysostom's dependence on earlier apologists, especially Eusebius of Caesarea, is expanded in the introduction to her translation of this work in *St. John Chrysostom. Apologist.*

and that this argument is directed specifically against the contemporary advocates of Greek culture.

The *Demonstratio*, as Paul Harkins has noted, is largely concerned with arguing that the successful spread of the Christian movement is a sign of a divine power at work. The logic of the argument, Harkins says, is that the widespread growth of the Christian movement is evidence of the fulfillment of prophecy, both the prophecies of the Old Testament and those of Jesus.[15] While Harkins is certainly correct that the argument from prophecy provides the structure of the treatise as a whole, another line of argument also is evident which corresponds to the ethical one which Chrysostom displays in his ascetical works. At several points in the treatise Chrysostom refers to the moral benefits brought into the world through the preaching of Jesus and the apostles. In the opening chapter of the *Demonstratio* Chrysostom writes:

> I shall show that Christ is God....I shall show that it is not the mark of a mere human to call men to such lofty deeds, especially men who were preoccupied with such strange customs or, rather, men who were caught in the trap of such an evil way of life.[16]

Chrysostom's argument is not simply that prophecy has been fulfilled; rather, the ability of Jesus' teachings to convert people to a moral way of life is itself considered evidence of his divine origin.[17]

Chrysostom then extends the same line of argument to the apostles. They, too, he writes, although ignorant, poor, and unlettered, overcame the influence of longstanding evil habit (συνήθεια) and pleasure (ἡδονή) in their converts.[18]

---

[15] Harkins, "Chrysostom the Apologist," 443-47.

[16] PG 48.813-14. Translated in Harkins, *St. John Chrysostom. Apologist* 189.

[17] The argument, of course, is not a new one in the history of Christian apologetics. Similar comments were made by most of the early Greek apologists. Origen of Alexandria in particular made the issue of ethics central in his response to the criticisms of the pagan Celsus. See H. Chadwick, "The Evidences of Christianity in the Apologetic of Origen," *Studia Patristica* 2 (TU 64; 1957) 331-39.

[18] The same linkage of "evil habit" and "pleasure" is found in the *Oppugnatores* 3.6: "Habit (συνήθεια) is a terrible thing, terrible enough to capture and rule the soul, especially when it has pleasure (ἡδονή) acting in conjunction with it."

> For two tyrannical factors opposed this change: habit and
> pleasure. For many years their fathers, grandfathers, great-
> grandfathers, their ancestors, their philosophers, and
> orators had given them a certain way of life. Yet people were
> persuaded to reject this, even though it was a difficult thing
> to do.[19]

It is significant that Chrysostom portrays the evil which must be
overcome in terms of the inherited values of a culture, passed down by
previous generations and confirmed by pagan education:
"philosophers and orators." References to the philosophers and
orators abound in this treatise and in the other apologetic work, *De
sancto Babyla*. It is very likely that Chrysostom had Julian and
Libanius in mind.[20] The former was well-known as a philosopher, the
latter famed as an orator.

The argument of the *Demonstratio*, therefore, is not simply that the
spread of the Christian movement has fulfilled prophecy. Chrysostom
also argues that the teachings of Christ and the apostles provide
superior moral pedagogy. The apostles replaced the old familial and
cultural values with a "new habit" (καινὴ συνήθεια): fasting instead of
luxury, poverty instead of love of money, temperance instead of
immorality, meekness instead of anger, kindness instead of envy.
Moreover, unlike the "philosophers and orators," who merely
confirmed the accepted values, the apostles achieved their notable
moral results without the supposed benefits of Greek culture:

> And these men were unlettered, ignorant, ineloquent,
> undistinguished, and poor. They could not rely on the fame
> of their homelands, on any abundance of wealth, or strength
> of body, or glorious reputation, or illustrious ancestry. They
> were neither forceful nor clever in speech; they could make
> no parade of knowledge.[21]

---

[19] PG 48.830. Translated in Harkins, *St. John Chrysostom. Apologist* 240, slightly
altered.

[20] See, for example, *De sancto Babyla* 11: "The philosophers and talented orators
had a great reputation with the public on account of their dignity and ability to speak.
After the battle against us they became ridiculous and seemed no different from foolish
children." Translated in Schatkin, *St. John Chrysostom. Apologist* 82. Schatkin, p. 82,
nn. 25 and 26, suggests that Chrysostom may have had Julian and Libanius in mind.

[21] PG 48.830. Translated in Harkins, *St. John Chrysostom. Apologist* 240.

The parallels between this apologetic work and Chrysostom's monastic treatises should be clear. Chrysostom argues that the resources for moral formation lie not in traditional Hellenic education, but in the Christian religion. Furthermore, the contemporary advocates of Greek culture, "philosophers and orators," are held responsible for moral turpitude.

The same interest in demonstrating the moral superiority of Christianity over the Hellenic tradition is also vigorously displayed in Chrysostom's apologetic treatise *On Blessed Babylas and Against the Greeks*. In this work, however, the polemic against the emperor Julian and the sophist Libanius is made explicit in a way that is not found in any of the works we have studied thus far. This treatise, therefore, will be especially valuable in determining the character of Chrysostom's apologetic argument and the identity of his opponents.

De sancto Babyla was composed in the form of a panegyric on the martyr Babylas, but in reality the work is an apology for Christianity.[22] It begins with the "ancient history" of Babylas, bishop of Antioch, who died as a martyr, probably during the persecution of the emperor Decius. But Chrysostom also uses the "modern history" of the martyr's tomb, which the emperor Julian tried to remove from Daphne, to demonstrate that "Hellenism has been overthrown by the power of Christ."[23] Chrysostom tells of the emperor Julian's frustration at the silence of the oracle of Apollo, owing to the presence there of Babylas' relics. He also describes the temple's destruction by fire, when the emperor Julian removed the martyr's relics to Antioch. Chrysostom also mentions Julian's abortive attempt to rebuild the Jewish Temple in Jerusalem as another sign of the power of Christ over paganism.[24]

Chrysostom is partly interested in the miraculous elements of the story. But the argument from miracles is not his sole concern.[25] He also wants to demonstrate the moral superiority of Christianity

---

[22] M. Schatkin, "The Authenticity of St. John Chrysostom's *De sancto Babyla*," 477.

[23] *De sancto Babyla* 15 (PG 50.537).

[24] *De sancto Babyla* 119 (PG 50.567-568). For a discussion of the place of this event in Chrysostom's apologetic work, see R.L. Wilken, *John Chrysostom and the Jews* 128-60.

[25] Indeed, the argument from an historical event as miracle had its limitations; the pagans could simply offer a different interpretation of the same historical fact. This is exactly what the emperor Julian did. In his *Misopogon* (361b-c) Julian suggests that Apollo had already left the shrine before the fire occurred, owing to his annoyance at the presence of the martyr's bones, and that the Christians had probably set the fire themselves.

through the cult of the martyr and his relics. In the process of doing so, Chrysostom explicitly attacks both the emperor Julian and Libanius. He does this in several ways. First, the martyr Babylas himself is portrayed as a noble philosopher, whose example of virtue "demonstrated that the philosophers, of whom they boast, are characterized by vainglory, impudence, and puerility."[26] Chrysostom argues that Babylas exhibited the virtue of παρρησία and compares him to the ancient Greek philosophers Diogenes, Zeno, Aristotle, and Plato, all of whom he criticizes on moral grounds. As Schatkin has noted, "Chrysostom uses the principles of Greek ethical theory to demonstrate that the Hellenic ideal of virtue is realized only among the Christians."[27]

A similar argument appears later in the treatise when Chrysostom treats the moral power of the relics and tomb of the martyr. He tells how the suburb of Daphne, the site of the temple of Apollo, had become a place notorious for immorality among the youth. He attributes the moral decadence specifically to the influence of the pagan myth of Apollo and Daphne, whose memory was perpetuated there.[28] The shrine of the martyr Babylas, Chrysostom tells us, was constructed intentionally to combat this evil moral influence. The presence of the martyr's tomb is "one more way which the philanthropic God has given to call us to virtue."[29] Chrysostom even provides a sort of psychological analysis of the moral benefit derived from seeing the tomb of a martyr, a power which he says is second only to that of words:

> For the sight of the coffin, entering the soul, acts upon it and affects it in such a way that it feels as if it sees the one who lies there joining in prayer and drawing nigh. Afterwards, one who has had this experience returns from there filled with great zeal and a changed person.[30]

---

[26] *De sancto Babyla* 45 (PG 50.545). Translated in Schatkin, *St. John Chrysostom. Apologist* 100.

[27] *St. John Chrysostom. Apologist* 42.

[28] After recounting the story of Daphne and Apollo, Chrysostom exclaims, "This is the myth; but the evil which followed from the myth was no longer a myth." See *De sancto Babyla* 68 (PG 50.552). Translated in Schatkin, *St. John Chrysostom. Apologist* 115.

[29] *De sancto Babyla* 65 (PG 50.550).

[30] *De sancto Babyla* 65 (PG 50.551). Translated in Schatkin, *St. John Chrysostom. Apologist* 112.

Chrysostom goes on to describe the martyr's tomb in Hellenic terms as a good pedagogue, whose very presence rebukes the rowdy youth and calls them to moral conduct:

> Just as a youth at a party, who observes his pedagogue nearby exhorting him by look to drink, eat, speak, and laugh with proper decorum is prevented from overstepping measure and thus injuring his reputation, likewise as soon as one arrives at Daphne and sees the martyr's shrine from the entrance of the suburb, he is chastened and, becoming more pious by the sight and imagining the blessed one, immediately hastens to the coffin; and when he comes there, he is affected with greater fear, renounces all cynicism, and departs on wings.[31]

Chrysostom's argument in *De sancto Babyla* appears to be parallel to that of the two monastic treatises: superior resources for moral formation are said to lie in Christianity and not in pagan religion. Instead of the monastic life, another current object of devotion—the cult of the saints—is adopted for Chrysostom's apologetic purposes. The oracle of Apollo at Daphne, whose worship the emperor Julian tried to restore, is held responsible for the moral decadence of young people; the veneration of the tomb of the martyr Babylas is credited with moral reformation. The aim of Chrysostom's argument is clear: to demonstrate that Christianity, not Hellenism, contains the more effective means of moral pedagogy.

One further point must be made regarding the treatise *On Blessed Babylas*. In this early apology Chrysostom does not simply attack an abstract "Hellenism" as it was represented in the figures of the ancient philosophers or in the myth of Daphne and Apollo. He also attacks specific contemporary pagans, the emperor Julian and the sophist Libanius. I already have mentioned his polemic against Julian's removal of Babylas' relics from Daphne and Julian's attempt to rebuild the Temple in Jerusalem. But Chrysostom also attacks Libanius for his oratorical efforts on behalf of Julian and the cult of Apollo.

---

[31] *De sancto Babyla* 70 (PG 50.552). Translated in Schatkin, *St. John Chrysostom. Apologist* 115-16.

In *De sancto Babyla* Chrysostom quotes extensively from Libanius' sixtieth oration, the *Monody* on Daphne. The sophist is roundly ridiculed for his lament over the pagan temple and for his defense of pagan religion. Libanius' oration was probably written soon after the events it describes, that is, in late 362 or early 363.[32] Chrysostom clearly was aware that the work expressed Libanius' sympathy for Julian's pagan restoration. *De sancto Babyla*, therefore, reflects the same concern evidenced in the two monastic treatises, that is, to respond to Libanius' defense of Julian.

It may be significant that Libanius previously had spoken of the oracle of Apollo at Daphne in his eleventh oration, the encomium on Antioch. In this work, which P. Petit has called "a manifesto of the pagan party provoked by the arrival of Julian to power," Libanius had given a pagan interpretation of the shrine.[33] He described the temple's establishment by Seleucus as an act of piety towards the gods which gained for Antioch divine favors. A series of miracles, Libanius tells us, convinced Seleucus that the myth of Apollo and Daphne was true.[34] Building the shrine was one more step in Seleucus' work of Hellenization: "He left bare no place that was suitable for receiving a city, but in his work of spreading Hellenic civilization, he brought the barbarian world quite to an end."[35] Libanius clearly takes the shrine of Apollo as a symbol of the moral and spiritual benefits of Hellenism.

What is especially interesting, from the point of view of this chapter, is that Chrysostom criticizes Libanius specifically on moral grounds. He cites Libanius' lament regarding the destruction of the temple: "O Zeus, what a resting place for a weary mind has been taken away from us! How devoid of turmoil the site of Daphne and the temple more so.... Who would not have put off disease here? Fear? Sorrow?" To this Chrysostom responds:

> What sort of resting place has been taken away from us, scoundrel? How is the temple more devoid of turmoil and a harbor sheltered from the waves, where there are flutes, kettledrums, headaches, revelry, and drunkenness? "Who would not have put off disease here?" he says. Actually, which of your sympathizers, even if he happened to be

---

[32] Schatkin, *St. John Chrysostom. Apologist* 32.
[33] Petit, *Libanius et la vie municipale à Antioche* 206.
[34] Or. 11.94-98.
[35] Or. 11.103. Translated in Downey, "Libanius' *Oration in Praise of Antioch*," 664.

healthy before, would not have contracted a disease here and
the most dire disease?[36]

Libanius called the temple a resting place for the soul, Chrysostom
says. But in reality it was a place of passion, storm, and confusion.[37]
Libanius' respect for the pagan shrine, Chrysostom tells us, is like
that of madmen, who "do not perceive the true nature of anything but
decide contrary to the realities."

Chrysostom's intentions are plain. The Hellenic tradition,
specifically its contemporary advocates, the emperor Julian and the
sophist Libanius, are being attacked for their religious views. But the
particular mode of Chrysostom's argument involves an ethical
dimension: the pagans are criticized for maintaining beliefs and forms
of worship that contribute to moral decadence, and the Christians are
endorsed for possessing superior forms of moral pedagogy. In the
following section of this chapter I will turn to the writings of Julian
and Libanius and examine the pagan position on its own terms. The
pagans' defense of their own tradition will reveal itself to be
remarkably similar to that of John Chrysostom. But the reverse claim
will be found there. The moral value of Greek education will be
asserted and the moral poverty of Christianity maintained.

3. The Pagan Argument

This discussion of the arguments of Julian and Libanius will begin
with two preliminary observations. First, one needs to distinguish the
personal religion of the emperor from that of the orator. Julian was a
philosopher, who self-consciously molded his way of life, even his
physical appearance, on the ascetical models in the Greek
philosophical tradition.[38] His conversion from Christianity to
paganism happened as a result of his contact with the Neoplatonist
doctrines of the philosopher Maximus of Ephesus, from whom Julian

---

[36] *De sancto Babyla* 104 (PG 50.562). Translated in Schatkin, *St. John Chrysostom. Apologist* 136.

[37] *De sancto Babyla* 113. Chrysostom goes on to mock Libanius' portrait of the god
Apollo as "no better than a licentious youth playing the zither at noon" (Schatkin 142).

[38] Julian's scraggly beard and ascetic demeanor earned him the ridicule of the
citizens at Antioch. See his *Misopogon* ("Beardhater") 338b-339b.

acquired a lifelong interest in theurgy.[39] Libanius, on the other hand, shows nearly no interest in philosophy for its own sake, nor any influence of Neoplatonism; he even seems to have remained aloof from Julian's attempts to restore sacrifices at Antioch.[40] As a recent scholar has noted, Libanius "unlike Julian, worshipped Culture and stopped there."[41]

Despite these differences, however, it is legitimate to treat the two men as allies in opposition to Christianity. Libanius seems to have been the only pagan at Antioch with whom Julian felt at home; Julian refers to Libanius with great respect on several occasions.[42] Furthermore, Libanius was an ardent supporter of Julian from the very beginning of his reign and well after his death. Chrysostom treated the two together in *De sancto Babyla,* and Libanius was remembered by the church historians of the fifth century for his efforts on behalf of Julian.[43] The two men shared a common reverence for the culture of Hellenism and a common antipathy towards Christianity. Whatever their differences in personal outlook, they can be treated together as representatives of the pagan resistance at Antioch to which Chrysostom responded.

Second, it should be noted that Chrysostom's moral critique of the pagans is highly rhetorical and exaggerated. Pagans such as Julian and Libanius were no less critical of immoral behavior than the Christian preacher. They, too, condemned the pursuit of unjust wealth.[44] They also abstained from the sexual promiscuity associated with the theatre, dancers, and mimes.[45] They, too, criticized the widespread practice of pederasty.[46] Julian, in particular, was almost prudish in his observance of sexual continence, as Libanius pointed

---

[39] Julian's religious evolution has been traced by G.W. Bowersock, *Julian the Apostate* (Cambridge, MA: Harvard University Press, 1978). See also R. Browning, *The Emperor Julian* (Berkeley and Los Angeles: University of California Press, 1976).

[40] See the story in Libanius' autobiography, or. 1.121-122.

[41] P. Athanassiadi-Fowden, *Julian and Hellenism* (Oxford, 1981) 207.

[42] See, for example, Julian's comments in *Misopogon* 340d-342c; 354cd. Cf. Libanius, or. 1.129-130.

[43] See, for example, Socrates, *Ecclesiastical History* 3.23.

[44] See, for example, Julian's unsuccessful attempt to establish fair grain prices, which were constantly undermined by greedy citizens at Antioch: *Misopogon* 357d, 368a-371b. Libanius defended Julian's actions in or. 16.23-24, or. 18.195-197, and or. 48.17-18.

[45] Julian, *Misopogon* 340a-342c; Libanius, or. 1.12.

[46] Julian, *Misopogon* 346a, 359d, 354cd. A collection of texts of Libanius on pederasty can be found in Festugière, *Antioche païenne et chrètienne* 198-206.

out.[47] While Chrysostom criticized the moral laxity of the citizens of
Antioch and associated it with pagan culture, Libanius and Julian
saw the problem in a different light. The pagans asserted the moral
value of the traditional culture and maintained that Hellenic religion
and education was the antidote to the moral decadence brought by the
Christians.

I first will treat the works of the emperor Julian and examine the
moral dimension of his defense of the Hellenic tradition. Several
aspects of Julian's polemic must be noted. First, like Chrysostom,
Julian was intensely aware of the apologetic value of moral behavior.
In several works Julian lamented that pagans sometimes fell short of
Christians in displaying charity; thus they render Hellenism subject
to criticism.[48] By devotion to the poor, Julian noted, Christians "have
led very many into atheism."[49] Like Chrysostom, Julian contrasted
pagan and Christian morality and used the deficiency of the pagans as
grounds to exhort them to improve.

Julian's concern with moral reformation led him even to plan a
reform of pagan priesthoods. In a letter to Arsacius, high-priest of
Galatia, Julian outlined his plans and acknowledged their specifically
apologetic intent: "Hellenism is not prospering as I desire, and it is the
fault of those who profess it."[50] He urged the priests to cultivate
philanthropy and care for the poor, so as not to be outdone by
Christians and Jews: "For it is disgraceful that, when no Jew ever has
to beg, and the impious Galileans support not only their own poor but
ours as well, all men see that our people lack aid from us."[51] He
ordered the priests of Galatia to establish hostels in every city for
strangers and assigned measures of wheat and wine to be distributed
to the poor. His aim, as his Christian contemporaries recognized, was
to imitate the charitable institutions of the Christian church and
thereby to challenge the Christian claim to moral superiority.[52]

---

[47] Libanius, or. 18.128: Julian was so chaste that he could place his bedroom next to
a temple. Cf. or. 18.179: Julian would have preferred not to have married at all, and
after the death of his wife he chose to remain celibate.

[48] See *Misopogon* 363a and ep. 89.290a.

[49] Ep. 89.305bc.

[50] Ep. 84.429c.

[51] Ep. 84.430d. Cf. Bowersock, *Julian the Apostate* 88: "It is evident that the
humanitarian program of Julian was a calculated part of his scheme to wipe out the
Christians rather than any reflection of a basic generosity of spirit on his part."

[52] See, for example, the criticisms voiced by Gregory Nazianzen in his invective
against Julian: oration 4.111-112 (SC 309.266-270).

Julian's attempt to reform the pagan priesthood, therefore, was based on similar grounds as Chrysostom's effort to mend the lives of Christians at Antioch: the two shared a belief that the moral life was a sign of the value of a religious tradition. But Julian did not let the matter rest there. He also turned the ethical argument into a polemic against Christianity. In his *Contra Galilaeos*, an attack on the Christian religion which Libanius said surpassed even that of Porphyry, Julian developed several different arguments impugning the moral value of scripture and asserting the moral benefits of Greek *paideia*.[53] He attacked the biblical image of a wrathful God as unworthy, partly for moral reasons. No one who imitates this God can become virtuous, Julian argued: to imitate the God of the Old Testament is to become angry, capricious, and jealous.[54] Julian also quoted 1 Corinthians 6:9-11 to prove from scripture that Christians have always lived base lives. Paul himself admits, says Julian, that within the Christian community are idolaters, adulterers, homosexuals, thieves, drunkards, and robbers.[55]

But the most significant argument in the *Contra Galilaeos*, for the purposes of this chapter, is Julian's attack on the Christians for reading Greek literature. Julian argued that Christians partake of pagan education because they realize the superior moral benefits present there:

> You yourself know, it seems to me, the very different effect on the intelligence of your writings as compared with ours; and that from studying yours no man could attain to excellence or even ordinary goodness, whereas from studying ours every man would become better than before, even though he were altogether without natural fitness. But when a man is naturally well endowed, and moreover, receives the education of our literature, he becomes actually a gift of the gods to mankind.[56]

---

[53] Libanius, or. 18.178.

[54] *Contra Galilaeos* 171d.

[55] *Contra Galilaeos* 245c; cf. 238e. In the *Contra Galilaeos* 213c Julian criticized Jesus for failing to convert his fellow Jews: "Could not this Jesus change the dispositions of his own friends and kin for their salvation?" In 205e he pointed out that Christians do not even know whether Jesus spoke of chastity.

[56] *Contra Galilaeos* 229d. Translated in W.C. Wright, *The Works of the Emperor Julian*. Loeb Classical Library. vol. 3 (Cambridge, MA: Harvard University Press, 1954) 385-87.

Julian's point is clear: Greek literature contains all the resources
necessary for moral education and is the property of the pagans.

Julian then turned to the topic of scripture and challenged the
Christians to produce the same ethical results with their literature:

> Choose out children from among you all and train and
> educate them in your scriptures, and if when they come to
> manhood they prove to have nobler qualities than slaves,
> then you may believe that I am talking nonsense and am
> suffering from spleen. Yet you regard those chronicles of
> yours as divinely inspired, though by their help no man
> could ever become wiser or braver or better than he was
> before.

Julian's argument attacked the Christians on two fronts. On the one
hand, he asserted the moral value of the Hellenic tradition and its
superiority over Christianity. On the other hand, he argued that
Greek literature had a specifically pagan character.

Julian's argument, of course, was highly rhetorical and even self-
contradictory. Like Chrysostom, he molded his presentation to
whatever issue was at hand. When addressing pagans he pointed to
the deficiencies of pagan behavior and urged them to mend their lives.
But in his apologetic works he argued that pagans possessed the
superior means of moral pedagogy and that the Christians were
inferior. The same contradictions are found in Chrysostom's works.
What is important to see, however, is that both pagans and Christians
accepted the notion that moral conduct had apologetic value, and both
sides claimed that the *paideia* on their own side produced the better
results.

Julian's defense of Hellenic literature and his attack on Christian
scripture might seem to be solely a rhetorical argument. But Julian's
assertions did not remain merely on the level of literary polemic. He
also tried to make his point by political action. On June 17, 362 Julian
issued his famous school law, forbidding non-pagans to take municipal
teaching posts.[57]   While the edict itself did not mention Christians
specifically, a subsequent rescript made it plain that Julian's primary
aim was to exclude Christians from the schools.[58] Both the rescript

---

[57] *Codex Theodosianus* 13.13.5.
[58] Ep. 61c.423d.

and the edict state that teachers should excel in morality as well as in eloquence. "A proper education," Julian writes, "results, not in laboriously acquired symmetry of phrases and language, but in a healthy condition of mind, I mean a mind that has true opinions about things good and evil, honorable and base."[59] By a "healthy condition of mind" Julian no doubt meant that a teacher should be committed to the cultural heritage of Greece and its specifically pagan convictions. Unless a person accepted the truth of the Hellenic tradition, Julian argued, he was unworthy to teach.[60]

Cultivated Christians were quick to reject Julian's identification of Hellenic language and literature with the religious traditions of paganism.[61] As Gregory Nazianzen noted, Julian used the term "Greek" ('Ελλην) "as if it were a word for religious worship rather than for a language."[62] Gregory argued that Hellenism was simply a language, "the common property of all rational beings."[63] If Julian wanted to exclude Christians from the polished speech learned in higher education, Gregory suggested, he should have forbidden them to speak Greek altogether.

Gregory's criticism of Julian's edict might seem to have a certain force; after all, for generations Christians had partaken fully of the benefits of Greek culture without endangering their Christian faith. But Gregory failed to address the full intent of Julian's action. As R. Browning has written, "Classical culture was not just a matter of grammatical forms and literary genres. It comprised both factual knowledge—such as mythology and history—and a whole structure of values and attitudes."[64] Hellenic education served moral and social functions which the Christian church did not. It shaped an entire way of life which included service to the city and the requisite civic virtues. Julian could be answered only by a more fundamental critique of the Hellenic way of life and by a rejection of the pagan claim to form virtue. This was the intent of Chrysostom's early works, and his defense of monastic life in particular.

---

[59] Ep. 61c.422a. Translated in Wright, vol. 3, p. 117.

[60] Chrysostom was aware of Julian's edict and its intentions. See his homily on the martyrs Juventinus and Maximinus, martyrs under Julian (PG 50.573).

[61] Even some pagans found the edict offensive. See Ammianus Marcellinus, *Res gestae* 22.10.17, who condemns the school law as "inhumane and worthy to be buried in eternal silence."

[62] Or. 4.5 (SC 309.92).

[63] Or. 4.4 (SC 309.92).

[64] *The Emperor Julian* 173.

Before proceeding to the final section of this chapter, a few
comments must be made about Libanius' extension of Julian's
argument. In chapter one I sketched the outlines of the sophist's
approach to education.[65] Libanius believed that rhetoric, city life and
traditional piety towards the gods were intimately connected in a
single fabric of life which was Hellenism. Here I wish to point out that
from the earliest days of Julian's reign, and for more than twenty
years afterwards, Libanius extolled the emperor Julian as the model
of the social, religious, and moral benefits of Hellenism.[66] He did this
in two ways. In his orations on behalf of Julian, Libanius attributed to
Hellenic *paideia* the formation of Julian's ascetic character as well as
his pagan convictions. In Libanius' works, therefore, the emperor
Julian lived on as a symbol of the Hellenic ideal.

First, in his Julianic orations, which, as we saw above, Chrysostom
knew and imitated in his defense of the monks, Libanius had argued
that Julian's conversion from Christianity to paganism occurred as a
result of his encounter with the philosopher Maximus of Ephesus.
After receiving true teaching about the gods and the nature of the
universe, Libanius remarked to Julian, "you quickly cast off your
error and, lionlike, burst your bonds, released yourself from darkness
and grasped truth instead of ignorance, the real instead of the false,
our old gods instead of this recent intruder and his baneful rites."[67]

Libanius went on to say that the study of rhetoric and first-hand
acquaintance with Plato confirmed Julian's opinion that pagan
religion must be restored.[68] Julian's efforts to purge the army of
Christians and to restore sacrifices, Libanius argued, have caused the
inhabitants of the earth to be transformed from mere swine into
human beings. "The cause of all this," Libanius maintained, "is
eloquence (λόγοι), and with eloquence of every type you have
furnished your intellect."[69] In Libanius' view Julian's pagan
education and his pagan religion were intimately linked: λόγοι and
ἱερά were akin, as he used to say.[70] Contrary to the experience of
many Christians who could study rhetoric or philosophy without

[65] See above, pp. 5-8.
[66] As late as oration 2, composed in the reign of Theodosius, Libanius combined an
attack on Christian morality and the monks with praise of Julian and his attempts at
reform. See or. 2.30-32, 58-61.
[67] Libanius, or. 13.12. Translated in Norman, vol. 1, p. 9.
[68] Libanius. or. 13.13.
[69] Or. 12.91-91. Translated in Norman, vol. 1, p. 91.
[70] Cf. or. 18.157 and or. 62.8, and the discussion above, pp. 6-7.

danger to their Christian faith, Libanius asserted that Greek *paideia* was a specifically pagan possession, and he used Julian's conversion to symbolize this fact.

Second, Libanius also employed Julian as a figure of the moral benefits of Hellenism. In several orations he placed great emphasis on Julian's ascetic way of life in regard to drinking, gambling, and sex.[71] He praised Julian's sleepless nights spent in study and work.[72] As we saw above, Julian's deportment was described in terms which Chrysostom later could apply to the Christian monks.[73] But the crucial difference in Libanius' presentation is that the formation of Julian's virtue and nobility of character is credited to Greek *paideia*. Homer, the orators, historians, and especially the philosophers are held responsible for Julian's humanity (φιλανθρωπία) and clemency (ἡμερότης):

> Above and beyond all else, those divine spirits Socrates, Pythagoras and Plato and all the effluents from them hold a place in your understanding. They have entered into it and have rendered it fine and beautiful, as physical instructors do with the bodies they train.[74]

Clearly, Libanius' defense of the emperor Julian, like Julian's own anti-Christian polemic, was an attempt to claim for Hellenic education both a moral and a religious function. Morally, *paideia* was to produce citizens who could benefit themselves and others in a commonwealth based on piety towards the gods; religiously, *paideia* was to convert a person from the "baneful rites" of Christianity and induce true reverence for the gods. As Libanius claimed in his funeral oration over Julian, the pagan emperor embodied both of these tasks:

> He washed a sour story clean with sweet discourse (λόγος), casting out all that earlier nonsense and in its place introducing into his soul the beauty of truth, no less than if he had brought into some mighty temple statues of gods that had been in times past befouled and besmirched.[75]

---

[71] Or. 12.18.
[72] Or. 18.175.
[73] Or. 13.44.
[74] Or. 15.28. Translated in Norman, vol. 1, p. 165.
[75] Or. 18.18. Translated in Norman, vol. 1, p. 291.

As the foregoing discussion has shown, the pagan revival of Julian, and its continued support by Libanius, was an attempt by the fourth-century Hellenists to claim the literary and cultural tradition of Greece as their own unique possession. Julian's arguments on behalf of Hellenism were perpetuated in the work of Libanius, but in a new way. Libanius took the emperor himself as a symbol of the moral benefits of Greek culture and its specifically pagan character.

When the pagan apologetics of Julian and Libanius are viewed in these terms, light is shed on Chrysostom's argument. Both in the monastic treatises and in the *Discourse on Blessed Babylas*, Chrysostom attempted to show that the quite un-Hellenic cult of the martyrs and the monastic movement were new modes of moral formation, which belonged specifically to the Christian tradition. He also attacked the moral claims on behalf of Greek *paideia* made by Julian and Libanius. Chrysostom's argument, therefore, was both dependent on that of his pagan predecessors, as well as innovative. The structure of his argument and the notion that virtue could be a criterion of the validity of religious truth seem to be derived from his pagan opponents. The idea that the monastic life and the martyr cult provide new and superior forms of moral pedagogy was Chrysostom's Christian contribution to the discussion.[76]

4. Pagan Criticism of the Monastic Life

In the final section of this chapter I wish to show that the critique which Julian and Libanius issued against Christianity also extended to the monastic life. It was precisely the pagan belief in the social and moral benefits of Greek culture that led them to oppose the Christian monks. Julian and Libanius, who saw in Christianity a return to barbarism and a rejection of culture, attacked the monks as the

---

[76] The apologetic use of the monastic life was not entirely Chrysostom's creation. The idea appears to be present already in Athanasius' *Life of Antony*, where the ascetic hero is portrayed in terms consciously derived from philosophical models. Chrysostom certainly knew the work of Athanasius. See homily 8.4-5 on Matthew (PG 57.87-88), where he refers to the *Life of Antony*. In his or. 4.71-73 against Julian (SC 309.182-190), Gregory Nazianzen had cited the monks as examples of virtue superior to the pagan philosophers whom Julian proposed to reverence. There is evidence that Chrysostom also knew this work of Gregory. See J. Bernardi, "La formule ποῦ εἰσιν: saint Jean Chrysostome a-t-il imité saint Grégoire de Nazianze?" *Studia Patristica* 1 (TU 63; 1957) 177-81.

supreme example of all that was wrong with the Christian tradition.[77]
The monks incarnated the spirit of all that was opposed to Hellenism:
a rejection of city life and the benefits of Greek culture. It was only
natural that the pagans should single out the monks for attack. As I
will suggest, when Chrysostom comes to defend the monks he seems to
have in mind this pagan critique.

I will treat Libanius first, then Julian. In one place Libanius
associated the monks with the emperor Constantius, whom he
despised for neglecting the cities, the cult of the gods, and λόγοι. In his
oration 62, "Against Those Who Criticize His Teaching System,"
Libanius blamed Constantius for excluding philosophers and orators
from his court and thereby creating a shortage of jobs for his students.[78] Instead of persons trained in rhetoric, Libanius complained,
Constantius took as his advisors "barbarians and pestilent eunuchs;"
he sought out the monks, "those pale men, the enemies of the gods,
who frequent the tombs."[79] In Libanius' eyes the monks are symptom-
atic of the neglect of culture encouraged by the rise of Christianity.

In various other works Libanius blamed the Christian monks for
the widespread desertion of farmland,[80] for the wanton destruction of
pagan shrines,[81] and for interference in judicial matters.[82] In his
famous *Oratio pro templis*, the sophist's "desperate, last-ditch defence
of the institutions of his religion,"[83] he mocked the monks for
presuming "to commune among the mountains with the creator of the
universe."[84] Monks, he pointed out, were once craftsmen and manual
laborers (and, therefore, devoid of culture); now they "claim to

---

[77] For a similar argument, see P. Canivet, *Histoire d'une entreprise apologétique au
Ve siècle* (Paris: Bloud and Gay, 1957) 92-94. Canivet believes that the criticisms of
Christianity by Julian, Libanius, and others lived on and shaped the apologetic work of
Theodoret of Cyrrhus in the fifth century.

[78] Or. 62.8. Libanius argued that Constantius' behavior was quite logical for a
Christian since λόγοι and ἱερά were related.

[79] Or. 62.9-10.

[80] Or. 2.32.

[81] Or. 30.8-10. A similar critique is found in Eunapius, *Vitae sophistarum* 472.

[82] Or. 45.26. The intervention of the monks was certainly influential at times. One
example is after the riot of 387. See above, p. 12, n. 56.

[83] A.F. Norman in *Libanius. Selected Works*, vol. 2, p. 98.

[84] Or. 30.48. Translated in Norman, vol. 2, p. 145.

discourse upon heaven and its occupants."[85] Libanius took the monks
as a symbol of the decline of Hellenism and its gods.[86]

The same argument is found, with perhaps even greater
vehemence, in the writings of the emperor Julian. Like Libanius,
Julian criticized the monks for their inordinate social influence, their
penchant for "uttering divine revelations," and their collection of alms
on specious pretexts.[87] But Julian also explicitly attacked the monks
for behavior which undermined the life of the city and was inimical to
the values of Hellenism. In his letter to the pagan priest Arsacius,
Julian accused the monks of "misanthropy," the opposite of that
"philanthropy" which for Julian and Libanius was the characteristic
trait of Hellenism:[88]

> Some men there are also who, though man is naturally a
> social and civilized being, seek out the desert places instead
> of the cities, since they have been given over to evil demons
> and are led by them into this hatred of their kind
> (μισανθρωπία). And many of them have even devised fetters
> and stocks to wear; to such a degree does the evil demon to
> whom they have of their own accord given themselves abet
> them in all ways, after they have rebelled against the
> everlasting and saving gods.[89]

Julian here attributed monastic "withdrawal" to the action of a
demon. Because the monks have rejected the pagan gods, he argued,
they are led by demons into the vice of misanthropy.

The pagan criticism of the monks, therefore, is two-fold. First, they
claimed that the monks embodied vices inherent in Christianity itself:
a rejection of the gods, a search for virtue outside of the inherited
culture, allegiance to the heavenly over the earthly city. The
contempt for the monks expressed by Julian and Libanius, then, is but

---

[85] Or. 30.31. Translated in Norman, vol. 2, p. 129.

[86] Libanius goes on in or. 30.31 to challenge the monks to reveal which god was
truly responsible for the success of the Roman empire: the Christian or the pagan.

[87] Or. 7.224b-c.

[88] P. de Labriolle, *La réaction païenne. Étude sur la polémique antichrétienne du Ier
au VIe siècle* (Paris: L'Artisan du Livre, 1934) 418-19. See also G. Downey,
"*Philanthropia* in Religion and Statecraft in the Fourth Century after Christ," *Historia*
4(1955)199-208.

[89] Ep. 89b.288b. Translated in Wright, *The Works of the Emperor Julian*, vol. 2, p.
297.

an extension of their hatred for the religion which was threatening
the culture, religion, and way of life of the Hellenes. But by naming
"misanthropy" as the monks' cardinal sin, Julian reveals that the
point at issue between the pagans and the Christians is not simply
whether Christianity or Hellenism produces better people. At the
heart of the rival claims and criticisms is a more fundamental
argument about what constitutes virtue. For the pagans, devotion to
the traditional gods and to the social institutions of the Greek city was
paramount in their definition of virtue. For the Christians, at least
for John Chrysostom, the monks could be taken as ideals of virtue
precisely because they demonstrated in their lives the secondary
value of the earthly city.

It probably is no accident that in his treatise *Against the Opponents
of the Monastic Life*, Chrysostom engages in a lengthy defense of the
"philanthropy" of the monks, in contrast to the "misanthropy" of those
engaged in worldly pursuits.[90] Chrysostom no doubt was familiar
with the pagan criticisms. In the *Oppugnatores* he tries to invert the
pagan argument and characterizes the monks as bearers of the true
virtue of philanthropy. In the third book of the treatise, addressed to
Christian parents, Chrysostom even argues that the values of the
Christians at Antioch represent a complete reversal of those espoused
by the monks:

> [You] dress up vice in fine sounding names, calling constant
> attendance at the racetrack and theatre "urbanity," and to
> be wealthy "freedom," and to lust for glory "magnanimity,"
> and madness "confidence," and prodigality "philanthropy,"
> and injustice "courage." Then, as if this fraud were not
> enough, you also call vice by contrary names, calling
> temperance "boorishness," fairness "cowardice," justice
> "weakness," modesty "servility," tolerance of evil "lack of
> strength."[91]

As this text shows, it was precisely those forms of behavior regarded
as civic virtues by the Antiochenes which Chrysostom considers

---

[90] *Oppugnatores* 3.7, 9-10. Translated below, pp. 138-39 and 143-47.

[91] *Oppugnatores* 3.7 (Dübner 45). In a passage strikingly similar to this one, the
emperor Julian had contrasted his own ascetic demeanor with the vices of the
Antiochenes: *Misopogon* 351b. The crucial difference between Julian and Chrysostom,
however, is that Julian attributed to Greek *paideia* his own formation in virtue.
Chrysostom, on the other hand, argues that the monks can form authentic virtue.

inimical to Christian life. Conversely, the monks, who to all observers were uncivil and misanthropic, are defended as civic "benefactors, patrons, and saviors," that is, as epitomes of civic virtue. Chrysostom's response to the Christian parents reveals that the basic problem he faced at Antioch was Christian attachment to traditional civic and social values.[92] The pagan portrait of the monk as misanthrope would have been shared by large numbers of Chrysostom's fellow Christians.

Chrysostom's defense of the monks, therefore, while it embodies apologetic motives and was largely shaped by the pagan critique, ultimately has his fellow Christians in view. It is the Christian citizens at Antioch who still lead lives inextricably connected to the culture and institutions of Hellenism.[93] And it was this culture, his pagan opponents had taught him, which was at root pagan.[94] By choosing the Christian monks as ethical models representing the highest achievement of a Christian "culture," Chrysostom intended both to answer the pagan claims and to critique the Christian practice. While the monastic "philosopher" was portrayed in the garb of Hellenic virtue, Chrysostom wished to redefine that virtue. In place of the Hellenic commitment to the city and its life, Chrysostom presented a rival, "heavenly" πολιτεία.[95]

---

[92] See A. Natali, "Christianisme et cité à Antioche à la fin du IVe siècle d'après Jean Chrysostome," in *Jean Chrysostome et Augustin*. Actes du Colloque de Chantilly 22-24 Septembre. Edited by C. Kannengiesser (Paris: Beauchesne, 1975) 41-59. Natali, however, stresses that civic life at Antioch evidences a "laicized" (i.e., non-religious) character. He overlooks, in my estimation, the impact of the pagan views regarding the inherited culture.

[93] For the negligible impact of Christian convictions on the way of life of most Roman citizens, see A.H.M. Jones, *The Later Roman Empire, 284-602. A Social Economic and Administrative Survey* (Norman: University of Oklahoma Press, 1964) 971-83. More recently, see R. MacMullen, *Christianizing the Roman Empire* (New Haven: Yale University Press, 1984) ch. ix, "How Complete Was Conversion?," 74-85. MacMullen also denies that Christianity had made much impact on the daily lives of Christians in the fourth century.

[94] Cf. A.J. Festugière, *Antioche païenne et chrétienne* 9.

[95] See homily 1.4 on Matthew (PG 57.18-20), where the monks are portrayed as displaying the efficacy of Jesus' moral teachings by revealing the πολιτεία of heaven in contrast to the *Republic* (πολιτεία) of Plato.

CHAPTER FOUR

TEXTS AND TRANSLATIONS

This translation of Chrysostom's *Comparatio regis et monachi* has been prepared from the Greek text edited by Bernard de Montfaucon.[1] The text of Montfaucon was reprinted by Migne in the *Patrologia Graeca*, volume 47, columns 387-392. It is this version which is the most readily available and which has been followed here.

The translation of *Adversus oppugnatores vitae monasticae* has been made from the edition of F. Dübner.[2] Dübner based his edition on that of H. Savile, which he emended according to his reading of several manuscripts.[3] Dübner also included several columns of critical notes at the beginning of his edition.[4] This edition, therefore, while it does not correspond fully to modern critical demands, is the best text currently available.[5]

Neither the *Comparison Between a King and A Monk* nor *Against the Opponents of the Monastic Life* has been translated previously into English. Both works, however, have been rendered into several modern languages. A German translation of both texts was published by J. Fluck.[6] A Spanish translation by D.R. Bueno also contained the two treatises.[7] *Against the Opponents of Monastic Life* alone can be found in

---

[1] Paris, 1718. Monfaucon's edition was reprinted with revisions by J.A. Gaume (Paris, 1834). It is the latter version which appears in Migne.

[2] *Sancti Joannis Chrysostomi opera selecta.* vol. 1 (Paris: Editore Ambrosio Firmin Didot, 1861) 1-75. No subsequent volumes appeared.

[3] Dübner, v-vi.

[4] See pp. vii-viii.

[5] Cf. the comments of C. Fabricius, *Zu den Jugendschriften* 22-23.

[6] *Die ascetischen Schriften des heiligen Johannes Chrysostomus* (Freiburg-im-Breisgau: Herder, 1864).

[7] *Obras de San Juan Crisóstomo. Tratados asceticos* (Madrid: Biblioteca de autores cristianos, 1958).

the Spanish translation of L. del Paramo[8] and in the French translation
of P. Legrand.[9] The latter occasionally has been consulted in my own
translation.

I have translated all biblical quotations directly from the Greek. My
notations to the text are deliberately eclectic. They cover matters of style
and rhetorical devices, points of historical and theological interest, and
textual questions. Parallels to other works of Chrysostom have been
noted where they serve to illumine the meaning of the text, and classical
allusions have been identified, where possible.

---

[8] *Tratados de San Juan Crisóstomo contra los perseguidores de los que inducen a
otros a abrazarse con la vida monastica* (Barcelona, 1918).

[9] *Saint Jean Chrysostome. Contre les détracteurs de la vie monastique.*
Bibliotheque Patristique de Spiritualité (Paris: J. Gabalda, 1933).

A COMPARISON BETWEEN A KING AND A MONK

1. Since I see that most people love and admire things that seem to be goods, rather than things which are by nature beneficial and truly good, I think that it is necessary to say a few words about both of them and to compare with each other both that which the multitude neglects and that which they zealously pursue. By thus coming to know the difference between the two, we will esteem the one as worthy of zeal and salvation and learn to despise the other as worthless.

So, then, on the one hand, people love power and glory, and the multitude considers blessed those who rule provinces, who ride in splendid coaches, who enjoy the shout of heralds and a great bodyguard. On the other hand, the life of philosophers and of those who have chosen the solitary way of life is despised.[1] When the former appear, they attract everyone's attention. When the latter appear, they draw to themselves the eyes of no one, or of just a few. And no one wants to become like the latter, but everyone wants to be like the former.

But to possess power and to have command of a province is difficult and even impossible to most people, and those who wish to rule would

---

[1]The word "philosophy" for Chrysostom and his contemporaries designated the ideal of Christian perfection. While the term sometimes refers specifically to the monastic life, especially in Chrysostom's early works, it by no means was restricted to that sense. See A.M. Malingrey, *"Philosophia"*: *Étude d'un groupe des mots dans la littérature grecque, des Présocratiques au IVe siècle après J.C.* (Paris: Klincksieck, 1961) 263-88, especially 284-86. See also G.J.M. Bartelink, " 'Philosophie' et 'philosophe' dans quelques oeuvres de Jean Chrysostome," *Revue d'ascétique et de mystique* 36 (1960) 486-92.

need a great deal of money; but to choose the solitary life and to spend
one's life in the service of God is easy and equally accessible to all.
Moreover, the power of office is utterly destroyed along with this life,
or rather it abandons those who desire it even while they live; indeed,
already it has led some into great danger or disgrace. But the solitary
life even now fills the just with many goods, and when this life is over,
it conducts them glorious and joyful to the judgment seat of God the
Father. Then the greater part of those who rule will be seen paying a
great penalty for the actions of their lives.

Come, then, let us compare the goods of philosophy and the
apparent benefits of power and glory in this life; let us examine closely
the difference between these two goods, for they will be clearer when
set side by side. Or, rather, if you wish, let us compare the greatest of
goods—I refer to kingship—with philosophy; let us see the fruits of
each possession, examining carefully that which the king commands
and that which the philosopher commands.

So, then, the king rules over cities and regions and many provinces;
with a nod of his head he commands generals and prefects and armies
and peoples and senates. But the person who has given himself to God
and who has chosen the solitary life rules over anger and envy and
love of money and pleasure and the other evils, ever vigilant and
watchful lest he allow his soul to submit to wicked passions and his
mind to become enslaved to bitter tyranny. Having placed the fear of
God in command over his passions, he constantly thinks only of the
loftiest matters. Therefore, the king and the monk rule in ways such
that it is fairer to call the monk a king than the one who wears a
shining, purple robe and crown and sits upon a golden throne.

2. For he is a king who truly rules over anger and envy and
pleasure, who commands all things under the laws of God, who keeps
his mind free, and who does not allow the power of the pleasures to
dominate his soul.[2] Such a one I would gladly see ruling peoples and
earth and sea and cities and peoples and soldiers. For the person who
has put the reasoning power of his soul in charge of his passions also

---

[2]Here Chrysostom borrows a phrase from Libanius' portrait of the emperor Julian.
See Libanius, or. 12.101 (Förster 2, p. 45) and the discussion of these quotations in the
introduction above, pp. 25-29. This is one of the several examples of such borrowings
discovered by C. Fabricius, "Vier Libaniusstellen bei Johannes Chrysostomos,"
Symbolae Osloenses 33 (1957) 135-36; id., *Zu den Jugendschriften des Johannes
Chrysostomos* (Lund: Gleerup, 1962) 118-21. See also my discussion in "Borrowings
from Libanius in the *Comparatio regis et monachi* of St. John Chrysostom," *Journal of
Theological Studies* n.s. 39 (1988) 525-31.

will more easily rule over men as well with the divine laws, so that he will be to the ruled as a father, frequenting the cities with all kindness. But the one who seems to rule over men, but who is enslaved to anger and the love of power and pleasures, first will appear quite ridiculous to his subjects, since he wears a crown of gems and gold but is not crowned with moderation, since his whole body shines with a purple robe, but he has a disarrayed soul.[3] Second, he will not even know how to administer his command. For if a person is unable to rule himself, how can he guide others rightly by the laws?

But if you wish also to see each one conducting himself in warfare, you will find the one fighting demons and prevailing and conquering and crowned by Christ.[4] For he enters into battle with divine help, fortified with heavenly arms, so that victory inevitably comes to him, whereas the king fights with barbarians. As much as demons are more formidable than men, so much more glorious is the one who conquers the former than the one who overcomes the latter.

But if you wish to examine the cause of war in each case, you will find a great disparity. For the one battles demons for the sake of piety and the worship of God, desiring to snatch either cities or villages from error. But the other combats barbarians for the sake of siezing places or mountains or money, for avarice and desire for unjust power call him to battle. In such wars many kings, lusting for greater things, often have lost even what was present. Therefore, the power of each and the enemies of each have revealed what a great difference there is between the king and the person who is eager to spend his life in the service of God.

You can recognize them clearly by looking at each one's way of life and at their conduct during the day. For, in truth, you will find the one engaged with the prophets, adorning his soul with the wisdom of Paul, continually jumping about from Moses to Isaiah, and from Isaiah to John, and from John to another. But the king is continually involved with commanders and prefects and bodyguards. But when a person is continually engaged with others, he becomes like them in character. Accordingly, the monk models his disposition after the characteristics of the prophets and apostles, but the king after those of

---

[3]Fabricius, *Zu den Jugendschriften* 119, sees in the words "disarrayed soul" (ψυχὴν ἀκόσμητον) the influence of Plato, *Gorgias* 506e.

[4]The monk as a warrior against demons was a popular theme in fourth-century monastic literature. See, for example, the combats described in Athanasius, *Life of Antony* 6-9 and Theodoret, *Religious History*, Prol. 4-6.

soldiers and bodyguards and armor-bearers, men who are enslaved to
wine, who gratify their pleasures, and who spend the greater part of
the day drinking, knowing nothing noble or more proper to do on
account of the wine.[5] Therefore, this is another reason why it is fitting
that the monastic life should be called blessed rather than the life
spent in power and kingship.

3. But if we wished also to examine the nighttime, we would see the
monk adorned with the worship of God and with prayers, singing
much earlier than the birds,[6] living with the angels, conversing with
God, enjoying the goods of heaven. But he who commands many
nations and peoples and armies, who rules over much land and sea,
him you will see stretched out on a couch snoring. For the monk feeds
on foods which do not demand a deep sleep, whereas luxurious food
puts the king to sleep, and drink keeps him in bed even until day.
Therefore, the monk has moderate clothing and food, and his table-
companions are athletes of virtue.[7] But the king needs to be adorned
with gems and gold; he must spread a glorious table and, if he is
imprudent, employ companions who are worthy of his own
wickedness. But if he is reasonable and temperate, perhaps they will
be good and just, but still quite inferior to the virtue of the monks.

Therefore, even if a king philosophizes, he will not be able to
approach even slightly the beauty and goodness of the monk.[8] For
even when travelling the king is burdensome to his subjects, when he
dwells in the city, both in peacetime and wartime, when he exacts
tribute and organizes armies and takes conscripts, when he conquers
and when he is vanquished. For when he is vanquished, he fills his
subjects with his own misfortunes, but when he conquers he becomes
unbearable, adorning himself with trophies, becoming haughty,
allowing his soldiers license to plunder, despoil, and injure wayfarers,
to beseige idle cities, to ruin the households of the poor, to exact each
day from those who have received him what no law allows, on the
pretext of some ancient custom, illegal and unjust. And the king does

---

[5]The addiction of soldiers to drink was proverbial, though perhaps not inaccurate.
See Libanius, or. 46.13-14 and the comments of R.A. Pack, *Studies in Libanius and
Antiochene Society under Theodosius* (University of Michigan, 1935) 17.

[6]"Singing much earlier than the birds" is another phrase which Chrysostom has
borrowed from Libanius' descriptions of the emperor Julian. See Libanius, or. 12.94
(Förster 2, p. 42) and the discussion above, pp. 26-27.

[7]Another echo of Libanius: or. 13.44 (Förster 2, pp. 78-79).

[8]"Beauty and goodness" (καλοκαγαθία) was a traditional description of noble
character. Cf. Plato, *Timaeus* 88c.

no harm to the wealthy with such evils, but he injures the poor, as if he were actually ashamed before the wealthy.[9]

But the monk does not act this way. As soon as he appears, he wins the favor of rich and poor alike; he approaches them each in the same way, using one cloak the whole year long, drinking water with greater pleasure than others drink marvellous wine,[10] asking of the wealthy no favor for himself, neither great nor small, but for those in need he continually seeks many favors. He is a source of profit, both to those who provide and to those who intend to receive. Thus he is the common healer of rich and poor alike, freeing the former from sins through a good warning, relieving the latter's poverty.[11]

But if the king orders a remission of taxes, he benefits the rich rather than the poor, whereas if he does the opposite he harms those who possess little. For harsh taxation would harm the wealthy a little, but it will sweep away the households of the poor like a torrent, filling the countrysides with lamentation. And tax-collectors pity neither the elderly, nor widowed women, nor orphaned children, but they make merry the whole time, the common enemy of the countryside, exacting from the farmers what the earth has not produced.[12]

4. But now let us examine the benefits which the monk and the king bestow on their subjects. The one has gold, but the other the grace of the Spirit. The king alleviates poverty, if he is good, but the monk by his prayers will set free souls who are tyrannized by demons. And if it should happen that a person is distressed by such calamities,

---

[9]On the difficulties experienced by the citizens of Antioch in supporting imperial armies, see Libanius, or. 49.2 and the discussion in J.H.W.G. Liebeschuetz, *Antioch. City and Imperial Administration in the Later Roman Empire* (Oxford: Clarendon Press, 1972) 161-66.

[10]Here Chrysostom borrows from Libanius' description of Socrates in declamation 1, the *Apologia Socratis* (Förster 5, p. 24). See the discussion in the introduction above, pp. 27-28. A similar description of Socrates appears in Chrysostom's *Against the Opponents of the Monastic Life* 2.5, translated below pp. 107-8.

[11]The social role of the monk as advocate for the poor has been admirably described by P. Brown, "The Rise and Function of the Holy Man in Late Antiquity." See the discussion above, pp. 12-13.

[12]In or. 2.32, dated 381, Libanius speaks of villages deserted because of harsh taxation. He adds, however, that the effects of the activities of the monks are worse: "Nowadays...you can go through miles of deserted farmland. The burden of taxation has emptied it and there is another and worse trouble besides,--that crew who pack themselves tight into caves, those models of sobriety, only so far as their dress is concerned." Tr. by A.F. Norman, *Libanius. Selected Works.* Loeb Classical Library, v. 2 (Cambridge: Harvard University Press, 1977) 27.

he bypasses the king as if he were dead and flees to the dwelling of the monks, just as someone escaping a wolf flees to the hunter who carries a sword in his hand. For prayer is to a monk what a sword is to a hunter. In fact, a sword is not so fearsome to the wolves as the prayers of the just are to the demons. Therefore, not only do we flee to the holy monks in times of need, but even the kings themselves flee to them when they are afraid, like beggars to the houses of the wealthy in times of famine.

Did not Achab, the king of the Jews, during a famine and drought have hope of salvation in the prayers of Elijah?[13] Did not Hezekiah, who held the same office and position, when he was sick and about to die, seeing death pressing upon him, flee to the prophet, as if he were mightier than death and a bestower of life?[14] And once, when war had broken out and Palestine was in danger of being razed to its foundations, the kings of the Jews abandoned the army and infantry and archers and horsemen and generals and centurions and fled to the prayers of Elisha.[15] For they thought that the servant of God could stand in place of many thousands. Hezekiah did the same thing when the Persian war was being fought: when the city had fallen into the greatest danger with respect to its foundations,[16] as those at the walls trembled and feared and shook, as if in expectation of thunder or an earthquake shaking everything, the king set the prayers of Isaiah in opposition to the many thousands of Persians.[17] And his hope did not deceive him! For as soon as the prophet raised his hands to heaven, God ended the Persian war with arrows from heaven.[18] Thus God taught the kings to regard those who serve him as the common saviors of the earth, so that being exhorted by the just to every good and charitable action, they might learn to honor their counsels and obey good admonitions.

---

[13]Cf. 1 Kings 17-18.

[14]Cf. 2 Kings 20: 1-11.

[15]Possibly a reference to 2 Kings 3, although the details given by Chrysostom differ significantly from the biblical account.

[16]Fabricius, *Zu den Jugendschriften* 119, has identified this clause as a borrowing from Demosthenes, 26.11. Libanius imitates the same passage in or. 16.5 (Förster 2, p. 162).

[17]Cf. 2 Kings 19: 1-4.

[18]Cf. 2 Kings 19: 35-36. Chrysostom refers to the destruction of the Assyrian army of Sennacherib. The accounts in 2 Kings 19 and 2 Chronicles 32 do not speak of "arrows from heaven," but rather of "the angel of the Lord." See also Isaiah 36-37.

Furthermore, not only do the foregoing considerations allow us to see the difference between the king and the monk, but also if it should happen that both of them should fall—the one deprived of virtue and the other of kingship—the monk would come to his senses more easily and, after quickly rubbing away his sins through prayer and tears and grief and care for the poor, he would easily return again to his previous rule. But if the king should fall, he would require many allies and a great quantity of soldiers, horsemen, horses, money, and dangers. And his hope of salvation lies entirely in others. But the monk will have salvation immediately consequent upon his own will, zeal, and conversion of heart.[19] *For the kingdom of heaven*, he says, *is within you.*[20]

And death is fearsome to the king, but painless to the one who philosophizes. For the person who despises wealth and pleasure and luxury, for the sake of which the multitude desires to live, will necessarily bear more easily the departure from that state.[21] But if it should happen that both of them are murdered, the monk will welcome dangers for the sake of piety, laboring for an immortal and heavenly life through death. But the king will have as his murderer some tyrant who lusts for power, and he will become a pitiable and horrible spectacle after the murder. But to see the monk murdered for the sake of piety is a sweet and saving spectacle. And the monk will have many who admire and imitate his goods and many disciples who pray to prove themselves his equal. But the king would utter many words in prayer, begging God that no one should appear desirous of kingship. Moreover, no one would dare to kill the monk, knowing that it would be impiety against God to snatch away such a person. But many murderers have attacked the king out of a desire for tyranny. That is why the king is guarded by soldiers, while the monk fortifies cities with his prayers, fearing no one. But the king lives in constant

---

[19]Like most of the Greek Fathers, Chrysostom has a positive estimation of the resources of human nature and the power of human choice (προαίρεσις) for the good. See the comments of J. Dumortier, "Les idées morales de saint Jean Chrysostome," *Mélanges de science religieuse* 12 (1955) 30-32.

[20]Luke 17:21. See Athanasius, *Life of Antony* 20 for a similar use of the Lukan text: "Greeks go abroad and cross the sea to study letters; but we have no need to go abroad for the Kingdom of Heaven nor to cross the sea to obtain virtue. The Lord has told us in advance: *The Kingdom of Heaven is within you.*" Tr. by R.T. Meyer, *St. Athanasius. The Life of St. Anthony.* Ancient Christian Writers, 10 (Westminster, Maryland: The Newman Press, 1950) 37.

[21]Another echo from Libanius, *Apologia Socratis*, decl. 1.3 (Förster 5, p. 15). See above, p. 28.

fear and anticipation of murder. For the one has a dangerous abundance, but the other a safe salvation.

Therefore, it seems to me that enough has been said about matters in the present life. But if we wished also to investigate the future contest, we will see the monk, glorious and admired, taken up into the clouds to meet the Lord in heaven, following the lead and instruction of all virtue and of that saving way of life. But even if the king appears to have administered his reign justly and with philanthropy (and this is very rare), he will receive the least degree of salvation and honor. For they are not equal; no, not equal are a good king and the monk who lives completely for the service of God. But if the king proves to have been wicked and ill-behaved, having filled the earth with many evils, who could tell the calamities which one could see afflicting him—burned, beaten, tortured, suffering such things which can neither be described in words, nor endured in reality?

Those who have pondered all these things and learned from them ought not to admire the wealthy. For the one who appears to be master of these things cannot approach even slightly the virtue of the monk. Therefore, whenever you see a rich man in fancy clothes, adorned with gold, riding in a carriage, making splendid processions, do not consider the man blessed. For wealth is transitory, and what seems to be good perishes along with this life. But when you see the monk walking alone, meek and humble and tranquil and gentle, emulate the man, show yourself to be an imitator of his philosophy, pray to become like the just man. For *ask*, he says, *and it will be given to you.*[22] For these things are truly good and saving and lasting, through the philanthropy and providence of Christ, to whom be glory and power for ever and ever. Amen.

---

[22]Matthew 7:7.

AGAINST THE OPPONENTS OF THE MONASTIC LIFE

Book One

When the children of the Hebrews had returned from their long capitivity and wished to rebuild the Temple in Jerusalem which had been razed to the ground many years earlier, certain cruel barbarians, who did not respect God for whom the Jews had erected the Temple, who did not pity the calamity of the people from which they had only recently been restored, who did not fear the punishment which God sends upon people who dare such deeds, first attempted on their own to hinder those rebuilding the temple.[1] But when these efforts failed, they sent a letter to their king in which they accused the city of Jerusalem of being rebellious, revolutionary and desirous of war, and they persuaded him to allow them to disrupt the building.[2] After receiving this charge from the king, and after providing themselves with a large cavalry, they interrupted the work for a while. Priding themselves on the great victory over which they ought to have grieved, they thought that their plot had come to a fine end.

But this was just the beginning, merely the prelude to the evils which were soon to befall them. For the work was completed and achieved an illustrious end. And those barbarians learned, and through them all learned, that whoever chooses to oppose those who desire to do something good—whether Mithridates or anyone else— opposes not simply human beings, but God himself who is honored by them.[3] Nor is it possible for someone who opposes God to come to a

---

[1] See Ezra 4:1-5. Cf. Josephus, *Antiquities* 11.19-30.

[2] The text of the letter is given in Ezra 4:11-16. It is addressed to Artaxerxes I (464-423 BCE.).

[3] Mithridates, one of the authors of the letter to Artaxerxes, was treasurer to Cyrus. See Ezra 1:8 and 1 Esdras 2:10, 15.

good end. Perhaps at the beginning of his reckless venture such a
person will experience nothing terrible; but if he does not suffer
immediately, God is calling him to repentance and allowing him to
recover, as if from drunkenness. But if he persists in his drunken fit,
deriving no profit from such forbearance, at least he will benefit
others in the highest way, teaching them by his own punishment
never to wage war against God, for no one escapes that invincible
hand.

In any case, the enemies of the Jews were immediately beset by
misfortunes so great as to obscure the tragedies in their scope.[4] For
after the bloodshed and immense carnage which they suffered at the
hands of the Jews who had once been hindered, the earth became
soaked to a great depth with the blood of the slaughtered men, and
from this blood a great mire was formed. The bodies of the horses and
the men were mingled together so that out of these bodies and out of
the wounds inflicted on them such a great swarm of worms was
produced that the earth was covered both with the pile of dead bodies
and with the swarm of worms which covered the bodies. Anyone who
saw this field would have said that there were not dead bodies lying
beneath it, but rather many streams which produced this type of
animal everywhere, for the swarm of worms gushed forth from that
putrification with greater force than from any fountain. And this
happened not merely for ten or twenty days, but for a long time.

Such was their punishment in this life. But what shall happen to
them in the next life will be much worse than this. For then it will not
be one thousand years, nor ten thousand, nor twice or three times that
number, but for endless ages their reanimated bodies will be subjected
to tortures and unspeakable suffering. And the blessed Isaiah knew of
this double punishment; so, too, did Ezekiel, the seer of incredible
visions; between them both they describe the punishments people
suffer: one told of the punishments in this life, the other told of the
hereafter.

2. But I have not recalled these events at this time for no reason,
but because someone has come and announced to us harsh and bitter

---

[4] The gruesome account which follows is found neither in the biblical version of
Ezra, nor in Josephus or 1 Esdras. Josephus, *Antiquities* 11.114-119, adds only that the
Samaritans were compelled to pay for sacrifices in the newly-rebuilt Temple. The battle
scene is entirely Chrysostom's own creation, an example of a rhetorical 'ἔκφρασις, or
elaborate description. Such devices were exercises (προγυμνάσματα) practiced by young
men in the rhetorical schools. Cf. the examples in Libanius, *Opera* (Förster 8, pp. 460-
546): land battles, horse-races, drunkenness, harbors, gardens, etc.

news, news which reveals great arrogance toward God. Certain people in our own day dare to do the very same deeds as those barbarians, indeed much more lawless deeds than they. On every side they drive away those who lead others to philosophy, and with many threats they forbid them to speak at all or to teach anyone anything like it. As soon as I heard this, I cried out and continually asked the messenger whether he said these things in jest. "Far be it from me," he said, "ever to joke about something like this! Nor would I even think of making up stories about such matters which I consider so important, and which I have prayed many times not even to hear now that they have happened."

Then I cried out more bitterly and said: "Truly, these events are even more sacriligious than the efforts of Mithridates and all the rest, inasmuch as this temple is much holier and more sacred than that one. But who are these people, tell me, and where do they come from, those who dare to do such things? Why do they do it, for what sort of reason? For what purpose do they throw stones against the God of peace? Samsas and the Pharasthians and the leaders of the Assyrians and all the rest were barbarians, as their names indicate, and they were trained in a manner far different from the Jewish way of life.[5] They did not wish to see their neighbors grow stronger, for they believed that the power of the Jews might in the future overshadow their own. But these people today, who have less freedom and more restricted license, have they any of the rulers as their accomplices in this bold undertaking? The opponents of the Jews had the Persian kings as their allies. But our rulers both desire and profess the opposite intentions, as I believe. That is why I am filled with so much distress when you say that such things were done in the middle of the cities while the emperors live in piety."[6]

Then he said, "If you think that is incredible, listen to this. Those who are doing such things pretend to be pious and call themselves Christian, and many of them have already been baptized. One of them, certainly inspired by the devil, even dared to say with his defiled tongue that he would withdraw from the faith and sacrifice to

---

[5] "Samsas" (Dübner: Σάμσας) is probably a reference to Shimshai (LXX: Σαμσαί Σαμψά), a scribe who wrote the letter to Artaxerxes cited in Ezra 4:11-16. See Ezra 4:8-9, 17, 23. The "Pharasthians" (Dübner: Φαρασθαῖοι) seems to refer to the "Apharsa-thacheans" (LXX: Ἀφαρασαθαχαῖοι) mentioned in Ezra 4:9.

[6] As noted above, the expression "to live in piety" (ἐν εὐσεβείᾳ ζώντων) probably means "to be a Christian." See above, pp. 40-41.

demons. For he was choked with rage to see persons who are free, well-born and able to live in luxury being led to this harsh life."

When I heard this, I was struck with an even fiercer blow; foreseeing the sort of evils which would come of this, I lamented for the whole world and said to God: "Take my soul from me,[7] relieve me of my distress, free me from this mortal life, and take me to that place where no one will ever speak to me about such a thing, nor will I ever hear of it. I know that one who departs this life enters the outer darkness where there is great wailing and gnashing of teeth. But I would rather hear teeth gnashing than people speaking words such as these."

Seeing me grieving so vehemently, he said: "Now is not the time for mourning. Your tears will never be able to recover those who have been lost or who are being lost, for I do not think that this horror will stop. But we must see to it that we do our part to extinguish the fire and stop the plague. And if you listen to me, you will put aside these lamentations and compose a speech which has advice for the sick and rebellious, for their own salvation and the common salvation of all people. And I will take this book and put it into the hands of the sick to serve in place of any other medicine, for many who are sick with this illness are friends of mine. They will allow me to approach them once, twice or frequently, and I know that they will swiftly be delivered from this plague."

"You are measuring our abilities," I responded, "according to the measure of your love. But I am not a skilled speaker and I would be ashamed to exercise my apparent talent for a purpose such as this.[8] For I am now forced to display our sins to all the pagans, both those who live today and those who shall come, the very ones I am always ridiculing for their teachings no less than for the laxness of their way of life.[9] If any of them should realize that among the Christians there are some people so hostile to virtue and philosophy that they not only refuse to labor for it, but do not even allow others to speak about it—indeed, not content with this degree of madness, if someone else should give advice and discuss this matter, they even drive him away

---

[7] An echo of 1 Kings 19:4.

[8] John's feigned reluctance to speak is an example of the rhetorical device, διαπόρησις. Such disclaimers served to call attention to the orator's eloquence, rather than to belittle it.

[9] Chrysostom's term Ἕλληνες has been translated throughout as "pagans," a term which bears Chrysostom's negative connotations more readily than the English word "Greeks."

on all sides—if the pagans should realize this, I am afraid that they will think that we Christians are not human, but beasts and wild animals in human form, some wretched demons, and enemies of the common nature, and they will make this judgment not only about those who are responsible, but about our entire people."

Then he laughed and said: "You are joking when you say this. For I will tell you something even more serious than this, if you are afraid that the pagans will learn from your words what everyone learned long ago from the deeds. As if some wicked spirit had filled the souls of all, this topic of conversation is on everyone's lips. Go into the marketplace, go into the doctors' offices, go anywhere in the city where those who wish to do nothing regularly gather, and you will see everyone laughing. The subject of their laughter and jests are these stories of attacks against the holy men. Just as warriors, who have won many battles and erected monuments, love to tell of their exploits, so also do these people rejoice over their rash deeds. You will hear one saying: 'I was the first to lay hands on so-and-so monk, and I struck him.' Another says: 'I found his hut before anyone else.' 'But I stirred on the judge more than the rest,' says a third. Yet another boasts of the prison and the terrors of the prison, and claims praise for having dragged these holy men through the marketplace. And on and on it goes. Then everyone breaks out in laughter at them. And these things happen in the gatherings of the Christians! And the pagans laugh both at the scoffers and at those who are scoffed at, at the former because of what they do, and at the latter because of what they suffer.

"Everywhere a sort of civil war reigns; indeed, it is much worse than civil war. For when those who have fought a civil war think back on it later, they utter many curses upon the ones who instigated it, and they attribute to some wicked demon everything which happened in the war. And the more involved a person was in that civil war, the more ashamed he is of his participation. But these people take pride in their accomplishments! And the present struggle is worse than civil war, not only because it is waged against holy persons who have done nothing wrong, but also because it is directed against those who do not know how to harm anyone and who are prepared only to suffer."

3. "Stop!" I said, "please stop! I have had enough of these stories, unless you want me completely to give up the ghost. But leave me while I have a little strength left. What you have enjoined on me by all means will be done. Only do not tell me any more stories, but go away and pray that the cloud of sadness over me will be lifted and that I will receive from God who is being attacked some strength so as to heal his attackers. He who loves all human beings will grant this, for

he does not desire the death of the sinner, but that he should repent and live."[10]

Having thus sent the man away, I began to write these discourses. If the only evil were that these holy and marvelous men of God are being dragged away and torn to pieces, drawn into the lawcourts, beaten and subject to the other outrages which I have just enumerated, and if no harm from these actions came to those who perpetrate them, I would not be upset at all about the matter, but I would find it amusing and enjoy a good laugh at their expense.

When little children strike their mothers without harming themselves, they provoke great laughter from those who are struck, and the angrier the child is when it does this, the more amused its mother becomes, until she breaks down and cries with laughter.[11] But if at some time the child strikes too often and too strongly and cuts its hand upon the sharp point of a broach fixed to the smock around its mother's waist, or upon a comb on her chest, then, to be sure, the mother stops laughing and feels greater pain than the child who struck her. And although first she heals the wound, she follows this with violent threats and forbids the child to do such things, so that it might not suffer that way again.

Therefore we would act as the mothers did, if we saw that the puerile anger and childish blows of these men brought no great harm to them. But in a short time, even if they do not realize it now because they are overcome by anger, they will weep and wail and lament, not as small children weep, but in the outer darkness and in the unquenchable fire. Therefore we will do as the mothers, with only this difference, that we will speak not with threats and violence as they did, but with cajolery and great indulgence towards these children, seeing that no harm comes to the holy men from them, but rather a greater reward and an increase of confidence. If we were to speak of future goods, you would laugh long and hard, since you are so used to laughing at such things. But even if you should love to laugh a thousand times over, you will not disbelieve in goods that are present.

---

[10] Cf. Ezekiel 18:23, 32. Chrysostom uses the single Greek word φιλάνθρωπος to describe God's love for the human race. On the significance of this expression in his works, see M. Zitnik, "Θεὸς φιλάνθρωπος bei Johannes Chrysostomos," *Orientalia Christiana Periodica* 41 (1975) 76-118.

[11] Metaphors from everyday life, especially the example of infants, were favorite rhetorical techniques of the philosophical diatribe. See A. Uleyn, "La doctrine morale de saint Jean Chrysostome dans le Commentaire sur saint Matthieu et ses affinités avec la diatribe," *Revue de l'Université d'Ottawa* 27 (1957), section spéciale, 10.

And even if you wanted to, you could not, since the facts themselves would contradict you.

You certainly have heard of Nero, for the man was notorious for his licentiousness; he was the first and only one in such high office to discover new modes of intemperance and immorality.[12] This Nero brought the same charges against the blessed Paul (for Paul was a contemporary of Nero) which you now bring against these holy men. For Paul had persuaded Nero's mistress, whom the emperor loved dearly, to accept his preaching of the faith, and likewise to cease from that impure intercourse. Nero brought the same charges against Paul and called him the same names which you utter, such as "corrupter" and "seducer" and the like. First he imprisoned Paul; and when he could not persuade him to stop advising the girl, he finally had Paul killed. But what harm came from this to the one who suffered wrong? And what benefit to the one who acted wrongly? What benefit did not accrue to Paul who was killed? What harm did not come to Nero who had him killed? Paul is honored everywhere on earth as an angel (for now I am speaking of the present life). But everyone considers Nero to be a corrupter and a vicious demon.[13]

4. As for the consequences in the next life, even if you are an unbeliever, I must speak for the sake of the those who are believers, although you ought to believe on the basis of punishments in this life. Nonetheless, however you are disposed to the matter, we will speak and keep nothing hidden. What, then, will happen in the next life? That wretched and miserable Nero, squalid and dejected, covered with shame and gloom, all bent over, will be banished to that place where the worm does not die and where the fire is never extinguished.[14] But the blessed Paul will stand with great confidence before the throne of the King, shining brilliantly, clothed in glory inferior to none of the angels and archangels, and he will receive the reward that befits a man who has given up his body and soul in order to please God.

---

[12] The use of historical examples is a typical feature of sophistic rhetoric. See H. Marrou, "Diatribe," *Reallexikon für Antike und Christentum* 3 (1957) 998. The details of Chrysostom's account of Paul and Nero are derived from the apocryphal *Acts of Peter and Paul.* See J. Rougé, "Néron à la fin du IVe et au début du Ve siècle," *Latomus* 37 (1978) 82. Cf. E. Hennecke and W. Schneemelcher, *New Testament Apocrypha*, v. 2 (Philadelphia: Westminster, 1965)575.

[13] According to Rougé, Nero was generally treated with disdain by both pagan and Christian historians in Chrysostom's day. See "Néron," 73-84.

[14] Cf. Mark 9:48, quoting Isaiah 66:24.

This is how the matter stands: a great recompense awaits those who do good works, but this reward is better and greater when those who do the good works have had to experience danger and great dishonor. Even if the same virtuous deed is accomplished by one person without a struggle and by another with struggles, nevertheless they will not be crowned with the same honor.[15] It is the same in the case of warfare. A soldier is crowned for raising the standard, but much greater honor is given to the soldier who is wounded in the process of raising the standard. And why do I speak about the living, when even those whose only act of virtue is to have died courageously in war, and who have done nothing else to benefit their countrymen, are honored throughout all of Greece as saviors and patrons?

But perhaps you also are ignorant of these matters, since your constant preoccupation is laughter and pleasure. But if the pagans, who have no sound understanding at all, bear witness to this practice, and honor with great honor those who have done nothing but die for them, how much more will Christ do this, who from his great abundance always offers surpassing gifts and rewards to those who undergo dangers for his sake? For he has offered a reward [for bearing] not only persecutions, beatings, prisons, murders, and slaughter, but also mere insolence and abusive language. These are his words: *Blessed are you when people hate you and when they set you apart and abuse you and reject your name as evil for the sake of the Son of Man. Rejoice on that day and exult, for behold your reward will be great in heaven.*[16]

So, then, if suffering physical and verbal abuse brings a greater reward to those who suffer it, the one who prevents them from suffering will benefit not the victims, but those who cause their suffering. Indeed, he harms the victims by eliminating their extra reward and removing the grounds for their rejoicing and exultation. So, for their sake we should be silent and allow to happen that which brings them a wealth of goods and a greater confidence. But, on the other hand, since we are members one of another, even if they refuse the favor once again, in view of our relationship we should not care for one part of the body and neglect another. For the virtuous will find another occasion to gain merit, even if they do not suffer evil now;

---

[15] Chrysostom's term for a "virtuous deed" (κατόρθωμα) is derived from Stoic ethics. See I. von Arnim, *Stoicorum veterum fragmenta*, v. 3 (Stuttgart: Teubner, 1903; reprinted 1979) 134, l. 24: κατορθώματα δ'εἶναι κατ' ἀρετὴν ἐνεργήματα, οἷον τὸ φρονεῖν, τὸ δικαιοπραγεῖν (Stobaeus, *Eclogues* II.85, 13).

[16] Luke 6:22-23.

whereas if these others do not stop their attacks, they will lose all hope of salvation.

For this reason, I will overlook the interest of the former and insist on yours, and I ask and beg you to listen to our exhortations and to stop thrusting the sword against yourselves. Do not kick against the goad, do not sadden the Holy Spirit, thinking that you merely torment humans. I know for certain that eventually you will approve this opinion of ours even if you do not do so now. But I want you to do this now, so that later you do not do so in vain.

That rich man, when he was still alive, thought that the law and the prophets and the exhortation which they contain were myth and nonsense.[17] But when he went to the next life, he so marvelled at their advice that even though he realized he could no longer benefit from praising them, he entreated the patriarch Abraham to send someone from Hades to carry the message to those on earth. He was afraid that others would suffer the same fate as he, that they would ridicule the sacred scriptures and marvel at them only when it was too late to benefit from marvelling. And yet that man did nothing comparable to what you are doing. If he did not share any of his goods with Lazarus, at least he did not prevent others who wished to share with him, nor did he drive them away as you are doing now.

And not only do you surpass him in this cruelty, but in another as well. Just as to refrain from doing good and to prevent others from doing good when they wish are not equal offenses, likewise it is not the same thing to deprive someone of bodily nourishment and to prevent someone with a great hunger for philosophy from being nourished by others. Therefore you outdo that cruel rich man in two ways: you prevent others from satisfying the poor man's hunger, and you display this inhumanity when a soul is being strangled.

The Jews also did this once, when they prevented the apostles from speaking to people words which would lead to salvation. But you are even worse than they. For they had assumed the role of enemies when they did all these things. But you masquerade as friends and act like enemies. At that time the Jews beat the holy apostles and insulted them and defamed them, calling them magicians and seducers. But such a punishment came upon them that no calamity could ever be compared to their sufferings. For they were the first and only people

---

[17] Cf. Luke 16:19-31. The parable of Lazarus and the rich man was an abiding source of Chrysostom's reflections on the moral life. See the *De Lazaro conciones* 1-7 (PG 48.963-1054) and *In quatriduanum Lazarum* (PG 48.779-84).

under the sun to have suffered in this way. Christ himself was a
trustworthy witness of these events when he said: *There will be a great
tribulation such as has not happened from the beginning of the world
until now, and never will be.*[18]

Now is not the time to go through all their sufferings, and yet we
should say a few things out of the many. But I will speak not my own
words, but those of a Jewish man who accurately recorded their own
affairs. What, then, did he say? When he had narrated the burning of
the Temple, he announced these new calamities:[19]

Such was the condition of affairs in the vicinity of the
temple. Meanwhile, the victims perishing of famine
throughout the city were dropping in countless numbers and
enduring sufferings indescribable. In every house, the
appearance anywhere of but a shadow of food was a signal
for war, and the dearest of relatives fell to blows, snatching
from each other the pitiful supports of life. The very dying
were not credited as in want; nay, even those expiring were
searched by the brigands, lest any should be concealing food
beneath a fold of his garment and feigning death. Gaping
with hunger, like mad dogs, these ruffians went staggering
and reeling along, battering upon the doors in the manner of
drunken men, and in their perplexity bursting into the same
house twice or thrice within a single hour. Necessity drove
the victims to gnaw anything, and objects which even the
filthiest of brutes would reject they condescended to collect
and eat: thus in the end they abstained not from belts and
shoes and stripped off and chewed the very leather of their
bucklers. Others devoured tufts of withered grass: indeed
some collectors of stalks sold a trifling quantity for four Attic
drachmas. But why tell of the shameless resort to inanimate
articles of food induced by the famine, seeing that I am here
about to describe an act unparalleled in the history whether
of Greeks or barbarians, and as horrible to relate as it is
incredible to hear? For my part, for fear that posterity might

---

18 Matthew 24:21.

19 Josephus, *Jewish War* 6.192-214. Translated by H. St. J. Thackeray, *Josephus*, v.
3. Loeb Classical Library (Cambridge, MA: Harvard University Press, 1928) 433-39.
Next to Plato, Josephus is the Greek prose writer most often cited by Chrysostom. See
P.R. Coleman-Norton, "St. John Chrysostom's Use of Josephus," *Classical Philology* 26
(1931) 85-89. [Reprinted by permission of the publishers and the Loeb Classical Library
from *Josephus*, v. 3, H. St. J. Thackeray, translator, Cambridge, Mass.: Harvard University
Press, 1928.]

suspect me of monstrous fabrication, I would gladly have
omitted this tragedy, had I not innumerable witnesses
among my contemporaries. Moreover, it would be a poor
compliment that I should pay my country in suppressing the
narrative of the woes which she actually endured.

Among the residents of the region beyond Jordan was a
woman named Mary, daughter of Eleazar, of the village of
Bethezuba (the name means "House of Hyssop"), eminent by
reason of her family and fortune, who had fled with the rest
of the people to Jerusalem and there become involved in the
siege. The bulk of her property, which she had packed up
and brought with her from Peraea to the city, had been
plundered by the tyrants; while the relics of her treasures,
with whatever food she had contrived to procure, were being
carried off by their satellites in their daily raids. With deep
indignation in her heart, the poor woman constantly abused
and cursed these extortioners and so incensed them against
her. But when no one either out of exasperation or pity put
her to death, weary of finding for others food, which indeed it
was now impossible from any quarter to procure, while
famine coursed through her intestines and marrow and the
fire of rage was more consuming even than the famine,
impelled by the promptings alike of fury and necessity, she
proceeded to an act of outrage upon nature. Seizing her
child, an infant at the breast, "Poor babe," she cried, "amidst
war, famine, and sedition, to what end should I preserve
thee? With the Romans slavery awaits us, should we live till
they come; but famine is forestalling slavery, and more cruel
than both are the rebels. Come, be thou food for me, to the
rebels an avenging fury, and to the world a tale such as alone
is wanting to the calamities of the Jews." With these words
she slew her son, and then, having roasted the body and
devoured half of it, she covered up the remainder. At once
the rebels were upon her and, scenting the unholy odor,
threatened her with instant death unless she produced what
she had prepared. Replying that she had reserved a goodly
portion for them also, she disclosed the remnants of her
child. Seized with instant horror and stupefaction, they
stood paralysed by the sight. She, however, said, "This is my
own child, and this my handiwork. Eat, for I too have eaten.
Show not yourselves weaker than a woman, or more
compassionate than a mother. But if you have pious scruples

and shrink from my sacrifice, then let what I have eaten be your portion and the remainder also be left for me." At that they departed trembling, in this one instance cowards, though scarcely yielding even this food to the mother. The whole city instantly rang with the abomination, and each, picturing the horror of it, shuddered as though it had been perpetrated by himself. The starving folk longed for death, and felicitated those who had gone to their rest ere they had heard or beheld such evils.

The horrible news soon spread to the Romans. Of them some were incredulous, others were moved to pity, but the effect on the majority was to intensify their hatred of the nation.

This is what the Jews suffered, and evils much worse than this, not only because they crucified Christ, but also because afterwards they prevented the apostles from speaking about our salvation.[20] This is the charge which the blessed Paul levelled against them when he prophesied that evil would befall them, saying that *the wrath has come upon them at last.*[21]

"And what does this have to do with us?," you say. "We do not drive them away from the faith or from preaching."[22] And what benefit is the faith, tell me, unless there is also a pure way of life? But perhaps you do not even know about this, since you are so ignorant of all our matters. But I will enumerate for you the declarations of Christ. Observe carefully if people are never blamed for their way of life, and if punishments are determined only for faith and doctrines. For when he had ascended the mountain and seen the great crowd flowing all around him, after issuing the other counsels, Christ said: *Not everyone*

---

[20] The destruction of the Jewish Temple was an event of considerable theological significance to Chrysostom, especially in his eight sermons against Judaizing Christians. For a recent discussion, see R.L. Wilken, *John Chrysostom and the Jews. Rhetoric and Reality in the Late Fourth Century* (Berkeley: University of California Press, 1983), especially 128-60.

[21] 1 Thessalonians 2:16.

[22] From this point on throughout the treatise Chrysostom will employ a dialogue technique of argumentation (διάλεξις). This was a question and answer method in which the orator pretended to argue with an imaginary opponent. The method is often associated with the diatribe of Stoic and Cynic preaching, but it also was widely used by the sophists, especially Libanius. See H. Hubbell, "Chrysostom and Rhetoric," *Classical Philology* 19 (1924) 261-76 and B. Schouler, *Libanios. Discours moraux* (Paris, 1973) 33-36.

*who says to me, "Lord, Lord," will enter into the kingdom of heaven, but
the one who does the will of my Father.*[23] And, *Many will say to me on
that day, "Did we not prophesy in your name and cast out demons in
your name and work many wonders in your name?" And then I will
confess to them, "Get away from me, you workers of iniquity, I do not
know you."*[24] And he said that a person who hears his words, but does
not put them into practice, is like a foolish man who built his house
upon sand, rendering it vulnerable to floods and rains and winds.[25]
And while discoursing in another place, he said: "Just as fishermen,
when they have drawn in their nets, separate out the poor fish, so it
will be on that last day when the angels throw into the furnace all
those who have sinned."[26] And when discussing people who are
licentious and impure, he said: *They will go to that place where the
worm never dies and the fire is never extinguished.*[27] And again, *A
king gave a wedding feast for his son and seeing a man wearing a dirty
garment, he said to him, "Friend, how did you get in here without
having a wedding garment?"* And the man had nothing to say. *Then,
he said to his servants, "Bind him hand and foot and cast him into the
outer darkness."*[28] This is how he threatens the licentious and
intemperate. Likewise, the virgins who were shut out by the
bridegroom suffered this because of their cruelty and inhumanity.[29]
And others for the same reason *have gone to the eternal fire prepared
for the devil and his angels.*[30] And those who speak rashly and
without purpose will be condemned. *For by your words*, he said, *you
will be justified, and by your words you will be condemned.*[31]

Do you think, then, that we are mistaken to be anxious about a way
of life, and to be so concerned about the more ethical part of
philosophy? I do not think so, unless you would maintain that Christ
said all this and more than this for no reason, for I have not said
everything. And if I were not afraid of prolonging my speech, I would
have taught from the prophets, from the blessed Paul, and from the
other apostles how much concern God himself has shown for the moral

---

[23] Matthew 7:21.
[24] Matthew 7:22-23.
[25] Cf. Matthew 7:24-27.
[26] Cf. Matthew 13:47-50.
[27] Mark 9:48.
[28] Matthew 22:2,12-13.
[29] Cf. Matthew 25:1-13.
[30] Matthew 25:41.
[31] Matthew 12:37.

life. But I think that what has been said is enough; or rather, even a small fraction of what was said should have been sufficient. For when God declares something, even if he speaks only once, what he says should be accepted as if it had been uttered many times.

7. "What, then?" you say, "are not those who stay at home able to accomplish the virtuous deeds needed to avoid punishment?" I myself have wished for this, no less then you, indeed, much more than you. Often I have prayed that there would be no need of monasteries and that such good order would reign in the cities that no one would ever be forced to flee to the desert. But now the reverse is the case, and the cities, where there are courts of justice and laws, are filled with much lawlessness and injustice, whereas the desert blossoms with the abundant fruit of philosophy. Therefore, you should not prosecute the persons who rescue those who desire to be saved from this storm and confusion and who guide them into the quiet harbor. Rather, you should indict those who render every city so difficult and unsuitable for philosophy that those who wish to be saved are compelled to seek out the desert places.

Tell me, if someone takes a lamp in the middle of the night and sets fire to a large house full of people, trapping those who are sleeping inside, who is the wicked person, in your estimation: the one who awakens the sleepers and leads them out of the burning house, or the one who set the fire in the first place and created the desperate situation for those inside and for the person leading them out? If someone sees a city suffering under tyranny, sick and rebellious, and persuades some of its inhabitants to flee to the mountain tops, and if, in addition to persuasion, he also assists their withdrawal,[32] whom would you accuse: the one who rescued the suffering citizens from that storm and led them into this quiet harbor, or the one who caused their shipwreck?

Do not imagine that human affairs are now in a better state than a city under tyranny; indeed, they are much worse.[33] For it is not a human being, but a wicked demon who has seized the entire world like

---

[32] "Withdrawal" (ἀναχώρησις) by Chrysostom's time was a technical term for departure into the monastic life. See G.W.H. Lampe, *A Patristic Greek Lexicon* (Oxford, 1961) 129. The term also had a long history in Greek philosophy. See the helpful discussion in A.J. Festugière, *Personal Religion Among the Greeks* (Berkeley and Los Angeles: University of California Press, 1954) 54-67.

[33] The following paragraph is another lengthy 'ἔκφρασις, combining the commonplaces of both tyranny and drunkenness. Both are τόποι found in Libanius' προγυμνάσματα (Förster 8, pp. 195-208, 477).

a savage tyrant and with his entire phalanx has invaded human souls. From there, as if from a fortress, each day he sends forth his polluted and accurst commands to all, not only tearing apart marriages, not only buying and selling, not only committing wicked murders, but also much worse deeds than these. He snatches souls which were once betrothed to God away from their union with Him and hands them over to his impure minions, forcing them to share in wicked intercourse. Once they take hold of the soul, they consort with it shamefully and arrogantly, as is the custom of the wicked demons who violently and madly desire our shame and ruin. They strip the soul of all its garments of virtue, and clothe it in the foul, torn and ill-smelling rags of wickedness, so that the soul is even more shameful clothed than naked; and when they have infected the soul with all their wickedness, they ceaselessly march against it with violence. And they are never satisfied with this disgusting and lawless intercourse. But just as drunkards, when they have imbibed a great amount of drink, are stimulated all the more, likewise these demons rage all the more and attack the soul more fiercely and more cruelly, the more they abuse it. They prick it and bite it on all sides, they pour their poison into it and do not stop until they have transformed the soul into their own image, or have seen it separated from the body.

Therefore, what tyranny, what capitivity, what ruination, what servitude, what war, what shipwreck, what famine could be worse than this? Who is so cruel and so vicious, who is so stupid and inhumane and lacking in compassion and unfeeling that he does not wish to free from this accursed madness the soul which suffers this outrageous abuse, as far as it is in his power, but who would instead allow it to suffer in this way? And if this is the action of a cruel and hard-hearted soul, where, tell me, shall we rank those who, in addition to neglecting the good, do something far worse? Not only do they not praise or approve holy men who are eager to leap into the midst of dangers, who do not refuse to lay hands upon the very throat of the wild beast, but who endure foul smells and dangers in order to draw up out of the very throat of the demon the souls who have already been gulped down—but they even drive them away on all sides and make war against them!

8. "What then?" is the reply. "Will all who live in the cities perish, tossed by a storm? Must everyone leave the cities and desert them to flee to the desert and populate the mountain tops? Is this what you are commanding, is this the law you are laying down?" Not at all! As I said before, it is exactly the opposite that I wish, and I pray that we would enjoy such peace and freedom from the tyranny of these evils

that not only would the city-dwellers have no need to flee to the
mountains, but also that those who inhabit the mountains, like
fugitives returning from a long exile, would return to their native
cities. But what can I do? If I rush to bring them home, I am afraid
that I will betray them into the hands of wicked demons instead and
that, in my desire to lead them out of solitude and flight, I will cause
them to fall from philosophy and tranquillity.[34]

But if, by referring to the great number of people who live in the
city, you think you can shame me and frighten me, so that I will not
have the courage to condemn the whole world, I will meet your objection by citing the decree of Christ. For you will not be so arrogant as
to oppose the decision of the One who is to judge us. What, then, does
Christ say? *Narrow is the gate and rough the road which leads to life,
and few are those who find it.*[35] But if those who find this road are few,
much fewer are those who are able to arrive at its end. For not everyone who sets out at the beginning will have the strength to reach the
end. Some will be thrown into the sea at the start of the voyage,
others in the middle, and others even as the ship enters the harbor.
Moreover, he says that many are called, but few are chosen.[36] When
Christ declares that the greater part will be destroyed and that only a
few will be saved, what quarrel do you have with me? This is what
you are doing: it is as if you were astonished at the story about
Noah—that all but two or three perished in the flood—and expected
this to silence us so that we do not dare to condemn the crowd. But we
will not change our mind, nor will we value the multitude more highly
than the truth.

What is happening now is no less serious than what happened in
the time of Noah; indeed it is more reprehensible because people today
have been threatened with gehenna, and yet their vices do not
decrease. For who, tell me, does not call his brother a fool? But this
renders a person liable to the fire of gehenna.[37] Who does not look at a
woman with lustful eyes? But this is equivalent to adultery, and the
adulterer must be thrown into the same gehenna.[38] Who has not
sworn an oath? But this is always from the evil one, and what is from

---

[34] According to Fabricius, *Zu den Jugendschriften* 126, the expression "to fall from
philosophy" (φιλοσοφίας . . . ἐκπεσεῖν) is rare; it is found only in Plato, *Republic* 496b-c
and in Plutarch, *Moralia* 47c and 52d.

[35] Matthew 7:14.

[36] Cf. Matthew 20:16.

[37] Cf. Matthew 5:22.

[38] Cf. Matthew 5:28.

that evil one is always worthy of punishment.[39] Who has never been envious of a friend? But this makes people worse than the Gentiles and tax collectors, and it is quite clear to all that those who are worse than these cannot escape punishment. Who has expelled from his heart all anger and forgiven the sins of all who have offended him? But no one who has heard Christ will deny that the person who has not forgiven must be handed over to the torturers. Who has not been enslaved to mammon? But to serve mammon requires that one abandon the service of Christ, and whoever renounces the service of Christ by necessity renounces his own salvation. Who has not secretly spoken slander? But even the Old Law commands such persons to be killed and slaughtered.

But what consolation is there in the recital of our own evils? That all have fallen into the pit of wickedness, as if by a prior agreement, this itself is the greatest evidence of the sickness which has now taken hold; but when we are consoled by the fact that our evils are shared, this is cause for even greater grief. For to have many companions in sin does not acquit us of accusations and punishments. And if someone feels discouraged by what we have said, let him wait a little while and then despair even more when we speak of things much worse than these, such as false oaths. For if swearing an oath is diabolic, what sort of punishment do you think misusing oaths will bring upon us? If calling someone a fool brings on gehenna, what punishment awaits the person who constantly abuses and insults the brother who has done him no harm. If only to remember past injuries merits punishment, what sort of torture awaits those who take vengeance?

But now is not the time for these matters; they will be treated in their proper place. To get to the point, is not the very event which compelled us to compose this speech alone sufficient to reveal the evil of the present disease? If ignorance of one's own sins and the ruthless pursuit of wrongdoing is the absolute height of wickedness, where shall we rank those new lawmakers of this recent and most strange legislation, who drive away the teachers of virtue with greater confidence than others drive away teachers of wickedness, and who attack those who try to live well rather than those who act wickedly? In fact, they never accuse or oppose wrongdoers, but they even enjoy their company, all but shouting through their words and deeds that one should embrace wickedness and never return to virtue, so that it

[39] Cf. Matthew 5:33.

is fine to take revenge not only against those who pursue virtue, but also against those who dare to utter a sound about it.

Book Two

To the Pagan Parent

1. So then, what we have said is enough to cause astonishment and shuddering. And if someone should apply these words of the prophet to this situation, that *heaven was astonished over this, and the earth shuddered exceedingly,*[1] and *there was astonishment and shuddering over the earth,*[2] this would be an appropriate description. But there is something even worse than this: it is not only strangers and those who are unrelated who become so upset and angry when the youth receive good advice, but parents and relatives who are enraged at this. I am aware that many people do not find it at all surprising that the parents act this way; instead they say that they are angered when they see persons who are neither parents, nor loved ones, nor relatives, nor friends, and who frequently even are unknown to those who choose to philosophize, suffering just as the parents do and even surpassing them in annoyance, opposition and accusations against those who persuaded them.

But the very opposite seems astonishing to me. For it would not be strange for those who are neither guardians nor friends to be distressed over another person's goods, conquered by envy and believing that the other's ruin is their own deliverance from misfortune—such thoughts are wretched and miserable, but so they think nonetheless. But when those who have borne children, who have raised them, who pray each day to see their children become more distinguished than themselves, who do and suffer everything for

---

[1] Jeremiah 2:12.
[2] Jeremiah 5:30.

advice from someone else, they set aside their own opinion concerning
their own children and follow another's suggestion. Therefore, they
should not be annoyed with us, if we say that we know better than
they what is beneficial for the children. And if we do not prove this
through our speeches, then they may accuse us, then they may attack
us as imposters, corrupters and enemies of the entire human race.

2. What, then, will be clear proof, and how will we know who really
sees what is beneficial, and who seems to see, but really does not see at
all? Let us force these words of mine, as well as the opposing
arguments, to undergo scrutiny and enter into combat,[5] and let us
submit them to examination by unbiased judges. Now, the rule of the
contest requires us to disrobe and to compete only against Christian
opponents, and it demands nothing more of us. As the blessed Paul
said: *For what have I to do with judging outsiders?*[6] But since it
happens that many of those who are drawn towards heaven are the
children of pagan parents, even though the rule of the contest exempts
us from doing battle with them, nonetheless we shall willingly and
enthusiastically prepare to compete against them first. And I wish
that our struggle were only against the pagans, although to fight
them is more difficult and more intricate.[7] *For the natural man does
not perceive the things of the Spirit, for it is foolishness to him.*[8]

This is our dilemma: we must persuade a person to desire a
kingdom when that person at the outset does not wish to believe that
the thing exists. However, even though our arguments must be made
within such narrow confines, I would prefer to do battle only against
the pagans. Against a Christian we have many legitimate arguments
at our disposal, and yet the excess of embarrassment far overshadows
the pleasure which comes from the abundance of fair grounds. For I
am ashamed to have to fight with a Christian over these matters.
This alone, I am afraid, gives the pagan a legitimate complaint
against me, for in other matters we easily conquer him by the grace of
God. But if he is willing to be reasonable, we shall quickly convert
him not only to a love of that way of life, but also to the same

---

[5] The phrase "to enter into combat" (συμπλακῆναι) refers to wrestlers locked in
combat. On the preponderance of athletic metaphors in Chrysostom, see J.A. Sawhill,
The Use of Athletic Metaphors in the Biblical Homilies of St. John Chrysostom
(Princeton, 1928).

[6] 1 Corinthians 5:12.

[7] Literally "has more holds" (πλείονας 'έχει λαβάς), another wrestling metaphor.
Chrysostom refers to the twists and turns of the argument.

[8] 1 Corinthians 2:14.

enthusiasm for the doctrines which are the foundation of this way of life. So far am I from being afraid of a contest with him, that I will enter the combat myself only after I first have presented my opponent in the most favorable light.

Imagine that this parent is not only a pagan, but is also the wealthiest of men, admired and possessing great power.[9] Suppose that he has many fields, many houses, thousands of talents of gold. Assume that he comes from a most regal homeland, and a most illustrious family. Imagine that he has no other children, nor hope of any more, but that he depends on this one child alone. And suppose that this young man also has good hopes, that he expects to rise quickly to power, to surpass his father in splendor, and to outdo him in all worldly matters.[10]

Then in the midst of these hopes, someone comes and discusses this philosophy with him. Imagine that he persuades the young man to laugh at all these things and to put on a rough cloak, to leave the city and flee to the mountains, and there to plant and irrigate and carry water and do all the other things which monks do which appear to be both low and shameful.[11] Suppose that he also goes barefoot and sleeps on the ground, and that this beautiful young man becomes thin and pale. Imagine that he who lived in such luxury and honor, who had such hopes, has put on a garment more vile than that of any of his slaves.

Have we now given our opponent sufficient grounds for accusation, have we adequately outfitted our antagonist? If this is not enough, we shall provide other arguments. After this, imagine the father devising countless ways to persuade his son to change, and all in vain,

---

9 The following three paragraphs employ the rhetorical device ἠθοποιία, a character sketch.

10 On the significance of the formula, "to surpass one's father," in Greek literature and especially in Libanius, see B. Schouler, "Dépasser le père," *Revue des études grecques* 93 (1980) 1-24, especially 19-24. The expression reflects Hellenic ideals of virtue (ἀρετή) and nobility (εὐγένεια).

11 In his treatise *De compunctione ad Demetrium* 1.6 (PG 47.403), Chrysostom revealed the difficulties which he as an urban Christian faced upon entry into the monastic life. See above p. 15. For the complaints of upper-class Christians that the monastic life was shameful and unworthy of the well-born, see Chrysostom's remark to the monk Stagirius: "Your father said that the thing made you shameful and unworthy of the brilliance of your ancestors, and that you were destroying his own glory as well, and that if the bonds of nature were not so compelling, he would quickly disinherit you" (*Ad Stagirium a daemone vexatum* 2.3 [PG 47.452]). Cf. the treatise *Ad Theodorum* 18 (SC 117. 194- 96).

while the child sits upon a rock and remains above the flood and rain and winds. See the father mourning and pouring forth tears, so that he stirs up greater wrath toward us. Then in the presence of everyone he meets, imagine him accusing us continually in these words:[12] "I bore him, I raised him. I worked hard all my life doing and suffering everything which tends to result from the begetting of children. I had fine hopes, I spoke with pedagogues, I called upon teachers, I spent money, I frequently stayed awake worrying about his good behavior, about his education, so that he would be inferior to none of his ancestors, so that he would appear more illustrious than all. I expected that he would be a comfort in my old age. I was thinking about a wife after a little while, and marriage, about a magistracy and political office.

"But suddenly, like a thunder-bolt, like a storm falling down from somewhere in the sky upon a trading ship loaded down with merchandise, which has just finished its journey over the great sea and sailed with a favorable wind and is, moreover, just about to enter the harbor, when the storm overwhelms the ship just outside the entrance, and it is feared that the storm will bring upon the head of such a wealthy man not only extreme poverty, but also a miserable death and destruction—this is what has happened to me now![13] These accursed corrupters and seducers (let him say these things, we will not differ) have carried off from such hopes the support of my old age and dragged him away to their dens like a band of robbers. They have so bewitched him with their songs that he prefers to stand nobly against the sword, fire, beasts, and everything rather than return to his former wealth.[14]

"And, what is worse, after persuading him to do this, they pretend to know better than we do what is in his interest. Houses are empty, fields are empty.[15] Farmers and household slaves are filled with grief and disgrace. My enemies delight in my misfortunes, my friends hide

---

[12] The lengthy speech which follows is an example of the rhetorical device προσωποποιία, the placing of a speech in the mouth of an imaginary character.

[13] Metaphors taken from the sea and from navigation are among the most popular rhetorical devices employed by the sophists. Cf. T.E. Ameringer, *The Stylistic Influence of the Second Sophistic on the Panegyrical Sermons of St. John Chrysostom.* (Washington, D.C.: Catholic University of America Press, 1920) 59: "Chrysostom in his liberal use of these terms rivals the most thoroughgoing of the rhetors."

[14] On the attraction of monastic singing, see Chrysostom, Homily 14.4 on 1 Timothy (PG 62.576). Cf. Libanius, or. 30.8, for a negative view.

[15] Libanius also blames the monks for the desertion of farms. See or. 2.32 and or. 30.48.

in shame. I have no thought now but to set on fire and to burn everything, houses, fields, herds of cattle and flocks of sheep. For what good are these things to me now, when the one who was to make use of them is not here, but has been taken captive and enslaved by wild barbarians in a slavery more bitter than any death? I have clothed my household in black garments, sprinkled their heads with ashes, set up a chorus of women, and ordered them to strike themselves more severely than if they had found him dead. Please excuse me for doing this. My grief is greater than if he were dead. Now the light of day greatly troubles me, and its rays are unpleasant to bear, whenever I conjure in my mind the image of that miserable child, whenever I see him clothed more dishonorably than the vilest of those farmers and sent out to more dishonorable works. Whenever I imagine his unbending resolve, I burn, I am torn apart, I burst!"

3. After saying these things, the father rolls forward before the feet of his audience, and scatters ashes upon his head; he disfigures his face with dust, entreats everyone to stretch out their hands, and covers his grey hair with dirt. We have probably portrayed our opponent well enough to inflame all his listeners and to persuade them to cast off a cliff those who have caused these things. In my speech I have tried to express the highest possible charges, so that nothing will be left to say when we have defeated this opponent by the grace of God. For when we have silenced the person who has all these grounds for complaint, the one who does not have them (and it is impossible for all of these conditions to converge) will easily concede the victory to us. Therefore, let him say all this and more. But I will beg the judges not to have pity on this old man now, but only when we shall show him grieving, while his son suffers no evil, but enjoys great goods, than which nothing greater can be found. For then he would be truly worthy of pity and tears, if he were unable to see the happiness of his child, but rather mourned while his child enjoyed the greatest goods.

How then shall we begin our speech to him? Let us begin with wealth and money, since this is what the parent mourns the most, and since the most fearsome thing of all seems to be that wealthy children are drawn to this way of life. Tell me now, whom does everyone call blessed and whom do we say is enviable: the person who is always thirsting and who, even before he has taken his fill of the first cup, is in need of another again, and who is constantly in this state, or the person who stands above this compulsion, and who remains ever thirstless and who is never compelled by the need of this drink? Is not the former like someone consumed by a fever, who is burdened by a most terrible compulsion, even if he should be able to drink rivers to their source? And does not the latter enjoy true freedom, and true health, and a superhuman nature?[16]

If someone who lusts for a woman should have intercourse with her continually and after this liaison should burn even more, but if another should stand beyond this madness and should not be seized by this evil, not even in a dream, who, once again, is enviable and blessed? Is it not the latter? Who is wretched and miserable? Is it not the one who suffers the sickness of this vain passion, who can never be extinguished, but who is afflicted all the more by the remedies that his mind conjures up? But if, in addition to what we have said, the person who is sick considers himself blessed, and does not wish to be freed from this compulsion, and if he weeps over those who have been freed from passion, as this father is doing now, will he not be more pitiable and more wretched? Such a person not only is sick, but also does not know that he is sick and for this reason does not wish to be freed and laments over those who have been freed.

Let us now speak about the possession of money, and we will see who is miserable and wretched, for [love of money] is more violent and more maddening than [carnal] passion. It can cause more suffering, not only because its flame burns more intensely, but also because it resists every conceivable remedy and is more unyielding than these [carnal passions]. For those who lust after drink or physical pleasure enjoy greater satisfaction after the act than those who are mad about money. That is why we had to illustrate these [carnal passions] in our speech, because they are not immediately apparent upon experience. But we can provide many examples of this sickness [of love of money] from reality itself.

Why, tell me, do you mourn for your son? Because he has been freed from such madness and turmoil, because he does not lust with an insatiable lust, because he stands above this struggle and battle? "But he would not have suffered this," you say, "nor would he have lusted for more, but he would have been satisfied to enjoy what he had. Above all," you say, "the thing is contrary to nature, so to speak."

---

16 Here and throughout book two, Chrysostom relies heavily on stock portraits of the philosopher derived from Stoic and Cynic ethics. The "freedom" (ἐλευθερία) and "self-sufficiency" (αὐτάρκεια) of the philosopher/monk is contrasted with the "compulsion" (ἀνάγκη) and slavery which passion and desire entail. A thorough discussion of Chrysostom's use of such τόποι can be found in A. Uleyn, "La doctrine morale de saint Jean Chrysostome," 5-25, 99-140.

So be it! We will grant that he would wish to add nothing to his present goods and that he would not be enslaved by this desire. Nonetheless, I will prove that he now enjoys greater comfort and pleasure. For what is easier: to be anxious about such things, and to be imprisoned by the slavery of guarding them, and to be afraid that any of one's goods might perish, or to be freed of these bonds? Granted that he has no desire for another's possessions; still it would be much better if he despised what is already placed before him. If not to be in need of more is admitted to be the greatest good, would there not be even greater happiness if he were also beyond the need of what is present? For the person who neither thirsts nor lusts (for nothing prevents us from going back to these examples) is demonstrably much happier, not only than those who always thirst and always lust, but also than those who suffer this [passion] for a short time and fulfill their desire, since he has not fallen into such a compulsion.

I will ask you another question: if it were possible to surpass all people in wealth and to be free of the evils which come from wealth, would you not choose this abundance a thousand times, so as not to suffer jealousy, slander, cares, or any other such things? If, then, we prove that your son possesses this and is now much wealthier, will you finally stop mourning and grieving so bitterly?

4. That he is free from care and from the other evils which wealth drags with it, you yourself will not deny; therefore, there is no need for us to speak with you on these matters. But you want to know how he is wealthier than you who possess such things. We will teach you this and we will prove that you yourself, who think that your son is now in extreme poverty, are the one who really is suffering poverty in comparison to him. And do not think that we are speaking about the goods that are in heaven and about things in the next life, for we shall make our demonstration from what is here at hand.

You are lord only over those things that are yours, but he is master over goods throughout the whole world. But if you do not believe me, let us go to him, and persuade him to come down from the mountains; or rather, even while remaining there, let him give a sign to someone who is very wealthy and pious to send him any amount of gold you wish. Or better, since your son will not allow this, have him order [the rich person] to give to someone in need, and you will see the wealthy man obeying and carrying out the order with greater zeal than any of your stewards. When the steward is ordered to spend money, he is downcast and sullen, whereas such a rich man, whenever he does not

spend, is afraid that he has given offense since he has received no such
order.[17]

And I could show you many persons, not only those who are famous,
but also those who are less prominent, who have such power. And if
your stewards squander what has been entrusted to them, you would
not have anyone to turn to, but immediately your wealth would be
transformed into poverty by their evil doing. But your son has no such
fear. For if he should become poor, he simply will ask someone else.
And if this [benefactor] should suffer a similar fate, he will go to
someone else; and the sources of rivers would probably run dry before
those who will follow his orders in these matters.

And if you shared our convictions, we would tell you many great
stories that are similar, both old and new. But since you prefer what
belongs to the pagans, I also find a paradigm there.[18] Listen to what
Crito says to Socrates:[19]

> I think that you've got enough of my money for yourself
> already. And then even supposing that in your anxiety for
> my safety you feel that you oughtn't to spend my money,
> there are these foreign gentlemen staying in Athens who are
> quite willing to spend theirs. One of them, Simmias of
> Thebes, has actually brought the money with him for this
> very purpose, and Cebes and a number of others are quite
> ready to do the same. So, as I say, you mustn't let any fears
> on these grounds make you slacken your efforts to escape,
> and you mustn't feel any misgivings about what you said at
> your trial—that you wouldn't know what to do with yourself
> if you left this country. Wherever you go, there are plenty of
> places where you will find a welcome, and if you choose to go

---

[17] On the influence of monks with wealthy Antiochenes, see Theodoret, *Religious History* 2.20, 3.22, 9.4, and 13.3.

[18] The use of noble philosphers as examples (παραδείγματα) was specially popular in the ancient rhetorical diatribe. See Marrou, "Diatribe," *Reallexikon für Antike und Christentum* 3 (1957) 998 and M. Aubineau, "Introduction," *Gregoire de Nysse. Traité de la virginité*. Sources Chrétiennes, 119 (Paris, 1966) 84. On the figure of Socrates specifically, see A.M. Malingrey, "Le personnage de Socrate chez quelques auteurs chrétiens du IVe siècle," in *Forma futuri. Studi in onore di M. Pellegrino* (Turin, 1975) 159-78.

[19] Plato, *Crito* 45 bc. Translation by H. Tredennick in *The Collected Dialogues of Plato.* Edited by E. Hamilton and H. Cairns. (Princeton, 1961) 30. [Original source: *Plato: The Last Days of Socrates*, translated by Hugh Tredennick (Penguin Classics, 1954, 1959), © Hugh Tredennick, 1954, 1959. Reproduced by permission of Penguin Books Ltd.] The length and accuracy of the quotation indicate that Chrysostom is not citing from memory. See Fabricius, *Zu den Jugendschriften* 134 and P. Ubaldi, "Di due citazioni di Platone in Giovanni Crisostomo," *Rivista di Filologia e Istruzione Classica* 28 (1900) 69-75.

to Thessaly, I have friends there who will make much of you
and give you complete protection, so that no one in Thessaly
can interfere with you.

What could be more pleasant than this abundance? But these
things have to do with a worldly man. If we wished to examine a
wealth which is more philosophical than this, perhaps you would not
follow the speech. Nonetheless we must speak on account of the
judges.

Such is the wealth of virtue, so much more pleasurable, so much
more desirable than yours, that those who have it would never
exchange it for the whole world, even if the world with its mountains,
seas, and rivers should be turned into gold. If this could happen, you
would know from direct experience that we are not merely boasting,
and that those who have found what is much greater and better
despise material wealth and would never exchange the one for the
other. And what do I mean by saying that they would not exchange
one for the other? They would not wish even to possess the two
together. Indeed, if someone should give you the wealth of virtue
along with money, you would receive it with open hands. Thus you
admit that this [wealth of virtue] is something great and wonderful.
But these [monks] do not even wish to possess your kind of wealth
along with their own, so well do they know that the thing is to be
despised. Once again, I will make this clear from your own
paradigms. How much money do you think Alexander would have
given to Diogenes, if Diogenes had wished to accept it? But he did not
wish to. But Alexander tried hard and did everything so as to be able
to approach the wealth of Diogenes.[20]

5. Do you wish to see your own poverty and the wealth of your child
from another angle? Go and take away his cloak, which is the only
one he has, drive him out of his cell, and destroy his hut, and even so
you will see him not at all annoyed or vexed; rather, he will thank you
for this, since you have impelled him further toward philosophy. But
if someone should take from you only ten drachmas, you never stop

---

[20] Chrysostom refers to the well-known meeting between Diogenes the Cynic and
Alexander the Great. The story occurs in several versions in Plutarch's *Alexander* 671,
and in Diogenes Laertius, *De clarorum philosophorum vitis* 6.32, 38, and 68.
Chrysostom tells a slightly different version of the story below in book two, section 5.
See P.R. Coleman-Norton, "St. John Chrysostom and the Greek Philosophers," *Classical
Philology* 25 (1930) 308-9 for further references to Diogenes in Chrysostom's works.

mourning and weeping. Who, then, is the wealthy one: the one who
cries over small things, or the one who despises all things?

And do not stop at this, but also drive him out of the entire region,
and you will see him laughing at this as if it were child's play. But if
someone simply drove you from your native city, you would believe
that this was the most terrible thing and would not bear the calamity.
But that son of yours, since all the earth and sea are his, would
migrate from one place to another as contentedly and painlessly as
you stroll through your own fields—indeed, even more contentedly
than you do. For even if it is possible for you to walk through your
own fields, you still must walk through fields that belong to other
people. But he travels through an entire world that is his own, and
everywhere pools and rivers and streams provide him drink in
abundance; his food is garden vegetables, herbs, and breads from
many places.[21]

I do not yet say to you that he also despises the whole earth since he
has a city in heaven. Even if he should have to die, he would bear
death with greater pleasure than he would your luxury, and he will
pray to die in that state more than you in your homeland and on your
bed. Thus one could say that the true wanderer and exile and
vagabond is the person who lives in a city and dwells in a house, and
not the one who is free of all these things. For you could not drive him
out of his homeland, unless you drove him from the entire earth. (At
least this is how I will speak now; for, if I were to speak the truth, you
send him to his homeland most of all when you drive him from the
earth. But I cannot yet say this to you who know nothing more than
what the eye sees.)

You could not show him to be naked, as long as he is clothed in the
garments of virtue; nor will you kill him by starvation, as long as he
knows what is true nourishment, whereas the wealthy are conquered
by all these things. And so, it would not be wrong to call the rich poor
and those who are very poor extremely wealthy.[22] For the person who
always can have plenty of food and drink and housing and relaxation
and who not only is not unhappy, but who lives more pleasantly in

---

[21] The image of the philosopher as a homeless exile was common among the Cynics
and associated especially with the figure of Diogenes. See Dio Chrysostom, or. 8.15-16
and or. 4.12-13; also Julian, or. 7.211d, "To the Cynic Heracleios," and the *Letter to
Themistios*, 256d, where Julian cites a maxim of Diogenes describing the "ideal man" as
the person "without a city, without a home, bereft of a fatherland."

[22] Such paradoxes were common in the moral preaching of the Cynics and Stoics:
Uleyn, "La doctrine morale de saint Jean Chrysostome," 20-23.

these conditions than you do in yours, clearly this person is wealthier than all you rich people who can find these things only at home.

That is why your son will never have to grieve about poverty. His wealth is superior to yours not only in its abundance and pleasure, but also because it will never fail and be turned into poverty. It is not subject to the uncertainty of the future, it does not breed anxiety or jealousy; rather, it produces admiration, praise and good repute. But the very opposite is the case for you. Not only do people not praise you for your wealth, but they hate you and turn away from you and envy you and plot against you. But when a person is wealthy with true wealth, he is especially admired for this and not envied or plotted against.

Now, then, in regard to health, who is better off? Is not your son vigorous and healthy in body like the wild animals,[23] since he enjoys the pure air and healthy streams and flowers and groves and pure, sweet smells, whereas the [wealthy] person, as if he were lying in a cesspool, is rather soft and sickly? And if your son has first place in health, clearly he enjoys superior pleasure as well. For who do you think lives in greater luxury, the one who lies on the high grass, beside a clear stream, under the shade of enormous trees, and who feasts his eyes on the sight and keeps his soul purer than the heavens and far from commotion and disturbance, or the person who is shut up in his house?[24] For marble stones are not purer than the air, nor is the shade of a roof more pleasant than the shade of trees, nor is a mosaic pavement more beautiful than a patch of multi-colored flowers.[25] You rich people yourselves testify to this: if it were possible to have trees and the comfort of meadows in the upper rooms of your houses, you would choose these rather than golden roofs and magnificent walls. For whenever you desire to take a vacation from your many labors, you leave the latter behind and hasten to the former.

But perhaps you are mourning about glory, that great and splendid glory which seems to be missing from the monastic life. You compare regal trappings with solitude, and the hopes in the one way of life with

---

[23] Fabricius, *Zu den Jugendschriften* 127, sees in the words "vigorous and healthy in body" (εὐσωματεῖ καὶ σφριγᾷ) an echo of Aristophanes, *Clouds* 799. On Chrysostom's reading of Aristophanes, see Q. Cataudella, "Giovanni Crisostomo, 'imitatore' di Aristofane," *Athenaeum* 18 (1940) 236-43.

[24] Fabricius, *Zu den Jugendschriften* 127, sees in the foregoing lines an imitation of Plato, *Phaedrus* 230b. There are several verbal reminiscences.

[25] For pictures and discussion of the elaborate mosaic floors of Antioch, see D. Levi, *Antioch Mosaic Pavements*. 2 vols. (Princeton, 1947).

those in the other, and you think that your son has fallen from heaven itself. Therefore, first of all, you must know that solitude does not make a person dishonorable, nor does kingship make him famous and illustrious. But before we come to reasoned argument, I will remove your suspicion by means of examples, examples taken not from among us, but from your own side.

Perhaps you have heard of Dionysius, the tyrant of Sicily,[26] and of Plato, son of Ariston. Who, tell me, has become the more illustrious? Who is praised and spoken of by all? Is it not the philosopher rather than the tyrant? And yet the tyrant ruled the entire world, lived in luxury, and spent his days amid great wealth, bodyguards, and other vanity, but Plato spent his time in the garden of the Academy, watering, sowing, eating olives, laying out a cheap table, and being free of all this vanity. And this is not yet the marvelous fact, but rather that after becoming a slave and being sold by order of the tyrant, Plato, far from appearing less honorable than the tyrant because of this, actually seemed admirable even to the tyrant himself.[27] Such is virtue! Not only through its actions, but also through the misfortunes it suffers, it prevents itself and those who practice it from being forgotten or consigned to oblivion.

And what of Plato's teacher, Socrates? How much more illustrious was he than Archelaus?[28] And yet Archelaus was a king who lived in great wealth, whereas Socrates lived in Lyceum and had only one garment and in this alone he was clothed winter and summer, and throughout the year.[29] He lived with his feet always bare and spent the entire day without food, eating only bread, and this was both his

---

[26] Dionysius I (c. 430-367 BCE).

[27] Chrysostom refers to the story widespread in antiquity (but not mentioned by Plato himself) that Plato had met Dionysius on his first visit to Sicily and that he had infuriated the tyrant by his outspoken condemnation of tyranny. In revenge, Dionysius handed Plato over to be sold by a Spartan envoy. See Diogenes Laertius, *De clarorum philosophorum vitis* 3.18-19. The historicity of the incident is questionable. See G.C. Field, *Plato and his Contemporaries. A Study in Fourth-Century Life and Thought.* 3rd ed. (London: Methuen, 1967) 17-18. Chrysostom refers to this story on several other occasions: homily 33.4 on Matthew (PG 57.392), homily 2.5 on Romans (PG 60.407), homily 4.4 on 1 Corinthians (PG 61.36). See P.R. Coleman-Norton, "St. John Chrysostom and the Greek Philosophers," 310.

[28] Archelaus was king of Macedon from 413-399 BCE.

[29] See the similar description of the monk in the *Comparatio* 3 and the parallel passage in Libanius, *Apologia Socratis*, decl. 1.18.

meat and meal. And he did not provide that meal out of his own resources, but he received it from others, so extreme was the poverty in which he lived.[30] Yet he was more illustrious than the king, so much so that, when the king frequently summoned him to appear before him, Socrates did not want to leave Lyceum and approach the king's wealth.[31] The way that each one lived is revealed by the glory which they now possess. For the names of those men, Plato and Socrates, are known to many, whereas Dionysius and Archelaus are virtually unknown.

And that man from Sinope, again another philosopher, was so much wealthier than these and a thousand other such kings, even though he lived in rags, that when Alexander was leading the army of Philip of Macedon into Persia, upon seeing Diogenes, Alexander left everything, approached Diogenes and asked him if he needed or wanted anything. But Diogenes did not reply.[32] Do you have enough examples now, or do you want us to recall still others? For these [philosophers] became more illustrious, not only than those who associated with kings, but also more than the king himself, although they chose the private life free of business and did not wish to get close to the government.

But even in the government you will see that those who become famous are not the ones who live in wealth, luxury, and abundance, but rather those who live a life of poverty, simplicity and modesty. Among the Athenians, Aristides,[33] whom the city honored with funeral rites upon his death, was so much more illustrious than Alcibiades who was outstanding in wealth, family, luxury, rhetorical

---

[30] The poverty of Socrates was a commonplace among writers of the diatribe such as Dio Chrysostom and Maximus of Tyre. It also appears several times in Libanius. See H. Markowski, *De Libanio Socratis defensore*. Breslauer Philologische Abhandlungen, 40 (Breslau: Marcus, 1910; reprinted New York/Hildesheim: G. Olms Verlag, 1970) 67-68.

[31] The call of Socrates by Archelaus was a well-known story, occuring in Aristotle, Seneca, Diogenes Laertius, Dio Chrysostom, Libanius and others. See Markowski, *De Libanio Socratis defensore* 107-8.

[32] See above, 2.4, p. 107.

[33] Aristides, Athenian statesman and soldier (fl. 490-467 BCE), became known in the tradition for his honesty and frugality. He was surnamed "the just" (ὁ δίκαιος). See the entry in Pauly-Wissowa, *Realencyclopädie der classischen Altertums-Wissenschaft* 2 (1895) 883. Plutarch, *Aristides* 27.1, records that Aristides' tomb is located at Phalerum and that "they say the city constructed it for him, since he did not leave even enough to pay for his funeral." Plato also attests to his character: *Menon* 94a and *Gorgias* 526ab.

power, bodily strength, nobility of birth and everything else, as much as a marvelous philosopher is more illustrious than some worthless child.[34] Among the Thebans, Epaminondas, a person who was called to the assembly but was unable to go because he had to wash his clothes and had nothing else to wear, nonetheless was more distinguished than all the generals who were there.[35] So do not speak to me of solitude or kingship. Fame and splendor do not reside in places or in clothes or in dignity or in power, but only in virtue of soul and philosophy.

6. But since the examples are not so persuasive, I will make my examination from your son himself. For we will find not only that he is now more illustrious, but also that he is more illustrious precisely because of the things which you say make him dishonorable and worthless. For, if you wish, we will persuade him to come down from the mountains and go into the marketplace, and you will see the entire city turning around and everyone pointing at him in wonder and amazement, as if some angel from heaven were now at their side. Do you think that glory is anything else but this? Because of those worn and worthless clothes, he will be more noble, not only than those in the king's service, but also than the king himself who wears the crown.

If he were dressed in gold, or even in purple with the king's crown upon his head, lying upon silken beds, being drawn by mules, and having bodyguards dressed in gold, he would not amaze everyone as much as he does now by being dirty and unwashed, wearing a rough garment, bringing no followers with him and being barefoot. The former are the rule for a king and are a matter of custom; therefore, if someone should say with admiration that the king is wearing a golden

---

[34] Alcibiades (c. 450-404 BCE), son of Cleinias, was an Athenian general and statesman. His physical beauty and moral decadence are amply attested in Plato's *Symposium* and in Plutarch's *Alcibiades*. See also the remark of Cornelius Nepos, *Liber de excellentibus ducibus exterarum gentium* 7.1.1: "In this man Nature seems to have tried to see what she could accomplish; for it is agreed by all who have written his biography that he was never excelled either in faults or in virtues." Translation by J.C. Rolfe, *Cornelius Nepos*. Loeb Classical Library (Cambridge, MA: Harvard University Press, 1929) 435.

[35] Epaminondas (d. 362 BCE), a Theban statesman and soldier, was famed for his frugality and the rectitude of his public life. Plutarch wrote parallel lives of Scipio and Epaminondas which are now lost. In his oration 4.71 against Julian, Gregory Nazianzen refers to the monks as contemporary "Epaminondases and Scipios" (SC 309.182; ed. J. Bernardi).

stole, not only would we not marvel, but we would even laugh at what
he said, since this is what we expect of a king.

But if someone should come and announce that your son has derided
his father's wealth and trampled underfoot worldly vanity and risen
above earthly hopes, that he has taken himself to solitude and put on a
cheap, wornout frock, immediately everyone would run together in
admiration, applauding him for his greatness of soul.[36] And, since
kings are constantly being denounced, golden clothes do not benefit
them at all, so impossible it is for clothes to make them admirable.
But your son's clothes gain for him great admiration. A robe like his
attracts more attention and notice than the robe of a king; even if no
one admired the king for his robe, everyone would marvel at your son
for wearing his.

"But," you will say, "what use to me is the opinion of the crowd and
their praises?" And yet, what else is glory but these things? "But,"
you will say, "I have no need of this; political power is what I want,
and honor." Certainly those who praise also give honor. But if you
wish for political power and position, we will find that the monks
possess this no less than the preceding goods. We could also make this
apparent from examples, but to argue in a way which is most likely to
persuade you, we will examine the case not in respect to other people,
but in regard to your son.

What do you say is a sign of the greatest power? Is it not to be able
to take revenge on all who harm you, to be able to repay those who do
good to you? But anyone can see that not even the king has this total
power, for many do him harm whom he cannot harm, and many serve
him well whom he cannot easily reward. Frequently in battle he
would like to avenge himself against enemies who harm him and
cause him countless evils, but he is powerless. And as for his friends
who displayed great accomplishments there, he is unable to reward

---

36 "Greatness of soul" (μεγαλοψυχία) is a classical virtue with both public and
private dimensions. According to Aristotle, *Nicomachean Ethics* 4.3.1123b, "that man
is thought to be 'great souled' who thinks himself worthy of great things and who is
truly worthy of them." Associated with both beneficence (εὐεργεσία) and courage
(ἀνδρεία), μεγαλοψυχία could also refer to the public acts of generosity on the part of a
civic official or patron. For the latter sense in Chrysostom's day, see the famous
depiction of this virtue personified in the fifth century mosaic of the Yakto complex at
Antioch: D. Levi, *Antioch Mosaic Pavements*, v. 1, 337-45. Libanius often used the word
to designate the spirit of one who had renounced wealth and material comforts in
exchange for the glory of the orator. See B. Schouler, *La tradition hellénique chez
Libanios* (Paris: Les Belles Lettres, 1984) 979-82.

them suitably because they already have fallen in battle and been
snatched away before the rewards are offered.

What, then, if we prove that your son has another power much
greater than that power which, as our discourse already has shown,
not even the kings enjoy? And let no one suspect that perhaps we are
talking about heavenly goods, in which you do not believe. We have
not forgotten our promises. But we shall prove our case from what
happens in this life. For if the greatest power is to be able to take
revenge on those who harm you, it is even greater still to achieve a
state of life in which no one can harm you, even if they wish to. The
superiority of the latter to the former will be clear and apparent to us
if we continue our speech with another example.

Tell me, which is better, to be so skilled in warfare that no one who
wounds us can escape unwounded, or to possess such a body that no
one can harm it, even if he should attack a thousand times? It
certainly is clear to everyone that the second form of power is the
greater and more godlike. And this is not all, but there is even
something far superior to this. What is it? To know the remedies by
means of which all wounds are done away with. Therefore, there are
three modes of power: the first, to be able to take revenge on
wrongdoers; the second, superior to the first, the ability to heal one's
own wounds (for the second does not always go with the first). But the
third is not to be subject to the power of any human being. We will
prove that your son possesses this third form of power which is beyond
human nature.

7. To prove that these words are not empty chatter, in our search we
have found something even better than this great power. For not only
will you not find anyone able to harm him, but not even anyone who
wishes to, and so he is safe on both counts. What could be more divine
than this life in which no one wishes to do harm, nor, if they wish, are
they able to do harm? Moreover, the lack of desire to harm comes not
from the inability (as is usually the case), but from the lack of any
reason to do harm. If it were simply the case that they were unable to
do harm, it would not be such a great thing, for great hatred is
engendered in those who wish to do harm, but who are unable
(although even this is no small kind of happiness). So then, we will
examine this point in particular, if you will. Tell me, then, who would
ever wish to harm a person who has nothing in common with other
people, neither contracts, nor land, nor money, nor business, nor
anything else? For what territory would someone dispute with him?
What slaves? What glory? What fears would there be? What causes
for annoyance? For we are moved to harm others either out of

jealousy, fear or anger. But this most regal man is above all things. Who would envy him who laughs at all the things which cause others to mourn and feel anxious? Who would grow angry with him who does no wrong? Who would fear him who has no suspicions? Therefore, it is clear that no one wishes to harm him.

Likewise, it also is clear that no one could harm him, even if he wished. For he provides neither opportunities nor occasions for someone to restrain him; rather, he is like the eagle which flies too high to be caught in the snares for the sparrows. How could anyone harm him? He has no money in order to be threatened with a fine. He has no homeland in order to be sent into exile. He longs not for glory in order to be led into dishonor. One thing is left—death. But in this, most of all, you can never harm him; rather, you would do him the greatest favor. For you would send him to the other life, which he desires greatly and which is the reason he does all that he does. And so, this would be deliverance from toil and not dishonor; it would be freedom from labor and rest.

Do you wish to know yet another way in which he is powerful, one much more philosophical than this? For even if someone should do countless, terrible things to him, beat him, and throw him into chains, his body would be injured because of nature, but his soul would remain uninjured because of his philosophy. He is not overcome with anger, nor constrained by hatred, nor conquered by enmity. And this is not the greatest feat, but there is something much more marvelous than this. For he loves those who do such things to him as if they were benefactors and patrons, and he prays for all goods to come to them. What comparable gift could you give him, even if you made him king of the world a thousand times over and extended his reign for a thousand years? Does he not possess something more honorable than any purple, any office, or any glory? What would you not sacrifice to possess such a soul? It seems to me that even those who are great lovers of their bodies would prefer this way of life.

Do you wish to see from yet another angle the more marvelous and most agreeable power of the man, from a point of view which is less exalted, but agreeable to you? What we have said thus far has proven that he is unconquered and invincible. But perhaps you are anxious to learn that he also exercises patronage for others and can guarantee their security.[37] The highest form of this patronage is to inspire in others the same zeal and thus to make them strong. But even if the others do not wish it and pursue instead this rather human and earthly way of life, even then you will see that he who has nothing is more powerful than you wealthy folk, precisely because he has nothing.

For who will address the king and censure him with greater power? You who have such great possessions and because of them are dependent even upon his slaves, you who tremble about everything, who provide countless occasions for him if he becomes angry and wishes to harm you, or the one who is out of the reach of his hands? For those who are free of all worldly things will address kings with exceedingly great power.[38] To whom would a person in power and engaged in imperial affairs more likely yield and obey, you who are wealthy and who, he suspects, frequently acts for the sake of money, or the person who has only one reason to give orders, namely philanthropy toward others? Whom will he honor and admire? The one about whom he could suspect nothing low, or the one who he thinks is baser than his own slaves? For just as when it is necessary to spend money, they prefer to obey those [holy] men, so also they urge them to be patrons.

8. But, if you wish, suppose that he accomplishes nothing through the medium of others, but only by himself. And let us bring someone who is suffering badly both to him and to you; or better, not to you, but to the emperor himself. Then we will see who is better able to care for the sufferer. First, let someone be brought who has suffered the most terrible calamity. Suppose that this person had only one son whom he has lost in the prime of his life. No ruler or king or anyone else could help him, especially not you. For you will give him nothing comparable to what he has lost. But if you bring him to your son, he will

[37] On the patronage (προστασία) exercised by Syrian monks, see Theodoret, *Religious History* 17.3, where the monk Abraham is invited to become the village patron after his intervention with tax-collectors. Later Abraham negotiated a loan for the village. On patronage in general, see Libanius, or. 47 *De patrociniis*, and Brown, "The Rise and Function of the Holy Man," *passim.*

[38] The "power" (ἐξουσία) of the holy man to address rulers was legendary. See Theodoret, *Religious History* 8.8, where the monk Aphraat rebukes the emperor Valens and a similar incident recorded about the monk Isaac of Constantinople in Theodoret, *Ecclesiastical History*, 4.34. After the riot of the statues at Antioch in 387, the intervention of the Syrian monks, especially Macedonius, was hailed by Chrysostom as a sign of the superiority of Christianity over Hellenism. See or. 17.1-2 *De statuis* (PG 49.172-175) and Theodoret, *Religious History* 13.7.

immediately uplift him, first of all by the sight, by the dress, by the dwelling, and he will persuade him to think nothing of human affairs. Then by his words he will easily dispel the cloud.[39]

But your house would cause him even greater grief. For when he sees that house of yours free of misfortunes, full of much happiness, and having an heir, he will burn all the more. But with your son he will be calmer, more philosophical. For when he sees your son showing contempt for such a great fortune, for such glory and splendor, he will not grieve so much about his dead son. For how will he be vexed by the loss of an heir to his goods, when he sees that someone else has despised all these things? And he will listen more readily when the person who speaks about philosophy proves his words true by his actions. But if you merely opened your mouth, you would cause him great anguish since you would be philosophizing about misfortunes that are not your own.

But your son, who teaches by his actions, will easily persuade him that death is nothing more than sleep. For he will not enumerate a host of parents who have suffered the same misfortune; rather, he will show that he himself each day undergoes death in his body and is ever prepared for it.[40] After rendering the doctrine of the resurrection more credible, he will send the man away freed from much of his grief, for his words supported by his actions will be much more effective at consolation than banquets and funeral meals.[41] And in this way, perhaps, the mourner will be healed.

Bring another to him, if you wish, someone who has lost his eyes after a lengthy illness. What will you be able to offer him? But your son, who is enclosed in a tiny dwelling, who is hastening towards another light, and who thinks that the present light is nothing compared to the future light, will prove that this illness is nothing terrible and will teach him to bear his misfortune with nobility. But will you be able to persuade those who are suffering calamity to

---

[39] The ability to offer consolation (παραμυθία) to those in mourning was considered to be one of the hallmarks of the true philosopher. See R. Gregg, *Consolation Philosophy. Greek and Christian Paideia in Basil and the Two Gregories.* Patristic Monograph Series, 2 (Philadelphia: Philadelphia Patristic Foundation, 1975) 4-6, and the literature cited there.

[40] The theme of "dying daily" was popular in monastic literature. See, for example, Athanasius, *Life of Antony* 19, 89, 91.

[41] Chrysostom often claims that the Christian fearlessness of death, shaped as it is by belief in the resurrection, distinguishes pagan from Christian. See F. Leduc, "L'eschatologie, une préoccupation centrale de saint Jean Chrysostome," *Proche-orient chrétien* 29 (1969) 109-37, especially 121-22.

philosophize? Certainly not, but you will cause them even greater grief. For we usually perceive our own misfortunes more clearly when we see our neighbors prospering. But your son will more easily restore these people. I do not mention the help that comes from prayer which is far better than anything else. I omit this since my speech is now directed to you.

But if you wish to be honored on account of your son and not to be despised (and it is likely that you desire this), I know no better way to achieve this than to have a child who surpasses human nature, whose glory shines throughout the earth, and who, despite such splendor, has no enemy. For if he were endowed with the power you desire, he would be honored by many, but he also would be hated by many. But, as he is, all who honor him take pleasure in doing so. For if humble people of humble origin, the sons of farmers and craftsmen, by embarking on this philosophy become so honored by all that no one in the highest ranks is embarrassed to go to their little hut and to share their conversation and table, but if they enjoy such fine treatment, as if they possessed the greatest goods (which, indeed, they do), how much more will they do this when they see someone from a splendid family, endowed with splendid possessions, who has such great hopes, approaching this virtue![42]

Thus the very thing which you regret, namely that he has gone from his former state to the present one, is that which more than anything else makes him illustrious. Moreover, this is what convinces everyone to regard him not as a man, but as an angel. For they will not have the same suspicions about your son which they have about the others, namely that he has chosen this path out of a desire for honor, a longing for money and a wish to become famous from a humble origin. Even if these false and evil words are said about the others, there could never be room for such suspicion in the case of your son.

9. And do not think that this happens only while the emperors live in piety. Even if the empire should undergo a change and the rulers should become pagans, the situation of your son would become all the more brilliant. For our status is not like that of the Greeks; it does not depend on the opinions of rulers, but it stands upon its own strength

---

[42] On the humble origins of monks as former craftsmen and farmers, see Libanius, or. 30.31 and or. 2.32. Visits to the monks by prominent citizens of Antioch were very common. See Theodoret, *Religious History* 3.9, 3.22, 6.6, 8.4, 13.3. Pagans frequently found this inordinate influence of the monks infuriating. See, for example, Eunapius, *Vitae sophistarum* 472 and Julian, or. 7.224ab.

and is more apparent the more it is attacked.[43] When a general is illustrious in peacetime, he will be even more famous at the onset of war. Therefore, even when the pagans are in power, it will be similar with your son, and his honor will be greater. For those who praise your son now will do so all the more when they see him prepared for battle, exercising greater confidence, and having many occasions for illustrious behavior.

Would you like us now to examine his attitude towards you, or is this topic superfluous? For he who is so gentle and kind towards others that he offers no one any cause for complaint will hold his father in even greater honor and will care for him much more than if he possessed worldly power. When someone comes to high office, it is uncertain whether or not he will despise his father. But now he has chosen a way of life through which he becomes more regal than the king and the most humble person in the world towards you. Such is the wisdom which exists among us: two things which seem to be opposites, namely a sense of moderation and a loftiness, meet in one soul.

Once there was a time when, desiring your money, he would have been pleased to see you dead. But now he even prays that you live a long time, so that even in this he might receive splendid crowns. For we shall receive no small reward if we honor our parents, and we are commanded to consider them as our masters, caring for them in word and in deed, as long as no harm is done to piety. *For what*, as the saying goes, *can you give back to them which is anything like what they have given to you?*[44] Know, then, that the person who in all other respects has reached the pinnacle of virtue will no doubt expend every effort to fulfill this duty as well. Even if he should have to die to save your life, he would not refuse, since not only does he care for you and honor you because of the law of nature, but above all because of God for whose sake he has come to despise all other things.

---

[43] Cf. the similar sentiments expressed in Chrysostom's treatise *On St. Babylas. Against Julian and the Greeks*: "When a Christian ascends the imperial throne, far from being shored up by human honors, Christianity deteriorates. On the other hand, when rule is held by an impious man, who persecutes us in every way and subjects us to countless evils, then our cause acquires renown and becomes more brilliant..." Translation by M. Schatkin, *St. John Chrysostom. Apologist.* Fathers of the Church, 73 (Washington, DC: Catholic University of America Press, 1983) 99. As Schatkin notes, p. 99, n. 82, "Chrysostom thus questions the advantage of the Constantinian alliance between the church and the Roman empire; his attitude is 'un-Byzantine'."

[44] Sirach 7:28.

Therefore, since he is now more illustrious, wealthier, more powerful, freer, and since in his loftiness of spirit he is now more your servant than ever, why, tell me, do you mourn? Because you do not fear each day that he might fall in battle or offend the emperor or incur the envy of his fellow soldiers? Do not the fathers of illustrious children have to fear these very things, and even more? Just as the person who places his child upon a high place must tremble lest he fall, so, too, must those who lead their children to high office.

"But the soldier's belt and the military cloak and the sound of the herald offer a kind of pleasure," [you object]. But how long does this last, tell me: for thirty days, or a hundred, or two hundred? And what then? Do not all these things pass like a dream or a myth or a shadow?[45] But now his honor will last to his death, and even beyond death, and much longer than that, and no one shall ever take this power from him, since it has been entrusted to him not by any human being, but by virtue itself.

But you wished to see him wearing luxurious clothes, riding on a horse, surrounded by a crowd of servants and supporting a retinue of flatterers and fawners? Why did you want these things? Was it not for him to take pleasure in all these things? If you heard him saying (for perhaps you will not trust us) that he considers his own life so much more pleasurable than a life of luxury, fornication, music, parasites, flatterers and other stupidity, that he would choose to die a thousand deaths rather than exchange the one type of pleasure for the other, what would you say to that? Do you not know how much pleasure there is in a life free of business? Perhaps no one else knows this since no one has ever tasted [this life] in its purity. But when this splendor is present, and when these other goods are found together in their entirety, I mean security and glory, what better way of life could there be?

"But," you will say, "why do you speak to me about this when I am so far from philosophy?" Why, then, do you prevent your son from drawing close to it? It is enough that the damage is done to you. Do you not think it is the greatest tragedy that people reach old age and are disgusted with their lives because they have done nothing worthwhile in their youth? "But surely," you will reply, "old age is a

---

45 The words "dream" ('ὄναρ) and "shadow" (σκία) echo a commonplace of Greek poetry: "Man is the dream of a shadow" (Pindar, *Pyth*. 8.99f). See M. Schatkin, *St. John Chrysostom. Apologist* 95, n. 69 for this and further classical parallels. The phrase is found several times in Chrysostom's early works.

burden because youth brought us great advantages." What great advantages? Show me an old man who possesses these great advantages. If he possessed them, and if they lasted any length of time, he would not be mourning now as if he were deprived of all these things. But if they have flown away and faded, why call them great advantages when they disappear so quickly?

But your son will not suffer this. If he should live to a great old age, you will not see him complaining, as you yourself do; rather, he will be full of joy, delight and contentment, for then his goods are in full flower. But the delights which your wealth procures, many though they may be, are limited to the first part of your life. Not so with your son; his wealth endures into old age and accompanies him even after death. That is why you feel discontented in your old age; despite the increase of your wealth and the abundance of occasions for glory and luxury, your age does not allow you to enjoy these things. That is why you tremble in the face of death and declare yourself to be the most miserable person in the world at the very hour of prosperity.

But your son will enjoy peace especially when he grows old, since he hastens to enter the harbor, and remains ever young, and never grows old. But you wanted your son to live in luxury which would have caused him a thousand regrets and grief in old age. We should not wish such luxury even on our enemies! But why do I speak about old age? In the space of a day those pleasures vanish—no, they do not last even for a day or an hour, but for the briefest moment. For what is pleasure? Is it not to fill one's belly, to partake of Sybaritic meals and to have intercourse with ripe young women, rolling around just like pigs in the mud?[46]

10. But let us not talk about this just yet. Let us first examine whether pleasure itself is not something insipid and cheap. If you will, let us deal first with what seems to be the most pleasurable, namely indulgence. Show me how long it lasts; show me how much of the day can be spent indulging. So little that it can barely be perceived. For as soon as a person has taken his fill, the pleasure is gone; even before satiety the pleasure passes more quickly than a flood; it disappears down his throat and does not last even as long as the food does. As soon as it passes his tongue, it already has lost its force. I will not mention the rest of the discomforts and turmoil which

---

46 The luxury of the inhabitants of Sybaris, a Greek colony on the gulf of Tarentum destroyed in 510 BCE, was proverbial in antiquity. Libanius refers to it several times. See Fabricius, *Zu den Jugendschriften* 135.

are produced by indulgence. Not only is the non-indulgent person more cheerful, but he is also lighter and will sleep more easily than the one who is distended by satiety. As the saying goes, *there is healthy sleep in a moderate stomach.*[47] Why speak of the sickness, the nausea, the misfortunes, the useless expenses? What of the complaints, the fines, the insults which arise from those banquets?

"But it is pleasurable to have intercourse with wicked women!" And what kind of pleasure would come from such a shameful action? We will not even speak of the quarrels between lovers, or the battles with rival lovers, or the damage to one's reputation. But let us suppose that there is someone who enjoys complete freedom in his debauchery; suppose that he has no rivals, that he is not neglected by his beloved, that he has an endless flow of money, although the concurrence of all these is an impossibility. (Indeed, the person who wishes to eliminate his rival must exhaust all his resources to surpass everyone else in munificence; on the other hand, the person who does not want to go bankrupt will be neglected and spit upon by his mistress.)

"But suppose nothing like this happens, and that everything goes according to his wishes." Can you still prove to us that he derives pleasure from this? For even in the act of intercourse there seems to be no pleasure, since the one who has consummated the union also has extinguished the pleasure; on the other hand, the one who is still in coitus does not experience pleasure, but rather tumult, confusion, frenzy, madness, great turmoil and violent shaking.

But the pleasure we enjoy is not like this. Far from it! It keeps the soul completely free of disturbance; it produces no tumult or confusion, but rather a kind of happiness, pure, chaste, honorable, endless, and much more powerful and robust than the pleasure which you have. Proof that our pleasure is superior to yours is that fear can take yours away. For if the emperor should send letters threatening death, most people will abstain from that pleasure; but in our case, even if someone could inflict a thousand deaths, he would not persuade us to despise this pleasure, but we would laugh all the more. This pleasure of ours is so much more imperious and more pleasurable than yours that there is no comparison between the two. Do not malign your child when he exchanges transient goods, or rather things which are not true goods, for those which are true and lasting goods. Do not mourn when he should be considered blessed, but do so

---

47 Sirach 31:20.

only when someone not like him is caught in this earthly life as if in a turbulent strait.

Now to the chief point. For even if you are an unbeliever and a pagan, nonetheless you will listen to what we say. You certainly have heard of the rivers Cocytos and Pyriphlegethontas, and the water of the Styx, and Tartarus which is as far from the earth as the earth is from the sky, and of the many kinds of punishments.[48]   Even if the pagans were unable to speak the truth about these things as they are, since they followed their own reasonings and certain teachings of ours which they misunderstood, nonetheless they have received a kind of image of the judgment. Among the poets, philosophers, orators, and all writers you will find speculations on these doctrines. You will hear about the Elysian Field, the Isles of the Blessed, the groves, the myrtle trees, the light air, the most pleasant odor, and the choruses who dwell there, garbed in white robes, dancing and singing hymns, and, in a word, the just desserts which await both the wicked and the good after death.

How do you think both the good and the wicked live after reflecting on these things? Are there not some persons who, even if they prosper in this life without pain and with great pleasure, upon reflection are struck, as it were, by the whip of conscience and by the expectation of the frightening things that await them? And, yet, good people, even if they should suffer a thousand misfortunes, have "a hope which nourishes" them, as Pindar says, and which does not allow them to feel the present misfortunes.[49]   Thus, even in this respect our

---

[48] Libanius puts on the lips of Socrates a similar description of the underworld in his declamation 2.36, *De silentio Socratis:* "But for those who have lived lawlessly and immorally, their souls filled with many impieties, there are Tartaruses, and Cocytuses, and Pyriphlegethons as receptions and terrible chastisements and eternal punishments in fire and darkness and wierd rivers driven in an unending course." Translation in M. Crosby and W.M. Calder, "On the Silence of Socrates," *Greek, Roman and Byzantine Studies* 3 (1960) 195. According to Calder, 199-201, Socrates functions in Libanius' discourse as a symbol of Greek paideia in the struggle against Christianity. Libanius presents pagan teaching on the afterlife as a rival to Christian teaching. See also Libanius' funeral oration over Julian, or. 18.272, where Julian's fearlessness of death is likened to that of Socrates and Tartarus and the Isles of the Blessed also are mentioned.

[49] Chrysostom quotes two words (ἐλπίδα κουροτρόφον) from fragment 214 of Pindar (Bergk; fr. 233, Boeckh): "With him liveth sweet Hope, the nurse of eld, the fosterer of his heart,—Hope, who chiefly ruleth the changeful mind of man." Translation by Sir John Sandys. *Pindar.* Loeb Classical Library (Cambridge, MA: Harvard University Press, 1937) 611. The fragment first was preserved in Plato, *Republic* 331a. See P.R. Coleman-Norton, "St. John Chrysostom's Use of the Greek Poets," *Classical Philology* 27 (1932) 217, for a discussion of the reference and its variants.

pleasure is greater than yours. For it is much better to begin with temporary labors and to end with eternal rest than to get a brief taste of things which seem to be most pleasurable and to end with the most bitter and burdensome evils. And when one acknowledges that even in this world the monk's life is more pleasurable, must we not do what I said at the beginning, that is, have pity on those who weep over such goods? Your child should not be mourned, but rather applauded and crowned, for he has entered upon a life without turmoil; he has arrived at the tranquil harbor.

But many fathers who have children engaged in the present life reproach you; some cry when they see you, and others laugh. Why are you not laughing at them or mourning over them? Pay no attention if they mock us, unless they do it with good reason. And if this is the case, we should mourn even if they did not laugh at us. But even if the whole world should laugh and mock us unjustly, we would still consider ourselves blessed and mourn rather for them, since they are the most miserable of all and no better than the insane. For it is typical of insane people and of those who are afflicted with this kind of illness to laugh at things which deserve praise and crowns. Tell me, if everyone praised you, marveled at you, and said that you were most blessed because your son was passionately excited over the madness of dancers and charioteers, would you not think that this was a laughing matter? So if they mock and laugh at noble and praiseworthy deeds, why do you not say that they are out of their minds? Let us do this even now; do not let your opinion about your son be determined by the views of the crowd, but by a careful examination of rational arguments. You will see that those who are laughing are the parents of children who are slaves in comparison with your son and not free men.

At the moment you are unable to see plainly because your mind is clouded by emotion. But when you are calmer and when your son has proven his great virtue, it no longer will be necessary to speak to you; instead you yourself will speak these words to others, and even more than these. My prophecy is not a groundless one, but it is based on my own experience. For I had a good friend whose father was a pagan, wealthy, illustrious and notable in every way. At first this father stirred up magistrates, threatened his son with prison, and, after stripping him of everything, left the young man in a foreign land lacking even necessary sustenance; he hoped by this to persuade him to return to the worldly life. But when he saw that his son did not yield to any of this abuse, the father was won over and sang the palinode, as it were.[50]   Now he honors and praises his son more than he does his own father. And although he has many other children who are illustrious, he says that they are not even worthy to be the servants of that son; now he himself is much more renowned on account of his son.

The same will happen in the case of your son, and the facts themselves will teach you that I do not lie. Therefore I will now be silent, asking only this of you: wait for but a year, or even less. Virtue among Christians does not require many days, since it grows by divine grace. You will see all that we have said displayed in actions. And then not only will you approve what has happened, but, if you are willing to rouse yourself even a little, you quickly will come to share your son's zeal, and he will become your teacher of virtue.

---

[50] That is, "he uttered a recantation." The term "palinode" first was used of an ode by the lyric poet Stesichorus in which he recanted his attack upon Helen. See the legend told in Plato, *Phaedrus* 243ab. The phrase "to sing the palinode" is found frequently in Libanius. See Fabricius, *Zu den Jugendschriften* 128.

Book Three

To the Christian Parent

1. Now let us teach the Christian parent that he should not attack those who urge his son to please God. Indeed, there is a danger that our speech might be superfluous and that the opposite of what I mentioned above might happen. Earlier I said that the rule of this competition did not require me to battle against a pagan. The apostle Paul, when he ordered us to judge only those within our own camp, allowed us to be free from doing battle with those on the outside.[1] But now, it seems, there is no need to argue with a Christian. For if previously it seemed shameful to discuss these things with a Christian, this is all the more the case now. For will not the Christian slink away and hide if he requires correction in this matter, if even the pagan had nothing to answer us?

What shall we do? Shall we be silent for this reason and say nothing? By no means! For if someone could promise and prove to us that no one would ever dare to do such things again, we then would have to keep silent and allow past offenses to be forgotten. But since no one can provide us with a trustworthy guarantee, it remains necessary to speak a word of admonition. For if our speech finds people sick with this illness, it will do its job; but if no one falls prey to this illness, then our prayers have been answered. For even doctors, after they have prepared medicines for the sick, ought to hope that the sick person will not continue to need these medicines. Likewise, we also pray that none of our brothers should need this correction. But if

---

[1] Cf. 1 Corinthians 5:12. See above, p. 97.

it should happen, God forbid, a "second sailing," as the proverb goes, will not escape them.[2]

Imagine, then, a father who is a Christian, one like the pagan in every way, except for his religious beliefs; suppose that he mourns like the pagan and rolls before the feet of all. Picture him displaying his grey hair and speaking of his old age, his solitude, and everything else; let him provoke the judges to anger as much as he wishes. But, in the case of this man, it is no longer before humans that judgment is passed. For he has heard the words which Spirit-filled persons have spoken among us concerning the horrid and fearsome tribunal in the next life. It is necessary, above all, to remember that day and the fire which flows like a river, the flame which is never extinguished, the sun which does not shine, the moon which is hidden, the falling stars, and sky turning round, the powers in confusion, the earth everywhere shaken and boiling, the terrible, alternating sound of the trumpets, the angels traversing the world, the thousands standing by, the myriads serving, the armies and powers arriving with the Judge, the sign shining before them, the ready throne, the opened books, the unapproachable glory, the fearsome and terrible voice of the Judge as he sends some into the fire prepared for the devil and his angels, as he shuts the gates to others after much labor for virginity, as he orders some of his servants to bind up the chaff and throw it into the furnace, while commanding others to bind the rest hand and foot, to strangle them with bare hands and drag them into the outer darkness and hand them over to the deadly gnashing of teeth. With the most violent and bitter punishment he afflicts one simply for gazing with impure eyes, another for laughing at the wrong time, another for condemning his neighbor without examination, another merely for slander. The one who will inflict these torments has spoken and warned that punishment also is delivered for these crimes.

2. All of us must approach this Judge in the next life and see that day on which all things will be laid bare—I do not mean words and deeds only, but even one's very thoughts. Although these acts seem to be insignificant now, on that day we shall suffer terrible chastisements. For the Judge demands of us with the same strictness

---

[2] A "second sailing" (ὁ δεύτερος . . . πλοῦς) was proverbial for "the next best way." It refers to the use of oars after the winds have failed. Cf. Menander, fr. 241.

both our own and our neighbor's salvation.[3] That is why Paul everywhere urges everyone to seek not merely their own interest, but also the interest of their neighbor. And for this reason he vigorously censured the Corinthians, because they did not show concern or care for the man committing fornication, but rather overlooked the wound which afflicted him.[4] And writing to the Galatians he said: *Brethren, if a person is overtaken in any trespass, you who are spiritual should restore him.*[5] And to the Thessalonians he had previously given the same admonishment, saying: *Therefore, encourage one another, just as you are doing,* and again, *Admonish the disorderly, encourage the fainthearted, help the weak.*[6]

Let no one say, "What business is it of mine to care for others? The one who perishes, let him perish! The one who is saved, let him be saved! Their doings are not my business; I am enjoined only to look after my own affairs." To prevent anyone from saying such things, to eliminate this savage and inhuman thought, Paul abolished it with these laws and commanded that a person should often neglect his own affairs to support those of his neighbors, and he determined that this strict way of life was to be observed everywhere.

Writing to the Romans, Paul ordered them to exercise great care in this matter, urging the strong to be like parents to the weak and persuading the former to be anxious for the salvation of the latter.[7] In this passage he speaks in the form of an exhortation and a counsel, but elsewhere he shakes the souls of his hearers with great vehemence.[8] For those who neglect the salvation of their brothers, he says, sin against Christ himself and tear down the temple of God.[9] And he does not say this on his own authority, but on instruction from the Teacher. For the Only-begotten of God, wishing to teach that this is a necessary duty, and that great misfortunes await those who do not wish to fulfill it, said: *Whoever should scandalize one of these little ones, it would be*

---

[3] The communal character of Christian salvation will become a persistent theme in Chrysostom's later preaching. See, for example, his homily 9.2 on Genesis (PG 54.623) and the discussion by F. Leduc, "L'eschatologie, une préoccupation centrale de saint Jean Chrysostome," 129-31.

[4] Cf. 1 Corinthians 5:1-5 and 10:24.

[5] Galatians 6:1.

[6] 1 Thessalonians 5: 11, 14.

[7] Cf. Romans 15:17.

[8] Chrysostom uses the rhetorical term "form" (τάξις) to refer to the style of Paul's discourse. This sort of rhetorical analysis is typical of Chrysostom's exegesis and in some ways anticipates certain modern critical approaches.

[9] Cf. 1 Corinthians 8:12.

better for him to have a great millstone fastened around his neck and to be drowned in the depths of the sea.[10] And the person who presented his talent is afflicted with the same punishment, not because he overlooked any of his own affairs, but because he neglected the salvation of his neighbors.

So, then, even if we live our own lives perfectly, we gain nothing, since that sin is sufficient to cast us into the depths of gehenna. For if nothing can save those who refuse to assist their neighbor in material needs and who have been cast out of the bridal chamber, even if they have practiced virginity, how is it possible that the person who has neglected what is much greater (for care of the soul is much more important) will not suffer every terrible punishment?[11] For God did not create man to provide only for himself, but to provide for many others as well. That is why Paul calls the faithful "lights," signifying that they are required to be useful to others.[12] For a light would not be a light if it shed its rays only upon itself.

That is why he says that those who neglect their neighbors are even worse than the pagans, speaking in this way: *If anyone does not provide for his relatives, and especially for his own family, he has disowned the faith and is worse than an unbeliever.*[13] What does he want to show when he uses the word "provide"? Is it to supply the necessities of life? I think he is talking about care for the soul. But if you are eager to disagree with me, my argument will be established all the more strongly. For if Paul speaks in this way about bodily needs, if he prescribes such a punishment for someone who does not provide this daily nourishment, if he says that such a person is worse than the pagans, where shall we rank the person who neglects a duty which is greater and even more necessary?

3. So, then, let us calculate the gravity of your sin; ascending step by step we will demonstrate that the greatest sin of all and the absolute height of wickedness is to neglect one's children. Now, the first degree of evil, wickedness, and cruelty is to neglect one's friends. No, let us begin our speech on an even lower level. Somehow or other I almost forgot that the old Law, which was given to the Jews, did not

---

[10] Matthew 18:6.

[11] Cf. Matthew 25:1-13. Chrysostom frequently refers to the parable of the "foolish virgins" to underscore the limited value of a merely physical virginity. See, for example, his treatise *On Virginity* 77. Later Chrysostom will apply this text particularly to the importance of almsgiving. See homily 78 on Matthew (PG 58.711).

[12] Cf. Philippians 2:15.

[13] 1 Timothy 5:8.

allow them even to neglect the beasts of burden of their enemies, whether they fell down or became lost, but the Law commanded them to lead back the lost and to raise up the fallen.[14]

Therefore, the first degree of wickedness and cruelty, beginning with the least important, is to neglect the flocks and animals of one's enemies when they suffer misfortune. The second degree, greater than the first, is to neglect one's enemies. For as much as a human person is more precious than an irrational animal, so much greater is this sin than the first. The third degree after this is to neglect one's brothers, even if they should be unknown. The fourth is to overlook one's own household. The fifth, when we disregard not only their bodily needs, but also the vital needs of their souls. The sixth, when we neglect not only our household, but also our children as they become corrupted. The seventh, when we do not seek out others to care for them. The eighth, when we even hinder and drive away from our children those who wish to care for them. The ninth, when we not only hinder them, but even attack them. And so, if such a great punishment is inflicted on the person in the first, second and third degrees of wickedness, how great a fire will befall you who stand in the ninth degree, which surpasses all the rest?

In fact, I would not be mistaken to call this not merely the ninth, or the tenth degree, but even the eleventh degree. Why is this? Because not only is this sin much greater by nature than those enumerated above, but it also is worse on account of the time. What do I mean by "on account of the time"? That we, who now commit the very same sins as those who were under the old Law, will not suffer the same torments, but rather much greater torments, for we have enjoyed a greater gift, partaken of a more perfect teaching, and received a greater honor. Therefore, since both nature and time make this sin so dreadful, consider how great a fire will fall upon the heads of those who dare to commit it.

To prove that what I have said is not mere conjecture, I will present factual evidence so that you may know that, even if we conduct all our own affairs properly, we shall receive the most severe punishment if we neglect the salvation of our children. I will not speak my own words to you, but I will rely on the sacred scriptures. There was a priest among the Jews, a moderate and temperate man, whose name was Eli. Eli was the father of two sons. When he saw them beginning to do evil, he did not restrain them or prevent them; or, rather, he

---

[14] Cf. Exodus 23:4-5.

restrained them and prevented them, but he did not do this with sufficient zeal.[15] The crimes of these children were fornication and gluttony. Scripture says that they ate before the holy meats were sanctified and before the sacrifice was offered to God. When their father learned of this, he did not punish them, but by verbal exhortation he tried to turn them from this wickedness; he continually spoke to them in this way: *Do not, my children, do not act in this way, for it is not a good report which I hear about you, that you cause the people not to worship the Lord. If a man should sin against a man, they will intercede for him to the Lord. But if a person should sin against the Lord, who will intercede for him?*[16]

Certainly, his words were quite severe; they were humiliating and capable of converting any sensible person. He pointed out their crime, showed its seriousness, and plainly declared the unbearable and terrible judgment which awaited them. However, since Eli did not do all that was required of him, he perished along with his sons. He should have threatened them, cast them from his sight, beaten them, and been much stricter and more severe. Since he did none of these things, he incurred God's wrath on himself and on his children; by sparing them at the wrong time, he destroyed his own salvation as well as that of his children.

Listen to what God says to him, or, rather, what he no longer says to him. For God has judged him to be no longer worthy of an answer; rather, as in the case of a household slave who has committed a most serious offence, God uses another to inform him of the evils which are to befall him. Such was the wrath of God at that time. Listen, then, to what he says about the teacher [Eli] to his disciple [Samuel]. To the disciple, and to another prophet, and to everyone God spoke concerning the evils to befall Eli, rather than speak directly to Eli, so thoroughly had God rejected him.

What, then, did God say to Samuel? *He knew that his sons cursed God, and he did not correct them.*[17] However, this is not exactly true because Eli certainly did correct his sons, but God says that his was not a true correction. God condemned his warning because it was not sufficiently forceful. Therefore, even if we show concern for our children, if we fail to do what is necessary, it will not be true concern, just as Eli's correction was not a true one. After God had stated the charge

---

[15] Cf. 1 Samuel 2:16 ff.
[16] 1 Samuel 2: 23-25.
[17] 1 Samuel 3:13.

against Eli, he added the punishment with great wrath: *For I have sworn*, he said, *to the house of Eli that the iniquity of Eli's house shall not be expiated by sacrifice or offering for ever*.[18] Do you see God's intense anger and merciless punishment? Eli must perish utterly, he says, and not only him and his children, but his entire household with him, and there will be no remedy to heal this wound. Except for the man's negligence in regard to his children, however, God had no other charge to make against the elder at that time; in all other respects Eli was a marvelous man.

One can measure his philosophy not only from the rest of his life, but especially from his behavior after this catastrophe. After hearing God's threats and realizing that he would face the most severe punishment, Eli showed no grief or bitterness. Nor did he say what the crowd usually does: "Do I control other peoples' choices? I am responsible for my own sins. The children have reached adulthood, and they alone should be punished." Eli did not say or think anything like this. But like a prudent servant whose only thought is to bear patiently whatever comes from the master, even if it should be painful, in this way Eli spoke words full of much philosophy: *The Lord himself*, he says, *will do what seems best to him*.[19]

This is not the only example of the man's virtue. Once the Jews were engaged in a war and someone came and announced to Eli the catastrophes which had occurred. When Eli heard that his sons had fallen shamefully and miserably in the battle, he remained silent. But when the messenger added, after announcing their death, that the ark had been captured by the enemy, then the old man, overshadowed with grief, *fell from his seat backwards against the door, and his back was broken, for he was an elder and heavy and honorable, and he had judged Israel for twenty years*.[20]

If, then, a priest, an elder, an honorable man, who ruled the Hebrew nation for twenty years without fault, who lived in times which did not require much perfection, could find no excuse in these actions; if he died a violent and miserable death because he did not care for his children with diligence; and if this sin of negligence, like a great, wild tidal wave, overcame all these actions and wiped out all his virtuous deeds, what punishment will be reserved for us who live in times which require much greater philosophy and who lack the virtue of Eli?

---

[18] 1 Samuel 3:14.
[19] 1 Samuel 3:18.
[20] 1 Samuel 4:18.

Not only do we not direct our children properly, but we even plot against and attack those who wish to do this, and we act more savagely than any barbarian towards our offspring. Indeed, the savageness of barbarians involves only slavery, destruction, captivity of the homeland, and evils of the body, but you enslave the very soul and, after binding it like some prisoner, hand it over to fierce and wicked demons and to their passions. For you are doing nothing else but this when you neither give them spiritual exhortation yourself nor allow others who wish to do so.

And let no one say to me that many people have neglected their own children more than Eli did and yet have suffered nothing comparable. Often many have suffered a worse fate than his on account of that sin. For whence come untimely deaths and serious and chronic illness, both our own and our children's? Whence come fines and calamities and insults and a thousand misfortunes? Do they not come from neglecting children when they are wicked? The sufferings of Eli the elder are enough to prove that this is not mere conjecture. But I also will say a word to you about these matters from a certain sage on our side. On the topic of children he has this to say: *Do not rejoice over impious children. Unless the fear of God is with them, do not count on their survival.*[21] For you will wail with untimely grief and you will see their sudden demise. Many, as I have said, often have suffered in this way. Even if some have escaped, they will not escape in the end, but they will suffer the greatest misfortune; for when they have gone to the next life, they will pay a more bitter penalty.

"Why, then," you ask, "is not everyone punished in this life?" Because God has established the day on which he will judge the world, and this day has not yet come; if it were otherwise, our entire race already would have been destroyed and exterminated. But so that this might not happen and so that the crowd might not become too lazy while awaiting judgment day, God takes certain people who are guilty of sin and punishes them in this life to teach the rest through them the measure of punishment which awaits them. [He does this] so that they might know that, even if they do not pay the penalty in this life, when they go to the next they will pay a penalty that is far more severe. Let us not be careless because God does not send a prophet today and does not threaten punishment as he did to Eli. For now is

---

[21] Sirach 16:1-3.

not the time for prophets; or, rather, he sends prophets even now,[22] for what was said to people in the past is said to us as well. Through Eli and his sufferings God speaks not only to Eli, but to all who sin as he did. For God is no respecter of persons, nor does he allow those who sin more grievously to go unpunished, when he destroys the one who sins less seriously along with his whole household.

4. This is not to say that the matter is unimportant to him; God shows great concern for the education of children. He has endowed nature with a powerful desire which by a kind of inescapable necessity leads parents to care for their children. Later, when he spoke to us, he imposed laws which prescribed care for them. When God established the feasts, he commanded that [the Jews] should teach their children the reason [for the feasts]. For example, when he spoke about the Passover, he added: *And you will announce to your son on that day, saying, "For this reason God did this for me, that I came out of Egypt."*[23] And in the Law he does the same thing; after speaking about the first-born, again he adds: *But if your son should ask you later on, "What does this mean?" you will say to him, "With a strong hand the Lord brought us out of Egypt, out of the house of slavery. For when Pharoah stubbornly refused to let us go, the Lord slew all the first-born in the land of Egypt, both the first-born of man and the first-born of cattle. Therefore, I sacrifice to the Lord all the males that first open the womb."*[24] All these commands were given to lead them to a knowledge of God. Even to children he gave many commands concerning those who had begotten them; he honored those who were well disposed, punished the arrogant, and thereby made them even dearer to their parents. When we are put in charge of another person, the honor imposes on us a great responsibility to care for that person. If nothing else, the fact that the fate of that person is entirely in our hands is enough to shame us, and we could not be brought easily to betray the one who has been entrusted to us. But if, as a result of negligence on our part, someone should become angry and disturbed with us more than people who are afflicted with insults, and if this person should punish us severely, this will draw us even more to our duty. This, then, is what God has done.

---

[22] At this point the *Patrologia graeca* text prints several words that are omitted in Dübner's edition: "What is the proof of this? *They have*, he says, *Moses and the prophets*" (Luke 16:29).

[23] Exodus 13:8.

[24] Exodus 13:14-15

In addition to these incentives, God has added a third bond, a natural one, which is, if you will, the most important. In order that parents might not despise God's injunctions, since they have been commanded to raise children, God has added the obligation imposed by nature. But in order that this bond, which is weakened when children are disrespectful, might not be broken, he established a bulwark of punishment both at his hands and at the hands of the parents, so as to render the children perfectly submissive and thereby to stimulate their parents' love.

And this is not all, but in another way, a fourth way, he has bound us tightly and firmly to our children. Not only does God punish children who behave badly toward their parents, not only does he receive favorably those who are good, but he also does the same thing to the parents, severely punishing those who neglect their children, but honoring and praising those who care for them. Eli the elder was punished simply for his negligence, although he was notable in other respects, and God honored the patriarch Abraham for his concern in this matter, no less than for his other virtues. Speaking of those many great gifts which he promised to give to him, and expressing the reason, God said: *I know that Abraham will put in order his sons, and his household with him, and they will keep the ways of the Lord God by doing righteousness and justice.*[25]

I say these things now so that we may realize that God will not easily tolerate those who neglect the ones who are so dear to him. He cannot labor on behalf of their salvation, while others disdain to show concern for them. However, he will not overlook it, but he will be most displeased and violently angry, as the facts have shown. That is why the blessed Paul continually speaks this exhortation: *Fathers, bring up your children in the discipline and instruction of the Lord.*[26] If we are commanded to watch over their souls so as to render an account, this is required much more of the father who bore and raised the child and who has him constantly at home. Just as one cannot excuse or apologize for one's own sins, so also there are no excuses for the sins of one's children. Once again the blessed Paul makes this very clear. When prescribing what sort of people were acceptable as leaders, besides all the other requisite virtues, he demands of them that they show concern for their children, as if we could find no pardon if they should turn out perverse, and right he was.[27]

---

[25] Genesis 18:19.
[26] Ephesians 6:4.
[27] Cf. 1 Timothy 3:4.

If wickedness were in people by nature, then one would have the right to make excuses. But since it is by free choice that we become either wicked or good, what specious excuse could a person offer, if he allowed the one he loved so much to become wicked and perverted?[28] Is it that he did not wish to make him a good person? But no parent would say this, for nature has appointed him to this task and continually urges him on to it. Was he unable to carry it out? This is no excuse. Since he received the child in his tender years, and since he was the first and the only one to have authority over him, and since he has the child at home with him all the time, his job as guardian is quite easy and manageable. Therefore, there is no other reason that children become corrupted than from madness over worldly things. When parents are concerned only with their own affairs and do not wish to give priority to their children's, they necessarily neglect their children, as well as their own souls.

I would say that these parents (and do not think that I am speaking out of anger) are even worse than those who kill their children. For the latter separate the body from the soul, but the former take the soul along with the body and throw them both into the fire of gehenna. By nature everyone must undergo [physical] death sooner or later; but the other death could be avoided, if it were not inflicted by the negligence of the parents. Moreover the death of the body will immediately end at the coming of the resurrection, but the death of the soul will find no such remedy. There will be no salvation in its future, only an eternity of inescapable punishments. It is not without reason, then, that we say that such parents are worse than those who kill their children. To sharpen a sword, take it in hand, and plunge it into the very throat of one's child, is not so terrible as to destroy and corrupt the soul, for to us there is nothing equal to this.

5. "What, then?" you say, "Cannot the person who lives in the city and has a house and a wife be saved?" Certainly, there is not one way of salvation, but there are many and varied ways. Christ said this in indefinite terms when he declared that there were many mansions in the Father's house.[29] But Paul speaks of this with some exactness when he writes: *There is one glory of the sun, and another glory of the moon, and another glory of the stars; for star differs from star in glory.*[30] What he means is this: some people shine like the sun, others

---

[28] On the notion of "free choice" (προαίρεσις) in Chrysostom's moral psychology, see the comments above, p. 75, n. 19.

[29] Cf. John 14:2.

[30] 1 Corinthians 15:41.

134 Two Treatises on Monastic Life

like the moon, others like the stars. And in this passage he did not stress the difference; rather, he shows that there is great variety within a single class of objects, a variety as great as the number of objects. *For star*, he says, *differs from star in glory.* Imagine, starting with the magnitude of the sun and going to the tiniest of all the stars, how many degrees one would descend in levels of dignity. If you were to lead your son to the imperial palace, and do and suffer all things, and persuade him to do likewise, so as to place him close to the emperor, and if you were to take into account nothing at all, neither the expense, nor the danger, nor death itself; but if, when the question of enrolling in the heavenly army is raised, you are not upset to see him take the last place and become the least of all, is this not absurd?

But, if you will, let us see whether it is possible for someone who is involved in worldly activities to obtain even this portion. The blessed Paul made a brief statement about this when he declared that those who have wives could be saved only if they lived with them as if they did not have them and only if they did not misuse the world.[31] But, if you will, let us examine this in our speech. Could you affirm that your son heard you teaching, or that he learned on his own, that the person who swears, even if he is faithful to his oath, offends the one God? And that the one who remembers injuries also cannot be saved? For Scripture says, *the ways of those who remember injuries lead to death.*[32] And that God so disdains the slanderer that he is forbidden to read the holy Scriptures? And that he will cast out the braggart and the arrogant from heaven and hand them over to the fire of gehenna? And that he punishes as an adulterer the person who merely gazes with impure eyes? And that sin which everyone has the opportunity to commit, namely judging one's neighbors, which merits the most severe punishment, have you ever warned him to avoid it and have you read to him the laws of Christ which were laid down about these matters? Or are you also unaware that such laws exist? How then will your son be able to conduct himself properly in these matters, when his father who should teach him does not know the laws?

I wish the only calamity were that parents give no useful advice to their children; this would not be so bad. But now you even push them in the opposite direction. When parents urge their children to study

---

[31] Cf. 1 Corinthians 12: 29, 31.
[32] Proverbs 12:28.

rhetoric, all they say are words like this:[33] "A certain man, of low estate, born of lowly parents, after achieving the power that comes from rhetoric, obtained the highest positions, gained great wealth, married a rich woman, built a splendid house, and is feared and respected by all." And another one says, "A certain man after learning Latin became illustrious in the emperor's service and he manages and administers all internal business."[34] And another one cites a third example. And they talk of those who become illustrious on earth, but no one ever mentions those in heaven; and if someone should attempt to mention this, he is chased away as a troublemaker.

6. Therefore, from the beginning whenever you sing songs for your children, teach them nothing else but what is at the base of all evils, inculcate in them what are the two most tyrannical lusts, I mean the love of money and—what is even more wicked— the love of vain and empty glory. Either of these alone is capable of subverting all things, but when both of them come together and attack the tender soul of a youth, like torrential rivers flowing together, they destroy all its virtues, gathering together so many thorns, so much sand, so much rubbish that they render the soul sterile and unable to produce any good.

Even the words of pagan writers will testify to this for us. The first of these passions [the love of money], even on its own and without the cooperation of the other passion, is called by one the "height" and by another the "chief" of evils.[35] If, considered separately, the first is the height and chief, when the one that is much worse and more powerful is added—I mean the madness for glory—and when it joins the first and attacks and puts out roots and seizes the soul of the youth, who, then, will be able to extirpate this disease, especially when even the parents do and say everything, not for these wicked plants to be

---

[33] The term λόγοι, translated here as "rhetoric," is quite broad in its range of meanings. Elsewhere I have rendered it as "literary studies" or "education." Λόγοι, as was noted above, p. 5, was Libanius' favorite term for his own educational system.

[34] Latin and law were rivals to Libanius' beloved λόγοι, and he constantly bemoans the flight of young men to the profitable careers afforded by these studies. See J.H.W.G. Liebeschuetz, *Antioch* 242-55.

[35] Love of money as the "height" (ἀκρόπολιν) and "chief" (κεφαλήν) of all evils was a well-known pagan sentiment, as Chrysostom has noted. Cf. his homily 63.4 on Matthew (PG 58.608). Further parallels in Greco-Roman literature can be found in Fabricius, *Zu den Jugendschriften* 136-37.

uprooted, but for them to be made secure?[36] Who is so senseless that
he does not despair of the salvation of a child who has received this
kind of education? They should want the soul to enjoy the very
opposite instruction and to avoid vice. But when the advantages of
money are always being touted and when damnable men are proposed
for emulation, what hope of salvation can there be? For those who
love money inevitably become envious, malicious, blasphemous,
perjurous, arrogant, abusive, deceitful, shameless, reckless, unfeeling
and full of all wickedness.

The blessed Paul gives trustworthy testimony on this matter, when
he says that the love of money is the root of evils in this life.[37] Before
him, Christ revealed the same thing, declaring that it is impossible
both to serve God and to be enslaved to that passion.[38] If, then, from
the beginning a young person is led into that slavery, how can he ever
become free, how can he resist the flood, when everything works
against him, when everything conspires to plunge him beneath the
surface and to force his death by drowning? If no one caused him
trouble, and if, rather, many people extended a hand, and if he were
able to rise up, to see clearly, and to wash off the brine of evil, would
this not be desirable? If, after a long time of singing the divine hymns,
he is able to banish the diseases that afflict people, would he not merit
a thousand praises, a thousand crowns?

Habit is a terrible thing, terrible enough to capture and rule the
soul, especially when it has pleasure acting in conjuction with it; but
that habit, toward which we are hastening and which we are eager to
attain, causes us to labor greatly. For this reason, when it was
necessary to cleanse the children of the Hebrews of their old habit of
vices which they had learned in Egypt, God took them alone into the
desert, removing them as far as possible from the corrupters. There in
the desert, as if in a kind of monastery, he completely molded their
souls, applying every means of healing, both harsh and gentle, and he
omitted nothing at all which could assist in healing them. However,

[36] Chrysostom's polemic against vainglory cannot be separated from his more
general attack on Greek culture. F. Leduc has suggested that Chrysostom's hostility to
the pursuit of glory is a direct reaction to the exaltation of glory by contemporary
pagans such as Julian and Libanius. See his "La thème de la vaine gloire chez saint
Jean Chrysostome," *Proche-orient chrétienne* 29 (1969) 3-32, and especially 21-32. The
preceding and following references to rhetorical education make this hypothesis very
likely.
[37] Cf. 1 Timothy 6:10.
[38] Cf. Matthew 6:24.

they did not reject evil, but in the midst of the manna, they sought onions and garlic and all the wickedness of Egypt. Such is the evil of habit! Then, after enjoying so much attention from God, after receiving a leader who was so great and noble, after being educated by fear and threats and favors and punishments and in every way, and after seeing such great wonders, the Jews did not become better.

But do you think that your young son who is in the midst of Egypt—or, rather, who is caught in the midst of the devil's troops— who hears no one giving him useful advice, who sees everyone leading him in the opposite direction, especially those who bore him and raised him, do you think that he can escape the devil's snares? How? From the warnings that you give? But you urge him on to the opposite things and do not allow him to pay heed to philosophy even in a dream. Rather, by turning the present life and its benefits over and over, you cause him to be tossed by even greater waves.

Can he do it on his own, all by himself? But certainly the young person cannot practice virtue all on his own. If, perhaps, he produces something noble, before it has time to grow it will quickly be drowned in the flood of words which comes from you. Just as the body which does not enjoy healthy foods, but is reared on sickly ones, cannot survive for long, so also the soul which has received such an education will never conceive anything noble or great. Inevitably it will become weak and soft, since it is continually attacked by evil as if by consumption, and eventually it will be thrown into gehenna to be destroyed there.

7. If you should say that things are not this way, and that it is possible to practice virtue perfectly even while living in the world, and if you should say this not in jest, but in earnest, do not hesitate to teach us this new and incredible doctrine. For I do not wish to undertake such great matters in vain, nor in the midst of such goods to abstain for no reason. But I am not able to learn this doctrine, for you do not permit it, and through your words and deeds you contradict this decree and teach an opposite doctrine. As if you desired to destroy your sons intentionally, you command them to do all the things which make it impossible for them to be saved.

Look at the matter once again. *Woe to you who laugh*, he says.[39] But you provide many occasions for them to laugh. *Woe to you who are rich*.[40] But you do everything so that they might make money.

---

[39] Luke 6:25.
[40] Luke 6:24.

Woe to you when all men speak well of you.[41]   But you frequently
deplete all of your resources for the sake of being esteemed by the
crowd. Again, the person who insults his brother is liable to gehenna.
But you think that they are weak and timid if they bear in silence
insults inflicted by others. Christ commands us to despise fighting
and litigation. But you constantly involve them in these evils. Many
times he commanded us to cut out the eye, if it should cause harm.
But you especially make friends with those who are able to give
money, even if they should teach the worst evil. He did not allow
divorce, except in the case of adultery. But you, whenever it is
possible to make money, also teach them to despise this precept. He
totally forbad oaths. But you laugh if you see any oath being kept. *He
who loves his life*, he said, *will lose it.*[42] But in every way you push
them towards this love. *If you do not forgive people their sins*, he says,
your heavenly Father will not forgive you.[43] But you reproach them if
ever they decline to defend themselves against injustice, and you urge
them to sieze that power quickly. Christ declared that the love of
glory renders all works vain, even prayer, fasting, and almsgiving.
But you do everything in order that they might gain glory. What need
is there to list all sins when those we have mentioned are enough to
merit a thousand gehennas, not only all these sins taken together, but
also each individual one? But when you gather them all together and
heap up an unbearable burden of sins, you send them into a river of
fire. How can they be saved, when they feed so much fuel to the fire?

And this is not the only terrible thing, that you instruct them in
ways contrary to the precepts of Christ, but you dress up vice in fine
sounding names, calling constant attendance at the racetrack and
theatre "urbanity," and to be wealthy "freedom," and to lust for glory
"magnanimity," and madness "confidence," and prodigality "philanthropy," and injustice "courage."   Then, as if this fraud were not
enough, you also call virtue by contrary names, calling temperance
"boorishness," fairness "cowardice," justice "weakness," modesty
"servility," tolerance of evil "lack of strength."[44] You act as if you

---

41 Luke 6:26.

42 John 12:25.

43 Matthew 6:15.

44 The actions which Chrysostom condemns all are associated in some way with
traditional Hellenic ideals of civic virtue. The emperor Julian had attacked the
pleasure-loving Antiochenes on similar grounds and argued that his own philosophical
virtues were considered vices by the populace. See Julian, *Misopogon* 351b, and my
comments above, pp. 65-66.

were afraid that the children would flee such outrage if they heard the true names of these things from others!

For to call vices by their bare and proper names helps to no small degree in avoiding them. It strikes sinners with such power that those who are famous for their shameful acts often do not take it well when they are called what they are, but they become angry and quite savage, as if they were suffering the most terrible misfortunes. For if you called a woman an adulteress and a boy a fornicator because of shamefulness of their behavior, you would become their irreconcilable enemy, as if you had committed the greatest injustice. And they are not the only ones who act this way, but you can see greedy persons, drunkards, braggarts, and all who do terrible and reckless deeds mourning and weeping, not so much because of their actions and the opinion of the crowd, as because of the names applied to their actions. And I know many who have become temperate and more reasonable as a result of being reproached. But you have removed even this remedy.

And, what is worse, you give this encouragement to them, not only through your words, but also through your deeds by building splendid houses, buying very expensive fields, and surrounding yourself with other forms of pomp, and in every way overshadowing their souls, as it were, with a kind of dense cloud. How can I be persuaded that they will be saved, when I see them being urged to do those things which Christ said would bring perdition on those who do them, when I see you despising their soul as if it were something incidental, while paying attention to truly superfluous things as if they were necessary and essential? You do everything for your child to have a servant, a horse and the most beautiful toga. But that he might become good, you never allow yourself even to think about this. Although you extend your zeal to wood and stones, you do not deem the soul worthy of the smallest bit of your attention. You endure all things so that a magnificent statue might be put in the house and so that the roof might be golden. But that the most honorable of all statues—the soul —might be golden, you do not wish to give a thought to this.

8. But I have not yet mentioned the greatest of the evils, nor have I revealed the chief catastrophe. Often I have begun to broach the subject and blushed; often I have been ashamed. What am I talking about? It is time to be daring and to speak. For it would be an act of great cowardice, if in our desire to cast out something evil we did not try to speak about this, as if silence by itself could heal the disease. Therefore, we will not remain silent, even if we must be ashamed and blush a thousand times. For the doctor who wishes to drain an abscess

does not hesitate to take a knife and insert his fingers deep into the wound. Therefore, we, too, will not hesitate to speak about this, inasmuch as this infection is worse.

What, then, is the evil? A new and lawless lust has invaded our life, a terrible and incurable disease has fallen upon us, a plague more terrible than all plagues has struck. A new and unspeakable crime has been devised. Not only written laws, but also the laws of nature have been overturned. Fornication now seems like a minor offense among forms of unchastity. Just as a more powerful feeling of grief can come and wipe out one's prior feeling of grief, so now the excess of this lewdness causes the unspeakable, I mean unlawful intercourse with women, no longer to appear unspeakable. For it is considered desirable to be able to escape these snares, and womankind is in danger of being superfluous when young men take their place in every activity.[45]

Even this is not as terrible as the fact that such a great abomination is performed with great fearlessness and lawlessness has become the law. No one is afraid, no one trembles. No one is ashamed, no one blushes, but they enjoy a good laugh. Those who are self-controlled are thought to be crazy, and those who admonish are considered fools. If they happen to be weaker, they are beaten; if stronger, they are mocked, laughed at, the butt of countless jokes. No benefit comes from law courts or laws or pedagogues or parents or attendants or teachers. Some are corrupted by money, others are concerned only about their pay. Some are more moral and pay attention to the salvation of those entrusted to them; but these are easily deceived and tricked, or else they fear the power of the unchaste. For it would be easier for a suspected tyrant to save himself than it would be for someone who tried to rescue [the youth] from these vile men to escape their hands. Thus, in the middle of the cities, as if in a great desert, males perform shameless acts with males.

---

[45] Chrysostom's lengthy tirade against pederasty sometimes is cited as evidence of its widespread practice especially among Christians at Antioch. See, for example, J. Boswell, *Christianity, Social Tolerance, and Homosexuality* (Chicago and London: University of Chicago Press, 1980) 131-32 and A.J. Festugière, *Antioche païenne et chrétienne* 198-210. While this may be true, one suspects that rhetorical excess has colored Chrysostom's attack on pederasty. Furthermore, pederasty in Chrysostom's mind was a vice intimately associated with Greek paideia and, therefore, this polemic is part of his more general attack on Greek culture. Cf. his treatise *De sancto Babyla* 49 (PG 50.546), where he criticizes Plato and Socrates for teaching that pederasty is "respectable and a part of philosophy."

But if some should escape these snares, only with difficulty will they avoid the reputation of those who indulge in such wicked behavior. First, because they are very few, they would easily be hidden by the crowd of evildoers. Second, because those vile and accurst demons, since they have no other way to punish those who despise them, try to harm their reputation. Since they are unable to deliver a mortal blow, or to reach the soul, they attempt at least to damage the exterior ornament which surrounds them and to destroy all good reputation.

For this reason I have heard many people wondering why a second shower of fire has not yet fallen in our own time, why our city has not yet suffered the fate of Sodom, for it is worthy of a greater punishment, since it has not yet learned from the misfortunes of Sodom. Although that region has cried out for two thousand years—its appearance speaking more loudly than words—to the whole world not to dare such a thing, not only have they not become more timid about this sin, but they have become more audacious, as if contending with God and trying to show by their actions that they will devote themselves more to these evils the more he threatens them.

Why, then, has not something similar happened; how is it that they dare to commit the sins of Sodom, but do not suffer the penalty of Sodom? Because another more terrible fire awaits them and a punishment which has no end. For although the crimes [of the inhabitants of Sodom] who lived at a later time were much more serious than the sins of those who were destroyed by the great flood, no such shower fell as a result of this. The argument is the same in our case. Why did people who lived near the beginning of time, when there were no law courts, when the fear of rulers did not hang over them, when there was no threatening Law or chorus of prophets to train them, no expectation of gehenna, no hope of the Kingdom, no other philosophy, no wonders which could raise up even stones, why did those people who enjoyed none of these advantages suffer such a great penalty for their sins?

On the other hand, why have people in our own day, who partake of all these benefits and who live in the midst of such great fear of both divine and human law courts, why have they not yet suffered the same as those in the past, although they are worthy of greater punishment? Is it not plain even to a child that they are being spared only to receive a more violent punishment? For if we are so angry and indignant, how could God, who cares for the human race most of all, who violently abhors and detests evil, allow these crimes to go unpunished? This is not the way things are, not at all! Without a

doubt he will strike them with his mighty hand, inflict an unbearable
blow, and apply torture so painful that what was experienced at
Sodom will seem like child's play.

What barbarians, what kind of beasts have they not surpassed in
that shameful union? There is in some irrational animals a great
passion and an unspeakable desire which is exactly like madness. But
although they do not understand this passion, at least they remain
within the bounds of nature; even if they should be in heat a thousand
times, they will not overturn nature's laws. But these persons who
are, so to speak, "rational," who have had the benefit of divine
instruction, who say to others what should be done and what should
not be done, and who have heard the scriptures which have come down
from heaven—these men have intercourse more fearlessly with young
boys than with prostitutes! As if they were not human, as if the
providence of God did not exist to judge events, as if darkness were all
around and no one could see or hear what they do, thus they commit
all these reckless deeds in utter madness.

But the parents of the children who are being violated bear it in
silence; they do not bury themselves in the earth along with their
children, nor do they think of some remedy for that evil. If it were
necessary to take the children to a foreign land to save them from this
sickness, or to the sea, or to the islands, or to an inaccessible land, or to
the world beyond us, should we not do and suffer all things so as not to
allow these defilements? If a place were diseased and plague-ridden,
would we not take our sons away from there, even if they were about
to make great profit, even if they were in the best of health?

But now, when such a great plague has spread everywhere, not only
do we ourselves drag them down into the depths, but we drive away
those who wish to set them free as if they were corrupters. What rage,
what thunderbolts do these crimes not deserve, when we are eager to
purify their tongue by means of pagan wisdom, while we not only
overlook the soul which lies rotting in the very mire of licentiousness,
but even prevent the soul which wishes to rise up? Who, then, still
dares to say that those who live in such great wickedness can be
saved? For those who escape the madness of unchastity (and these are
few) do not escape those tyrannical desires which corrupt all things,
namely the love of money and of glory. But most people are afflicted to
an even greater degree by both of these desires, as well as by
fornication.

Further, when we wish to educate them in rhetoric, we not only
remove any obstacles to their instruction, but we also provide support
by hiring pedagogues and teachers, by spending money, by providing

leisure from other activities, by shouting to them more frequently than coaches do in the Olympic games that poverty comes from lack of education and that wealth comes from education. We do and say all things, on our own and through others, to lead them to the goal which demands all these efforts and frequently we do not even succeed.

Do we believe, then, that moral virtue and the careful observance of an outstanding way of life will develop by themselves, even when there are such great obstacles to these things? What could be more illogical than this: to attach such honor and importance to what is easy, as if it could not be achieved without great effort, and yet to think that what is much more difficult will come upon us as we sleep, as if it were something cheap and unimportant? For philosophy of soul is more difficult and more laborious than rhetorical education, just as doing is greater than speaking, and deeds require more effort than words.

9. "But," you say, "what need is there of philosophy and a strict way of life for our children?" This is it, this is the very thing which destroys everything, that a matter which is so necessary, which encompasses our whole life, seems to be superfluous and secondary. If someone should see your son lying sick with a physical illness, he would not say, "But why does he need good and fine health?" No, he would take every trouble to restore him to such good health that he would not be sick again. But when the soul is sick, they say that there is no need for medicine, and with these words they dare to call themselves parents!

"What then? Shall we all become philosophers," you say. "Shall we let everything that pertains to this life go to ruin?" It is not philosophy, my good man, but the failure to philosophize which destroys and corrupts everything. Who, tell me, really corrupts the present situation: those who live moderately and morally, or those who devise new and illicit modes of luxury?[46] Those who try to possess everything, or those who are satisfied with what they have? Those who have phalanxes of servants and who parade around with a swarm of flatterers and parasites, or those who think that only one servant is enough for them (for I am not treating the height of philosophy, but only what is accessible to most people)? Those who

---

[46] In the remainder of this paragraph Chrysostom employs the rhetorical device ἐπαναφορά, the repetition of a word or words at the head of successive cola, in this case the article οἱ. On this device see T.E. Ameringer, *The Stylistic Influence of the Second Sophistic* 30: "Hermogenes informs us that the sophists employed it with a view to δεινότης and ranges it among the figures that give beauty to style."

love humanity, who are gentle and who have no need of the honor of
the multitude, or those who demand honor from their fellow citizens
more than any debt, who cause countless calamities for anyone who
does not stand up in respect, greet them first, bow down and act like a
slave in their presence? Those who practice obedience, or those who
desire political positions and offices and who are willing to do and to
suffer everything for this? Those who say that they are better than
everyone else and who, therefore, think that they can do and say all
things, or those who count themselves among the least and who,
therefore, reproach the irrational power of the passions? Those who
live in splendid houses and who prepare richly laden tables, or those
who desire nothing more than the necessary food and shelter? Those
who carve out for themselves thousands of acres of land, or those who
think it unnecessary to own even one little plot? Those who compile
interest upon interest and pursue the unjust path of all commerce, or
those who tear apart these unjust contracts and aid the needy out of
their own resources? Those who reflect upon the worthlessness of
human nature, or those who do not wish to see this and who with
consummate arrogance reject the thought that they are mortal?
Those who keep mistresses and wreck other people's marriages, or
those who abstain even from their own wives?

Does not the one group, like tumors in the body and raging winds at
sea, grow upon the community of the world and through their
incontinence toss like a storm those who could be saved if they were
left alone? Do not the others, like lights shining in deep darkness, call
those who are in the midst of shipwrecks into their own security and,
by raising the lamps of philosophy on high, thus lead those who are
willing into the harbor of the unencumbered life? Do not the former
cause wars, conflicts, battles, the destruction of cities, slavery,
servitude, captivities, slaughter and countless misfortunes in this
life—not only what happens among people by human agency, but also
what comes from above, such as droughts, heavy rains, earthquakes,
landslides, the flooding of cities, famine, plagues, and everything else
which heaven sends us?

10. And so, these are the ones who overthrow the community, who
corrupt the interests of all. These are the ones who cause innumerable
calamities for others, who torment those who wish to live in peace,
who drag them from every place and attack them. They are the reason
we have lawcourts, laws, penalties, and various types of punishments.
Just as in a household where many are sick and few are healthy, you
could see many medicines, many doctors going in, so, too, in the world
there is no people, no city, where there are not many laws, many

rulers and many penalties. For the medicines alone are not able to heal the sick person, but there must also be people to apply the medicines; such are the judges who force the sick, willingly or unwillingly, to accept the healing. However, the sickness has become so powerful that it has defeated even the skill of the doctors and has attacked even the judges. It is as if a person, oppressed by fever, dropsy and countless other more dreadful sufferings, could not overcome his own misfortunes, but turned to others to free him, while they themselves are afflicted by the same terrible diseases. For a flood of wickedness, like a torrent which has burst through all obstacles, has been violently poured forth into human souls.

And why do I speak only of the overthrow of the community? The danger is that the plague created by these wicked men might discredit those who speak about God's providence. Thus it goes forth, spreads and hastens to encompass all things; it has turned everything upside down; finally, it makes war upon heaven itself, arming men's tongues to speak no longer against their fellow servants, but now against the Master himself who rules all things. For why, tell me, is there so much talk everywhere about Fate?[47] Why does the multitude attribute events to the irrational movement of the stars? Why do some people pay honor to Fortune, or to Chance?[48] Why do they think that all things move without rhyme or reason? Is it the fault of those who live chastely and moderately, or of those who, as you say, keep the community together, but who, as I have shown, are the common scourge of the world? Clearly the latter are at fault. For no one becomes irritated when a person philosophizes or when someone is fair and moderate and temperate and despises the things of this life; but they feel this way when someone is wealthy, when he lives in luxury and is greedy and rapacious, when he is wicked and full of countless evils, when he is famous and prospering. These are the things that those who do not believe in God complain about and attack. These are the things that offend the multitude; whereas, for the sake of those who live moderately, not only will they not say anything like this, but

---

[47] "Fate" (Εἱμαρμένη) derives from the verb μείρομαι and refers to "an allotted portion." Fate was seen as a general scheme ruling the world and often associated with ideas of astral determinism.

[48] "Fortune" (Τύχή) was a tutelary deity of Antioch. See P. Petit, *Libanius et la vie municipale à Antioche* (Paris, 1955) 192. J. Misson has discussed Libanius' special devotion to Fortune: *Recherches sur le paganisme de Libanios* (Louvain, 1914) 50-66. See, for example, Libanius' *Autobiography* (or. 1.12), where he attributes his "incorruptible virtue" not to his teachers but to "the providence of Fortune" (προνοίᾳ Τύχης).

they would even condemn themselves, if they were induced to accuse
the providence of God.

And if everyone, or even the majority, wished to live properly, no
one would have ever thought to talk in this way, and the chief of these
evils would have been avoided, namely to inquire into the origin of
evil. For if evils did not exist, or were not apparent, who would have
been led to investigate the source of evil and to give rise to the
thousand heresies which result from this investigation? For this is
how the ideas of Marcion, Manes, Valentinus, and most of the Greeks
originated.[49] But if everyone philosophized, there would be no need to
investigate these things. If nothing else, the excellent state of society
would teach everyone that we live under a God and King who administers and governs our affairs according to his wisdom and prudence.

This is happening even now, but it is not readily apparent because
of the great cloud which these people have spread over the whole
world. But if this were not the case, the providence of God would shine
forth for all, as if at high noon and in the bright, calm air.[50] If there
existed no law courts, no accusers, no sycophants, no tortures or
punishments, no prisons or penalties, no confiscation of property or
fines, no fears or dangers, no enmities, no plots, no injuries or hatred,
no famine or pestilence, nor any of the other terrible things which
could be mentioned, but if everyone lived with proper moderation,
what living creature would have doubted God's providence? Not one,
of course!

But today it is as if, in the midst of a storm, the ship's pilot is doing
his work and saving the ship, but his diligence and experience are not
apparent to the sailors on board because of the confusion, fear, and
anxiety caused by the threat of catastrophe. Even now God rules this

---

[49] Marcion of Sinope (died c. 160) taught at Rome and founded a Christian sect
whose teachings included a rejection of the Old Testament and its God and the
endorsement of several Pauline letters and an edited version of Luke as his canon.
Manes (or Mani) was born c. 216 near Seleucia-Ctesiphon, the capital of the Persian
empire. First influenced by the Elkesaites, a Jewish-Christian sect with Gnostic
leanings, Manes developed a full-blown Gnostic system which included an
uncompromising cosmic dualism, an elaborate salvation myth, and a severe asceticism.
Manicheism spread widely and rapidly. See P. Brown, "The Diffusion of Manicheism in
the Roman Empire," *Journal of Roman Studies* 59 (1969) 92-103. Valentinus (c. 100-
175), a native of Egypt who later taught at Rome, authored the Gospel of Truth and was
a leading figure in the second-century Gnostic movement. See B. Layton, *The Gnostic
Scriptures* (Garden City: Doubleday, 1987) 217-22.

[50] A echo of Homer, *Odyssey* 10.94 and Plato, *Phaedrus* 242a. See Fabricius, *Zu
den Jugendschriften* 128, for parallels in Dio Chrysostom, Libanius, and others.

universe, but it is not apparent to most people because of the storm which agitates the world and the confusion which these people more than any others cause. In this way not only do they overthrow the community, but they also destroy piety. It would not be a mistake to call these men the enemies of humanity, who live in a manner opposed to the salvation of others, who by their polluted teachings and impure lives cause those who are sailing with them to suffer shipwreck.

11. But in the monasteries nothing like this can be seen; even if such a storm should arise, they alone live in tranquility, in the harbor, in great security, observing the shipwrecks of others, as if from heaven. For they have chosen a way of life which befits heaven, and they have attained a state inferior in no way to that of angels.[51] Just as among the angels there is no inequality, nor do some enjoy prosperity while others experience misery, but all of them share one peace, one joy, one glory, so it is likewise in the monasteries. No one reproaches poverty, no one exults over wealth. That "yours" and "mine" which overturns and upsets everything is utterly banished. All things are held in common—food, housing, clothing. And why is this surprising, when they even share one and the same soul?[52]

All are noble with the same nobility, all are servants with the same servanthood, all are free with the same freedom. There you find one wealth for all, the true wealth—one glory, the true glory. For in that life the goods are present, not in name, but in reality. One pleasure, one desire, one hope for all; indeed everything is perfectly regulated as if by a norm and rule. There is no inequality, but order, proportion, harmony, deep and exact agreement, and constant grounds for contentment. Thus everything that they do and suffer is a source of joy and contentment. Only in that life can one see this happen perfectly, nowhere else; not only do they disdain worldly goods, not only have they put away every reason for discord and fighting, not only have they splendid hopes concerning the future, but also they think that whatever happens to anyone of them, for good or for ill, happens to all of them. Sadness disappears more easily when all share equally the burden of the individual; likewise, they have many

---

[51] The notion that the monastic life imitated the life of angels was a popular theme in monastic literature. See Theodoret of Cyrus, *Curatio affectionum graecarum* 3.91-92 and *Religious History* Prol. 2, 3.15, 4.9, 21.3, and 26.23. See also the discussion by R.M. Price in *A History of the Monks of Syria* (Kalamazoo, MI: Cistercian Publications, 1985) xxx-xxxi.

[52] A passage nearly identical to this can be found in Chrysostom's homily 72.3 on Matthew (PG 58.671-73).

reasons for good cheer, since they rejoice not only over their own good fortune but no less over the good fortune of others.

What would our own life be like, if we all imitated them? For now our world is ruined and corrupted by those who live in a manner far different from these monks. But when you cast your vote for the opposing side, you are acting like a person who says that a lyre, which is perfectly tuned, is useless for music, but who says that another lyre, which is out of tune and broken and ruined by too much loosening or stretching of its strings, is suitable for making music and delighting the audience. We could find no better example of musical ignorance than the person who speaks this way; nor could we find any clearer specimen of envy and misanthropy than those who cast their vote against the monks.[53]

But what do the more reasonable parents say? "Let them learn letters first," they say, "and then, after they have achieved the power of oratory, let them take up this philosophy; then no one will prevent them." But is it certain that they will reach adulthood at all? For many have passed on, snatched away by an untimely death. But, granting that this is certain, let us assume that they will reach adulthood. Who will be responsible for all of the first part of their life? I am not at all speaking out of a love of disputation, for if someone could give me a guarantee about this, I would not lead them out even after they have been educated. On the contrary, in that case especially, I would order them to remain, and I would not praise those who urge them to take flight. Rather, I would turn them away like common enemies of society, since by hiding the lamps and leading the saviors away from the city into the desert they deprive of the greatest goods those who dwell therein. But if no one will promise us this, what use is it to send them to teachers where they will learn wickedness before letters, and, while they wish to achieve what is less, they will lose what is greater, namely all strength and vigor of soul?

"What then? Shall we completely eliminate education?" you say. I do not say this, but let us not destroy the edifice of virtue nor bury the soul alive. When the soul is self-controlled, no harm will come from a lack of knowledge of rhetoric; but when the soul is corrupted, the greatest damage will result, even if the tongue is quite sharp; indeed,

---

[53] By refering to the "musical ignorance" (ἀμουσία) of the opponents of the monks, Chrysostom is playing on the double meaning of the term "music." The word can refer to an ignorance of music per se or to a more general lack of education. A "museum" (μουσεῖον) could refer to a school of rhetoric. Chrysostom's point is that true ignorance is to oppose the monks.

the damage will be greater the more skilled in rhetoric he becomes. For when wickedness gains experience in speaking, it does far worse deeds than ignorance.

"What if, after going there," you say, "in addition to having an idle tongue, they also fall from that virtue?"[54] What if, after staying here, I reply, in addition to destroying the soul, they make no progress in eloquence in school? And my response is more justified than yours. Why? Because, if in both cases the future is uncertain, in yours it is more uncertain. Why is this? Because the pursuit of rhetoric requires good behavior, but good behavior does not require the assistance of rhetoric. It is possible to live a life of self-control without a literary education, but no one could ever achieve oratorical power without good behavior, since all of his time would be spent in wickedness and immorality.[55] Therefore, your fears of failure are much more appropriate in the case of rhetorical education, because failures are more frequent there and much greater interests are in danger. And in the monastic life one need only to devote oneself to one matter, but in education two things must be achieved, since it is impossible to achieve one without the other, that is, to learn rhetoric without self-control.[56] But, if you wish, we will grant that the impossible is possible. What good will come to us from expertise in letters when we are struck with a mortal blow? What harm will come from a lack of knowledge if we live properly in the most important matters? Such opinions are held not only by us, who laugh at pagan wisdom and think that it is foolishness, but also by pagan philosophers. That is why many of them cared little for education. Some even completely despised it, remained ignorant, and spent their entire life in the

---

54 The parents' objection here is not merely rhetorical. In his treatise to the lapsed monk Theodore, Chrysostom tells the story of a young man, Phoenix, who had abandoned his education to join the monks. When he later failed to persevere and wanted to return to civic life, Phoenix was considered unfit "because he had prematurely interrupted his rhetorical studies and was unable to derive any benefit from them" (*Ad Theodorum lapsum* 18; SC 117.195).

55 Nearly identical sentiments are expressed in Chrysostom's homily 21 on Ephesians (PG 62.152): "Study not to make him an orator, but train him to be a philosopher. The lack of the former causes no harm at all, but if the latter is lacking, all the rhetoric in the world will be of no advantage."

56 Libanius likewise stressed the importance of moral rectitude as a prerequisite for accomplishment in rhetoric. See Festugière, *Antioche païenne et chrétienne* 113-14.

branch of philosophy concerned with behavior.57 And yet they lived a
brilliant life and became famous. Anacharsis, Crates and Diogenes
paid no attention to letters.58 Nor did Socrates, some say. We will cite
as evidence the words of a man who far surpassed all practitioners of
this art and who knew better than anyone the circumstances of
Socrates' life. When he led him into the courtroom to make his
defense, [Plato] put these words on Socrates' lips:59

> But from me you shall hear the whole truth—not, I can
> assure you, gentlemen, in flowery language like theirs,
> decked out with fine words and phrases. No, what you will
> hear will be a straightforward speech in the first words that
> occur to me, as I am confident in the justice of my cause, and
> I do not want any of you to expect anything different. It
> would hardly be suitable, gentlemen, for a man of my age to
> address you in the artificial language of a schoolboy orator.

He said these things to show that it was not because of laziness that
he did not learn or practice rhetoric, but because he did not think it
was very important. For rhetoric is not appropriate for philosophers,
or even for grown men; rather, it is an ostentatious display of
adolescents at play.60 This is the view of the philosophers, and not
only the other philosophers, but also him who far surpassed them all
in this matter. For Plato would not allow his teacher to be decked out
with that sort of finery since he believed that such decoration was

------

57 Here and in the following paragraphs Chrysostom relies on an ancient
philosophical commonplace, the hostility between rhetoric and philosophy. The
opposition was developed especially in Plato's *Gorgias*. Among Chrysostom's
contemporaries, Synesius of Cyrene in his *Dio* made abundant use of this commonplace.

58 Anacharsis, Crates, and Diogenes were revered figures among the Cynics. A
recent discussion, with an edition and translation of letters ascribed to these figures,
can be found in A. Malherbe, *The Cynic Epistles* (Missoula, Montana: Scholars Press,
1977).

59Plato, *Apology* 17 bc. Translated by H. Tredennick in *The Collected Dialogues of
Plato*. Edited by E. Hamilton and H. Cairns (Princeton: Princeton University Press, 1961) 4.
[Original source: *Plato: The Last Days of Socrates*, translated by Hugh Tredennick (Penguin
Classics, 1954, 1959), © Hugh Tredennick, 1954, 1959. Reproduced by permission of Penguin
Books Ltd.] Fabricius, *Zu den Jugendschriften* 138, has pointed out that the same passage of
Plato is quoted by Theodoret of Cyrus in his *Curatio affectionum graecarum* 1.30 and by
Isidore of Pelusium (PG 78.1082) who also paraphrases Chrysostom's comment on the text.

60 Chrysostom's term φιλοτιμία, here rendered as "ostentatious display," can bear
both a positive and a negative meaning. Cf. Plato, *Republic* 553, where the word is
linked with θυμοειδές (a "high spirit") to express an ideal of civic service in a timocratic
society as opposed to private money making.

shameful for the philosopher. But these are things better said to a pagan than to a Christian. For if those, who chase after the glory of the crowd and who are unable to become famous from any other source but pagan wisdom, should think this [eloquence] is nothing, would it not be absurd if we so marvel at it and admire it that we despise the essentials in order to achieve it?

12. Therefore, the preceding argument is sufficient for the pagan, but for the Christian we must produce examples from our own side. What kind of examples? Those great and holy persons, those at the beginning, who did not know letters; then, the ones who came after them, who knew letters, but who were not yet skilled in rhetoric; and, finally, after them those who both knew letters and were skilled in rhetoric. The first [Christians] were ignorant in both areas; not only were they not trained in rhetoric, but they were even illiterate. Nonetheless, in those very areas where the power of rhetoric seems to be most necessary, they surpassed the most skilled orators, making the orators look worse than uneducated children. For since persuasiveness is the essence of rhetoric, and since the philosophers have not won over a single tyrant, but since the unlettered and ignorant have overturned the whole world, it is quite clear that the unlettered and ignorant have won the prize of wisdom, not those who have a perfect knowledge of letters and rhetoric. Thus true wisdom and true education is nothing other than the fear of God.[61]

And no one should think that I am mandating that children should be unlearned! If someone could guarantee that the essentials would be cared for, I would not object to their receiving an education in addition to this. Just as when the foundations of a house are being shaken and the entire building is in danger of falling down, it would be the height of folly and madness to run to the painters and not to the builders, so, conversely, it would be inappropriate and arrogant to prevent someone from painting the house, as long as the walls are standing securely and firmly.

To show you that I am speaking from the heart, I now will tell you a story which illustrates what I have already proven by the facts. A young man who was very rich once came to live in our city to receive an education in Latin and Greek literature. He had with him a pedagogue whose sole task was to form the young man's soul. I went

---

[61] The ability of the apostles to spread the gospel, despite their lack of the benefits of Greek culture, is a favorite apologetic argument of Chrysostom. See, for example, his treatise *Quod Christus sit Deus* (PG 48.830) and our comments above, pp. 48-50.

to this pedagogue (for he was one of those who live in the mountains)
and tried to find out why, after having achieved such great wisdom, he
had lowered himself to take the position of a pedagogue. But he said
that he had only a little time left in that occupation and told us the
whole story from the beginning.[62]

"This young boy," he said, "has a severe and harsh father, who is
passionately devoted to worldly concerns, but his mother is moderate,
temperate, and chaste and looks only towards heaven. The father,
because he was an accomplished soldier, wanted his son to follow in
his footsteps; but the mother did not desire or want this, and she even
vigorously prayed that it would not happen. She prayed and longed to
see him shine in the monastic way of life. But she did not dare to say
these things to the father; she feared that if he suspected this he would
enslave the child in the bonds of life prematurely, that he would
deprive him of this zeal, that he would lead him into the army and into
the whole lax way of life which comes from the army, and that he
would render the child unable to live an upright life afterwards.

"And so she contrived another stratagem. She called me to her
house and told me everything; then she took the child by the hand and
entrusted him to me. When I asked why she was doing this, she said
that the only way left for us to save the child was for me to agree to
take the position of a pedagogue and go there to take charge of him.
[She said that] she herself would persuade the father that a training
in rhetoric would be beneficial, even when he entered the military. 'If
I succeed', she said, 'you will be able to take him away alone to another
place, where you can enjoy full freedom to form him without
interference from his father or any of the household, and where you
can make him live as if he were in a monastery. But give your
approval and promise that you will play along with me in this
pretense. I am not speaking about something insignificant; the soul of
my child is at stake and in danger! Do not allow him whom I love
more than everything to be endangered, but deliver him from the
snares, the storms, the waves which surround him on all sides. If you
do not wish to grant me this favor, I now call upon God [to stand]
between us, and I give witness that I have left nothing undone which

---

[62] In the following paragraphs Chrysostom borrows classical views on the moral
role of the pedagogue and applies these to the monks. See the similar descriptions of the
educative function of the pedagogue in Plutarch, *Moralia* 439F and Libanius, or. 58.7-9.
See also the emperor Julian's tribute to his pedagogue Mardonius in *Misopogon* 353c.
Cf. the comments of Libanius on Julian's pedagogue: or. 12.27 and or. 18.11.

might have assisted the salvation of his soul, but I am innocent of the blood of that child! But if it should happen that he suffers the kind of misfortune which can happen to a young man who lives in such great luxury and laxity, it is from you and from your hands that God will require the soul of that child on that great day!'

"Pouring out these words and more than these, with violent and pathetic weeping, she persuaded me to undertake this charge, and with these orders she dismissed me." The mother's plan was not without success. In a short time that noble [monk] trained this child so well and kindled in him so ardent a desire for this life that he cast off everything at once and ran to the desert, so that he needed another bridle to lead him from an excessive zeal to a moderate asceticism. It was feared that by his zeal he might prematurely reveal the plot and that he might stir up serious trouble for his mother, his pedagogue, and monks everywhere. For if his father learned of his flight, he would stop at nothing to drive away those holy men, not only those who took his son into their charge, but all the others as well.

Then I took the child and told him all these things and more. I allowed the desire for this philosophy to remain, indeed I even increased it, but I asked him to live in the city and to apply himself to the study of rhetoric, for in this way he could do the most to benefit his companions and escape the notice of his father as well. I thought this was necessary not only for the sake of the monks, his mother and the pedagogue, but also for the child himself. For if his father had attacked him at the beginning, it is likely that he would have shaken the shoots of philosophy, which were still tender and recently planted. But if a long time went by and he became well rooted, I was quite confident that whatever happened, he could never harm his son.

This is exactly what happened, and my hope was not deceived. When his father attacked him later, after much time had passed, and rushed against him with great force, not only did he fail to make any impact at all on the building, but he even made it appear to be stronger. Many of his fellow students profitted so much from his company that they came to share his zeal. Since he always had at home someone to train him, like a statue which constantly profits from the hand of a craftsman, each day he received some addition to his beauty of soul. And what is truly marvelous is that, when he appeared in public, he seemed no different from the crowd. For he had no wild and rough demeanor, nor did he wear an unusual cloak, but he was like the rest in clothing, expression, voice, and all other respects. For this reason he was able to capture many of his comrades within his nets, since on the inside he concealed much philosophy.

But if you saw him at home, you would think that he was one of those who live in the mountains. His house was arranged according to the discipline of every monastery, where there is nothing but the essentials. All his time was spent in reading the holy books; although he was quite sharp in his studies, he spent only a brief part of his day in pagan learning and devoted the rest to frequent prayer and the sacred scriptures.[63] He spent the entire day without food—and not only one or two days, but many days. His nights were spent in the same way: in tears, prayers, and such reading. All these things his pedagogue reported to us in secret. For if the child had found out that any of these things had been disclosed, he would have been quite indignant. His pedagogue said that he had made for himself a garment out of hair and that he slept in it at night, having found that this was a clever way to [ensure that] he arose quickly. In other ways, too, he perfectly followed the discipline of the monks and continually gave glory to God who had put on him the light wings of this philosophy.

So, then, if someone even now should show me such a soul, if he should provide such a pedagogue, if he should promise that everything else will be taken care of in the same way, I would pray a thousand times that this might happen, even more than the parents themselves. An even greater booty would be ours, since through their life, their age, and their constant company such youth would be able to capture their companions. But there is no one who can promise this, no one who will do it. Since there is no one, it would be the ultimate cruelty to allow someone who is unable to defend himself, who lies exposed to countless wounds causing others to become weaker, to be cut down in the midst of the battle, when he should have been allowed to retreat. Similarly a commander would be punished if he led away from the battleline those who were able to fight, but ordered those who were wounded, prostrate, and a hindrance to others to remain constantly in the midst of the battle.

13. But since most parents persist in their desire to see their children live a life of letters, as if they knew for certain that they would reach the summit of eloquence, let us not argue about this, let us not say that he will fail to obtain his goal. Rather, we will grant for the sake of argument that the child will fully achieve the goal of his

---

[63] Chrysostom frequently describes a conversion to the ascetic life as a turning from pagan to Christian literature. See *Ad Theodorum lapsum* 1.48 (SC 117.50) and *Ad Stagirium a daemone vexatum* 1.2 (PG 47.427). See also the description of the monk in the *Comparison Between a King and a Monk*, translated above, p. 71.

study and reach the acme of success. But suppose we are faced with a two-fold choice: either he frequents the school-rooms and enters the contest for knowledge, or he goes to the desert to struggle on behalf of the soul. Tell me, where is it better to excel? If it should happen in both areas, I am quite in favor of that. But if one or the other must be sacrificed, it is better to choose what is superior.

"Yes," you say, "but how will we know for certain that he will stand firm and persevere and not change for the worse, for many have fallen?" But how do we know that he will not stand firm and persevere, for many have stood firm, even more than have fallen? Therefore, we must be encouraged by the success of the latter, rather than discouraged by the failure of the former. But why are you not afraid of failure in the matter of rhetorical studies, where there is the greatest reason to fear? For among the monks only a few out of the many have failed, whereas in rhetorical studies only a few out of the many have succeeded.

And this is not the only reason, but there are many other reasons to fear in regard to rhetoric. The child's lack of ability, the ignorance of teachers, the negligence of pedagogues, the father's want of leisure, the inability to pay fees and salary, the difference of characters, the wickedness, envy and ill will of his fellow students, and many other things will deter him from his goal. And this is not all, but even after reaching the goal, there will be further obstacles. For when he has overcome everything and reached the pinnacle of education, if he has not been prevented by any of these obstacles, other traps still lie in wait for him. The ill will of rulers, the jealousy of fellow workers, the difficulty of the times, the lack of friends, and poverty frequently frustrate his ultimate success. But it is not this way among the monks; there only one thing is necessary—a noble and good desire; if this is present, nothing can prevent him from reaching the summit of virtue.

Would it not be unjust, therefore, to fear and tremble when the best hopes are clear and near at hand, and yet, when such hopes are rather remote and hindered by many obstacles, not to fear but to have even greater confidence when the difficulties are greater and more manifest? When it comes to rhetoric, why should one ignore the misfortunes which often happen and look only at the successes which seldom come about, but in the case of the monks do the opposite? Why acknowledge only the misfortunes, where there is great hope for true goods, but where the hope concerns opposite things, to consider only the successes? However, in the case of rhetoric, just when everything has worked out to his benefit, frequently an untimely death strikes

him at the moment of his success and snatches away the athlete after
his countless labors before he receives his crown. But in the monastic
life, even if this should happen in the middle of his struggles, he will
depart in the greatest splendor, with an especially beautiful crown.

If, then, you fear the future, you should especially fear it in the case
of rhetoric, where there are many obstacles to his reaching the end.
When it comes to rhetoric, you sit waiting a long time, looking only to
the end, and paying no attention to what happens in between, such as
the expenses, hardships, and uncertainty. But when it comes to the
monastic life, although the child has not yet entered the front door,
although he has not yet taken hold of this beautiful philosophy, you
immediately are afraid and tremble and admit thoughts of despair.

Earlier you yourself said to me: "What then? Is it impossible for the
person who lives in the city and has a house to be saved?" If, therefore,
he can be saved with a city and a house and a wife, how much more is
this possible without these things! For it would be a contradiction to
be confident of salvation, even when one is enslaved to worldly
business, and yet, when one is free of all this, to tremble and fear that
an illustrious life is impossible without these things. If, as you say,
the person who lives in the city can be saved, how much more is this
possible when he dwells in the desert. Why, then, are you afraid that
this is impossible in the monastery, but you are not afraid when it
comes to rhetoric, where there should be greater fear?

14. "But it is not the same," you say, "when a person in the world
sins and when someone does so who has dedicated himself once and for
all to God. They do not fall from the same height; therefore, their
wounds are not equal." You certainly deceive yourself and are greatly
mistaken if you think that there is one set of requirements for the
person in the world and another for the monk. The difference between
them is that one is married and the other is not; in all other respects
they will have to render the same account. For the person who
becomes angry with his brother without cause, whether he is a person
in the world or a monk, will offend God in the same manner. The
person who looks lustfully at a woman, no matter what his state of
life, will be punished in the same way for that fornication. And, if we
might be allowed to add an argument from our own reasoning, the
person in the world will suffer a more severe punishment. For it is not
the same thing for the man who has a wife and who enjoys such
consolation to be brought to ruin by a woman's beauty, and for a man
who has withdrawn from all this help to be conquered by sin.
Similarly, the person who swears, no matter what state of life he is in,
will be condemned in the same way.

When Christ gave prescriptions and laws about these matters, he did not make any distinction, nor did he say, "If a monk should swear, the oath is wicked; but if he is not a monk, it is not the same." No, he spoke simply and at one time to all people: *I say to you, do not swear at all.*[64] Again, when he said: *Woe to you who laugh,*[65] he did not add "to you monks," but he legislated simply and for all. In all the other great and marvelous commandments he did the same. When he said, "Blessed are the poor in spirit, those who mourn, the meek, those who hunger and thirst for justice, the merciful, the pure in heart, the peacemakers, those who are persecuted for the sake of justice, and blessed are those who for his sake hear evil spoken and unspoken from the pagans,"[66] he did not specify either monk or secular by name; this distinction was introduced by human speculation.

Nor do the scriptures know anything like this, but they want everyone to live the life of monks, even if they should happen to have wives. Listen to what Paul says (and when I speak of Paul, I speak of a second Christ). Writing to men who had wives and who were raising children, he demanded of them all the perfection which is proper to the monks. Forbidding all luxury with respect both to clothing and to food, he wrote these words: *Women should adorn themselves modestly and sensibly in seemly apparel, not with braided hair or gold or pearls or costly attire.*[67] And again, *she who is self-indulgent is dead, even while she lives.*[68] And again, *if we have food and clothing, with these we shall be content.*[69] What more than this could anyone ask of the monks?

When he was instructing others to control their tongues, he again gave strict regulations, such as even monks find it difficult to obey. Not only did he forbid lewd behavior and foolish speech, but even jocularity; not only did he proscribe anger and wrath and bitterness, but he even banished shouting from the mouths of believers. For he said: *Let all anger and wrath and shouting and slander be put away from you, along with all malice.*[70] Do these seem like small matters to you? Wait a moment and you will hear much greater commandments which he addressed to all concerning the pardoning of injuries: *Let not*

---

[64] Matthew 5:34.
[65] Luke 6:25.
[66] A paraphrase of Matthew 5:3-12.
[67] 1 Timothy 2:9.
[68] 1 Timothy 5:6.
[69] 1 Timothy 6:8.
[70] Ephesians 4:31.

the sun, he says, *go down on your anger.*[71] *See that none of you repays
evil for evil, but always seek to do good to one another and to all.*[72]   And
again, *Do not be conquered by evil, but conquer evil with good.*[73]   Do
you see how he extends philosophy and forbearance to reach the
highest possible point?

Listen to what he prescribes concerning love, the chief of goods.
After extolling it and speaking of its great virtues, he declared that he
demanded of people in the world the same love which Christ
demanded of his disciples. Just as the Savior said that the greatest
love was to lay down one's life for one's friends, so Paul hinted at the
same thing, saying: *Love does not insist on its own way;*[74] and he
commanded that they should pursue this kind of love. If this were all
that he said, it would be sufficient proof that he demands of people in
the world the same behavior which is required of the monks. For the
love, which in this passage he describes partially, is the bond and root
of much virtue. What could a person seek which is greater than this
philosophy?

For when he commands us to be above anger, wrath, noise, love of
money, gluttony, extravagance, vain glory and other worldly pomp,
and to have nothing in common with the earth, when he demands that
we put to death our members, it is quite clear that he demands of us
the same perfection which Christ demanded of his disciples and that
he wishes us to be dead to sin, as if we were already dead and buried.
That is why he says: *For he who has died is free from sin.*[75]   There are
even places in his exhortations where he urges us to imitate Christ,
and not only the disciples. Whenever he exhorts us to love, and not to
remember injuries, and to be moderate, he produces the example of
Christ. Therefore, when Paul orders us to imitate not only the monks,
not only the disciples, but Christ himself, when he decrees the
greatest punishment for those who do not imitate them, how can you
say that this [way of life] is a greater height? For all people must
reach the same point! And this is what overturns the whole world, the
idea that only the monk is required to show a greater perfection, while
the rest are allowed to live in laxity. But this is not true! It is not!
Rather, he says, the same philosophy is demanded of all. And I myself

---

[71] Ephesians 4:26.
[72] 1 Thessalonians 5:15.
[73] Romans 12:21.
[74] 1 Corinthians 13:5.
[75] Romans 6:7.

would affirm this most vehemently, indeed, not I, but the One who is to judge us.

If you are still surprised and in doubt, come again, let us flood your ears with the same streams, so that all the wickedness of your unbelief might finally be washed away. I will demonstrate my case from the punishments to be inflicted on the day of Judgement. The rich man was punished so severely, not because he was a cruel monk, but because (if I must express my personal view), being a worldly man who lived in wealth and purple raiment, he neglected Lazarus in his extreme poverty. Moreover, I would add no qualification at all, but I would simply say that he was punished so severely in the fire simply because he was a cruel man.

And the virgins were ejected from the bridal chamber because they were deficient in charity. And if I might again express my own opinion, not only did they not receive greater punishments because of their virginity, but perhaps their punishments were even milder because of that. For they were not told, *Depart to that fire prepared for the devil and his angels*,[76] but only, *I do not know you*.[77] But if someone should say that the two passages mean the same thing, I will not contradict him. For at the moment my concern is to demonstrate that the monastic life does not incur harsher punishments and that people in the world are subject to the same punishments when they commit the same sins as the monks. The person who was clothed in the soiled garments, and the one who demanded a payment of one hundred denarii did not suffer what they suffered because they were monks; the former perished because of fornication, and the latter because of his refusal to grant pardon.[78] And if you make a review of all those in the gospels who were punished, you will see that they received their penalties only in proportion to their sins.

And what is true of the punishments is also true of the counsels. For when Christ said: *Come to me all who labor and are heavily burdened, and I will refresh you. Take my yoke upon and learn from me, for I am meek and humble of heart, and you will find rest for your souls*,[79] he said this not solely to monks, but to the entire human race. When he commanded that one should enter through the narrow gate, he addressed this not only to the monks, but to all people. And when

---

[76] Matthew 25:41.
[77] Matthew 25:12.
[78] Cf. Matthew 18:23-35.
[79] Matthew 11:28-29.

he commanded everyone to hate their souls in this world, and when he delivered all the other precepts, he did likewise.

But when he is not speaking to everyone or legislating for everyone, he makes this clear to us. For example, when he spoke about virginity, he added: *He who is able to receive this, let him receive it.*[80] And he did not add "all," nor did he phrase this in the form of a commandment. And Paul did the same, for in all respects he appears to imitate the Teacher. When dealing with the same subject, he said, *Now concerning virgins, I have no command of the Lord.*[81] Therefore, I think that not even the most quarrelsome and impudent person will deny that both the person in the world and the monk are required to reach the same height and that both will receive the same wounds when they fall.

15. Now that this has been demonstrated clearly, let us examine another point: who is likely to fall more easily? Certainly, in this matter there is no need for an examination. The person who has a wife will practice self-control more easily, because he enjoys great consolation. But in the other matters it is not so clear. Moreover, even when it comes to self-control, we see more married people failing than monks. For the number of monks who leave the monasteries to marry is not as great as the number of married persons who rise from the marriage bed to fornicate. Now if married people fall so frequently where the contests are easy for them, what will they do in the face of the passions which torment them more than the monks? Carnal desire affects the monks more violently since they do not have intercourse with women. But the other passions cannot even approach the monks, whereas they violently attack people in the world and turn them upside down.

If, then, when they are faced with a more violent combat, the monks conquer more frequently than those who do not suffer in this way, it is clear that they will prevail much more easily in other matters where they are not so troubled. The love of money and the desire for luxury, power, and all the other goods are naturally conquered more easily by the monks than by people in the world. In warfare we say that the battle is lighter where the casualties are few and rare, not where the dead continuously fall one after the other; so, too, we should have the same opinion in these matters. Avarice will be conquered more easily, not by the person who is caught in the midst

---

[80] Matthew 19:12.
[81] 1 Corinthians 7:25.

of worldly activity, but by the one who lives in the mountains. The former will more easily be vanquished, and once vanquished by avarice, he must be numbered among the idolatrers. But if the monk has money, he would not neglect his household, but he would readily provide everything for them; the person in the world, however, will not only neglect them, but will also mistreat them no less than he would strangers. This second kind of idolatry is far worse than the first.

Why should I mention all the other vices which are easy for the monks to conquer, but which strike people in the world with great violence? Why, then, do you not fear and tremble when you are leading your son to a place where he will more quickly be captured by evil? Or does it seem to you that it is a small matter to be an idolatrer, to be worse than unbelievers, to deny the service of God through his conduct? But those who are enslaved to the world are more subject to these things than are the monks. Do you see that your fear is only an excuse? If it were necessary to fear, one should fear not for those who are escaping the waves, or for those who are hastening into the harbor, but for those who are being tossed in the storms and gales. Shipwrecks happen more quickly in the world, because the sources of trouble are more numerous and because those who must resist them are lazier. But in the monastic life there are no such floods, but there is a great calm and a greater zeal on the part of those who have to struggle. This is why we draw them into the desert, not simply that they may put on a sackcloth, wear a collar, or lie among ashes, but above all else that they may flee evil and choose virtue.[82]

"What, then?" you say. "Will all married people perish?" I do not say this, but they must expend greater effort if they wish to be saved, because of the constraint imposed on them. For the person who is free of bonds will run more easily than the one who is enchained. Will the latter then receive a greater reward and more glorious crown? Not at all! For he placed this constraint upon himself when he was free not to. Therefore, since we have clearly demonstrated that we bear the same responsibilities as the monks, let us run upon the easier road; let us lead our sons upon it; let us not throw them into the sea, let us not lead them into the depths of evil, as if we were their enemies and opponents.

---

[82] Such unusual practices as the wearing of chains and iron collars was not uncommon among the Syrian monks. See Theodoret, *Religious History* 3.19, 4.6, and *passim*. These eccentricities earned the ridicule of the emperor Julian: ep. 89B.288b.

If other people acted like this, it would not be so terrible. But when it is the parents, who have enjoyed a full worldly life, who have learned from experience that earthly pleasures are cold, when it is they who are so mad that they lead others to these pleasures, when they are too old to indulge themselves, when it is they who should have proclaimed themselves miserable because of their prior experiences, but who instead throw others onto the same road, when they themselves are already close to death, judgment, and punishments, what excuse will be left to them, what pardon, what pity? They will pay the penalty not only for their own sins, but also for the wicked deeds of their children, whether or not they succeed in upsetting them.

16. But perhaps you long to see your children's children? How is this, when you are not yet parents yourselves? For the act of begetting does not a parent make. And this is agreed upon by those parents who, when they see their sons reach the height of wickedness, reject and disown them as if they were not their own, and neither nature, nor birth, nor any such bond can restrain them. Therefore, those who are far inferior to their children with respect to philosophy should no longer be considered parents; only when they also have given birth to them in this way should they desire grandchildren; only then will they be able to see them. For the monks also have children; they are born *not of flesh and blood nor of the will of man*, but they have been begotten *of God.*[83] Such children as these have no need to torment their parents over money, or marriage, or any such thing; on the contrary, they allow them to be free of all care and provide them with a greater pleasure than their natural parents enjoy. They are not born and raised for the same purposes as natural children, but for a much greater and more splendid destiny. Thus they delight their parents even more.

Besides these considerations, I also will add one more: it is not unreasonable that those who disbelieve in the resurrection should grieve about having descendants, since this is the only consolation left to them. But we, who think that death is a sleep, who have been taught to despise all things in this life, what pardon would we merit if we mourned about such matters and desired to see children and to leave them behind in this place, from which we are hastening to depart and in which we groan when we are present? This is what we would say to those who are more spiritual. But if there are some who

---

[83] John 1:13.

are lovers of the body, who are quite attached to the present life, I would say this to them: first, it is not certain that a marriage will produce children at all; second, if children do come, there will be even greater discouragement. For the happiness which children bring us is far outweighed by the grief which comes from the daily care, anxiety, and fear which they cause.

"And to whom," you say, "will we leave our fields, houses, servants, and gold?" For I also hear you lamenting about these things. The child who previously was to inherit these goods will now be a much safer guardian and master of the property than before. Previously many things threatened to ruin his property: moths, the length of time, robbers, sycophants, jealous persons, the uncertainty of the future, the unstable character of human affairs, and ultimately death would have robbed your son of both his money and these possessions. But now he has stored his wealth beyond all this; he has found a safe place where none of the obstacles we have mentioned can intrude. This place is heaven, which is free of all treachery, more fertile than any land, a place where those who have deposited their wealth are allowed to reap the fruit of this deposit. Since this is the case, there is no need for you to make these complaints; but if your child wanted to live in the world, then you should lament and complain: "To whom shall we leave our fields, our gold and the rest of our goods?" Now our dominion over these goods is so extensive that not even after death will we lose control over them, but we will enjoy their fruit most when we have gone to the next life.

But if you wish to see someone who is master of his goods even in this life, you also could see this happen more to the monk than to the person in the world. Who, tell me, is the more lordly: the one who spends and gives with great fearlessness, or the one who does not dare to touch anything on account of his parsimony, but who hoards these goods and keeps away from his own property as if it were another's? The one who spends rashly and without purpose, or the one who does this only when necessary? The one who sows on earth, or the one who plants his seeds in heaven? The one who is not allowed to give all his goods to whomever he wishes, or the one who is free of all who demand such high taxes? The farmer and the businessman are set upon from all sides by many who compel them to pay tribute, each one demanding part of their property. But you would never see anyone threatening him who desires to give to the needy; thus, even in this life he is more lordly.

If he spends his money on prostitutes, gluttony, parasites, and flatterers, if he puts his glory to shame, destroys his salvation, and

becomes a buffoon, you say that he is master over what he spends. But
if he spends the same amount with great prudence for what is truly
glorious, useful, and pleasing to God, do you no longer say this? It is
as if, upon seeing someone spend his money on pipes for aquaducts,
you would say that he is master of his possessions, but upon seeing
someone do this for necessary purposes, you would lament that he does
not have power over his own resources. In fact, the persons of whom
we speak are more rightly compared, not to those who spend without
purpose, but to those who spend and bring ruin upon themselves. The
one kind of spending makes a person more illustrious, wealthier, and
more secure; the other kind makes him not only shameful and worthy
of reproach, but also liable to every type of ruin.

17. "Why is it not possible," you say, "for them to take up this
philosophy after marriage and children, when they have reached an
old age?" First, who will promise us that we will reach a ripe old age;
second, who will promise that we will preserve the same resolve when
we have reached old age? For we have no control over that appointed
day. Christ taught us this when he said: *The day of the Lord will come
like a thief in the night.*[84] Moreover, our thoughts do not always
persevere in the same good intention. That is why a certain wise man
gave this advice: *Do not delay to turn to the Lord, do not postpone it
from day to day, lest you be wiped out while you delay, and at the time
of vengeance be utterly destroyed.*[85]

But even if the future were not uncertain, it would not therefore be
right to hold your sons back, or to ignore the great harm which results.
It would be utterly senseless, when the young man is in need of help
and when the enemy is violently attacking him, to force him to engage
in worldly affairs and thus to be easily overcome, but to dress him for
battle and raise him up, when he has sustained countless wounds and
has nothing healthy about him, when he already lies sick and
prostrate.

"Exactly," you say, "for then the wrestling will be easy, then the
battle will be light, when his lusts have been extinguished." But what
kind of battle is it, when there is no one to spar with us? On this
account the crowns will not be bright in the end. For *blessed is he who
bore the yoke in his youth. He will sit alone and be silent.*[86] He is
worthy of countless praises, blessings, and laudations, who bridles his

---

[84] 1 Thessalonians 5:2. Chrysostom has mistakenly attributed this saying to Jesus
rather than to Paul. He may have been thinking of Matthew 24:43.
[85] Sirach 5:8.
[86] Lamentations 3:27-28.

nature when it is raging and who preserves the ship at the very height of the storm.

But let us not argue over this point; if you wish, we will grant that the battle will be in the future. If it were in our power to establish the time for the contest, we would do well to defer it. But if we must do battle throughout the whole of life, it is necessary that he begin as soon as he reaches maturity, at about ten years old. From this age a person is responsible for his sins, as we are shown in the story of the boys who were devoured by the bears for laughing at Elisha.[87] If the combat begins at this age, when the battle threatens to rage against us, how can you determine the time for the contests? If you were master of the devil and could order him not to attack or strike, then this advice of yours would make some sense. But if you allow him to fight and to strike, while ordering me to be quiet and even to submit willingly, what could be worse than this spiteful abuse: to strip the fighter of his arms while the enemy rages and thus to betray him into the hands of his opponent?

Is the young man feeble? For this reason there is need of greater security; and where there is need of security, there is need of greater caution. Such a youth must live in complete peace and tranquility; he must not be thrown into business or tossed into the fray, where there is great confusion and turmoil. But just when the battle is more difficult on account of their age, weakness, inexperience, and the perversity all around them, you draw them into the thick of it as if they were already well accomplished and strong, and you do not allow them to go for training in the deserts. It is as if someone would order a warrior, who could erect countless trophies, to study about warfare in tranquility, but would command a person, who is inexperienced and unable even to glance at a battle, to enter into battle, thereby piling up obstacles which make success more difficult.

Moreover, we must consider that it is not possible for a man to be master of himself when he has a wife, but either of two things must happen: either he has intercourse with his wife throughout his life, if she wishes this; or, if she does not wish this, he falls into adultery by refusing to live in continence.[88] What need is there to mention the other difficulties which children cause, domestic concerns, which are

---

[87] Cf. 2 Kings 2:23-25.

[88] Montfaucon's text (PG 47:379) differs slightly from Dübner's at this point. I have followed Dübner who adds the negative (μὴ) before the participle βουλομένης ("if she does not wish this").

capable of dulling all one's enthusiasm and inflicting great torpor of soul?

18. For this reason it is better to prepare him for battle from the earliest age, when he is in control and unencumbered, not only because of what we already have said, but also, and no less, because of what we are going to say. The person who enters this philosophy towards the end of his life spends all of his time washing himself clean of the sins he accumulated earlier in life, if this is possible, and all of his zeal is consumed in doing this. Often there is not enough time, and the person departs bearing the traces of his wounds. But the person who has stripped for the battle from the earliest age does not spend his time doing this, nor does he sit nursing his wounds, but he receives his rewards immediately. The former is delighted if he wins even the smallest battles, but the latter will erect trophies from the very start of the race and will add victory to victory. Like an Olympic athlete who goes from youth to old age amid proclamations of victory, so he will depart this life, his head crowned with countless crowns.

Where do you wish your son to be? Among those who are able to gaze with great confidence even upon the archangels, or among those who stand with the crowd and occupy the last place? For the last place is all they will be allotted, and this only if they can surmount all the obstacles which we just now have enumerated: if an untimely death does not overtake them, if later on they are not prevented by a wife, if they are not so wounded that their old age is not long enough to enable them to be healed, if they keep throughout their whole life a firm and steady resolve. When all these conditions concur, then they scarcely will be ranked in the last place. Do you wish your son to be among these, or among those who shine in the front of the phalanx?

"Who," you say, "is so cruel that he wants the former rather than the latter for his children? But we miss their company and we want them to be with us." I myself also want this and I pray no less than you, their parents, that they will return to their father's home and make recompense for their upbringing, something they could not find equalled anywhere. But let us not demand this of them now. Is it not absurd that, when we send them to study rhetoric, we banish them from their homeland for a long time, or that when they must learn some type of mechanical skill or something even more vile, we bar them from their own homes and order them to eat and sleep in the home of a teacher; but, when they wish to approach not a human science, but rather the heavenly philosophy, that we immediately draw them back before they can accomplish what we hope for? Even a person who is being taught to walk across a tightrope will spend a long time away from his family; but when they are learning how to fly from earth to heaven, we shut them in with their parents! What could be more senseless than this? Do you not see that farmers, even if they are in a great hurry to receive the fruit of their labors, would never allow themselves to reap the fruit before its time?

So, then, let us not take our sons away from their sojourn in the desert before it is time; let us allow the teachings to penetrate them and the roots to be firmly planted. Even if they must be raised in the monastery for ten years, or even twenty years, we should not be upset or grieved. The longer he exercises in the gymnasium, the stronger he will be. Or better yet, if you agree, let us not fix a definite time; the only limit should be that which brings to maturity the fruits which have been planted in him. Then he may return from the desert, but not before. For we have nothing to gain from haste in this matter, except that he will never reach maturity. The person who is deprived prematurely of the nourishment which comes from the root ultimately will be useless when the proper time arrives.

In order that this might not happen, let us patiently endure the separation; not only should we not urge them to return, but we should even prevent them if they wish to return before it is time. If he has been trained to perfection, he will be a profit shared by father, mother, home, city and nation; but if he returns incomplete, he will be a laughing stock and an object of reproach, harmful to himself and to others. Let us not create such a monster! Even when we send our sons far from home, we wish to see them again only after they have managed to accomplish successfully that for which they were sent away. But if they return before this, we are more disheartened by their return than gratified, because they have returned fruitlessly. Would it not be the greatest stupidity not to display as much zeal for spiritual matters as we show concerning worldly matters? Is it not foolish to endure separation from our children so philosophically when it comes to worldly pursuits that we hope this separation will be prolonged, if there is some profit to be made, and yet, when it comes to monastic life, to be so cowardly and distressed at their departure that we destroy the greatest goods by this meanness of spirit? And we do this, even though we have these many consolations: not only that they have stripped themselves for greater [contests], that they will successfully reach the end, and that nothing obstructs their hopes, but also the temporary character of the separation itself.[89]

For when the children are far from home, it is not easy to meet with them, especially if the parents are advanced in age; but in the monastic life it is always possible to visit them. Let us do this when they are not yet able to visit us. We ourselves should walk to them, be with them, talk with them. We will derive great profit and pleasure from this. Not only will we be gladdened by the sight of our beloved children, but we shall return home having received the greatest fruits; indeed, often we will remain with them, conquered by the love of philosophy.

Therefore, let us call them back only when they have become strong and able to render service to others. Let us bring them back only so that they might be a light to all, so that they might be a lamp set upon a lampstand. Then you will see what sort of children you have begotten, what sort of children cause their parents to be considered happy by you. Then you will see the benefits of philosophy, when they heal people suffering with incurable diseases, when they are hailed as benefactors, patrons and saviors to all, when they live like angels among people on earth, when everyone turns to look at them. Moreover, whatever we might say would be nothing compared to what actual experience and the facts themselves can reveal.

If things were as they should be, the lawmakers would not have waited until the young men were grown up to instill fear in them, but they would have educated them and molded them while they were still young. Then there would have been no need for the youth to be threatened later by the laws. But now it is as if a doctor would say nothing to a sick person and would not show him how to be relieved of his illness, but would write out countless prescriptions once the sick man had perished and become incurable. For the lawmakers instruct us only when we already are perverted! But Paul was not this way, but he set teachers of virtue over the young people from the beginning, from the earliest age, to prevent wickedness from gaining a foothold. The best instruction consists, not in first allowing wickedness to gain the upper hand and later seeking how to eliminate it, but rather in doing and working in every way so that our nature becomes inaccessible to evil. That is why I urge you not only not to prevent

---

[89] Dübner has emended the text πρὸς αὐτὸν to read πρόσκαιρον ("temporary"). Cf. PG 47.380

those who wish to do this, but even to give them assistance, to save the ship, and to make it ready to sail with a favorable wind.

If all of us should adopt this point of view, if we should lead them to virtue above all else, knowing that this is our task and that all other tasks are secondary, such great goods would result that I would seem to be boasting if I should speak about them now. But if someone should wish to know, the facts themselves will teach him well, and he will render great thanks to us, but even more to God, when he sees the heavenly way of life blossoming on earth and the doctrines about the future goods and about the resurrection finding credence here below even among the pagans.

19. Here is the proof that we are not merely boasting. Whenever we speak to pagans about the way of life of those who are in the deserts, they have nothing to say in objection to this, but they imagine that their case is strengthened and that they can argue about the small number of those who live a virtuous life.[90] But if we grew this fruit in the cities, if good behavior received its beginnings there and had the force of law, if we instructed the children to be friends of God above all else, if we taught them spiritual teachings instead of and above all other things, every reason for sorrow would vanish, the present life would be free of countless evils, and all of us would achieve in this life what is said about the future life—that sadness, grief and groaning are absent. If neither the love of money nor that of vain glory enters us, if we do not fear death, if we believe that neither poverty nor the bearing of evil brings us harm, but rather that it offers the greatest profit, if we know not what it is to be hated or to hate, neither our own passions nor those of others would ever attack us, but the human race would become nearly like the angels.

"But what person," you ask, "has achieved this level of virtue?" Naturally, you do not believe because you live in the cities and are not conversant with the sacred scriptures. But if you knew those who live in the deserts and those who lived long ago, who are mentioned in the spiritual books, you would learn that the monks, and the apostles before them, and before the apostles the just, practiced this philosophy with all perfection. But so that we do not quarrel with you, we will grant that your son will achieve the second or third rank after these; even here he will enjoy no small goods. He will not come before Peter

---

[90] For a similar argument see Chrysostom's homily 26.4 on Romans (PG 60.643-44), where he reports the complaint of a pagan that Christians in the city fail to live Christian ideals properly.

or Paul; indeed, he will not come close to them. Is this a reason for
depriving him of an honor inferior to theirs? When you talk like this,
it is like saying, "Since it is not possible to be a precious stone, let him
remain a piece of iron, let him not become silver or gold."

Why, then, do you not adopt this attitude when it comes to profane
matters, instead of taking the opposite view? When you send your son
to study rhetoric, you do not expect to see him reach the top;
nonetheless, you do not deter him from these studies because of this,
but you do everything in your power and think it desirable if he should
reach the fifth or sixth rank from the top in rhetorical skill. If your
sons serve in the emperor's army, you do not at all expect them to
reach the rank of provincial governor. But you do not order them to
take off the military belt or forbid them to approach imperial office; on
the contrary, you do everything possible so that they do not depart
from that way of life, thinking that it is enough to see them numbered
in the middle ranks.

Why, then, in one case, even if it is not possible for them to reach the
higher rank, do you wear yourself out and labor for lesser things, even
if the hope for these things is uncertain, but, in the other case, you
hesitate and draw back? It is because you have great enthusiasm for
what is inferior, but care not the slightest for what is greater; then,
being ashamed to admit this, you have thought up excuses and
pretexts. If you truly wanted it, none of these things would have
prevented you. This is how the matter stands. When a person truly
desires something, even if he cannot achieve it all or the highest part,
he would choose to reach the middle part, or even what is far below
this. And a person who loves wine and other drink, even if he is
unable to have wine with an agreeable taste and a rich bouquet, will
never disdain more ordinary wine. And, again, the lover of money, if
he receives a gift of silver, will be very grateful, even if it is not gold or
precious stones.

This is the way desire is: it can dominate and persuade whomever it
captures to suffer and endure all things for its sake. Therefore, if your
words were not mere excuses, you would have cooperated and lent a
hand. A person who wants something to happen will not prevent it
from happening, but will do everything to make it happen. When
people enter the Olympic games, although they know that only one
out of such a great crowd will achieve the victory, nonetheless they
labor hard and exert themselves. However, there is a great difference
between the athletic example and our own case, not only because the
two contests differ in their ends, but because in the case of the
Olympics only one person can leave with a victory crown. But in our

case, superiority and inferiority consist, not in whether one receives a crown or not, but in greater and lesser degrees of glory, a glory in which all share.

In short, if we wished from the beginning to mold the children and to entrust them to those who wish to educate them, it would not be unlikely that they would attain the highest rank in the army. For God would not ignore such enthusiasm and zeal, but he would give his assistance and take the statue in hand. With this hand at work, it is impossible that any effort should fail; indeed, it is impossible not to reach the very summit of splendor and glory, if only we do what is in our power. For if women are able to persuade God to cooperate with them in caring for their children, so much more shall we be able to do this, if we wish. In order not to prolong my speech, I will pass over the other women, although there are many to speak of, and we shall call to mind only one of them.

20. There was a Jewish woman named Anna.[91] Anna gave birth to one child and did not expect to have another. Indeed, she had scarcely given birth to him, and this after many tears, for she was sterile. When she saw that her rival frequently insulted her because of this, she did not act as you do, but after bearing that son she allowed him to remain with her only as long as was necessary for him to be weaned. When he no longer needed to be nursed, she immediately took him and offered him up to God, and she ordered him to return to his father's house no longer, but to live continually in the temple of God. Whenever she desired to see him, as a mother does, she did not summon the child to her own house, but she went up to him with his father, keeping her distance from him as if he were a votive offering.

This young man became so noble and great that when God had turned away from the race of the Hebrews because of their profuse wickedness and no longer spoke to them in oracles or appeared in any vision, he won back God's favor through his virtue and persuaded him to supply what had been given previously and once again to restore the prophecy which had vanished. And he was able to do this not when he reached a mature age, but when he was still a small child. As scripture says: *There was no frequent vision and the word [of the Lord] was rare.*[92] But although this was the situation, God continually delivered oracles to him. Such is always the reward for giving our possessions to God and for disowning all things, not only money and

---

[91] Anna was the mother of Samuel. See 1 Samuel 1 ff.
[92] 1 Samuel 3:1.

possessions, but also our very children. For if we are commanded to do this in the case of our own souls, how much more is this the case with everything else.

The patriarch Abraham also did this, indeed something much greater than this, and that is why he received his son back with greater glory. Then do we most truly possess our children when we have entrusted them to the Master. For he will govern them much better than we, since he feels greater concern for them. Do you not see the same thing happening in the homes of wealthy people? For even there the servants who live at an inferior rank with their parents never become very famous or achieve great power. But those children whom the masters have taken from their parents and assigned to serve them and to watch over their treasuries, these enjoy greater goodwill and confidence; they are more illustrious than their fellow servants, just as masters are superior to their household slaves. But if human beings are so kind and benevolent towards their servants, much more so is the Infinite Goodness, that is God.

So, let us allow them to serve at a higher rank, by leading them not to a temple like Samuel, but to heaven itself with the angels, with the archangels. For everyone knows that those who have undertaken this philosophy will surely serve and minister with them. And they will govern not only themselves, but also you with greater confidence. For if some people have received some consolation because of their fathers, much more so will fathers be consoled on account of their children. In the first case there is only the privilege of nature, but in the second case there is also the privilege of upbringing, which is much greater than that of nature.

We will confirm both of these for you from the sacred scriptures. Hezekiah was a pious and virtuous man, but he did not have such great confidence from his accomplishments that he could stand against so great a danger. Therefore, God said that he would save Hezekiah because of the virtue of his father. *For I will defend this city to save it*, he said, *for my own sake and the sake of my servant David.*[93] And when Paul wrote to Timothy concerning parents, he said that *they will be saved through bearing children, if they remain in faith and love and holiness, with modesty.*[94] And scripture praises Job not only because he was just and truthful and reverent, but also because of his concern for his children. But Job's concern was not to gather gold for

---

93 2 Kings 19:34.
94 1 Timothy 2:15.

them, nor to make them glorious and famous. What was it? Listen to what scripture says: *When the days of the feast had run their course, Job sent for them and sanctified them, and rising early in the morning he offered burnt offerings according to the number of them all, and one calf for sin on behalf of their souls. For Job said in his heart, "It may be that my sons have conceived wicked thoughts against God in their minds."*[95]

What excuse, then, will be left if we dare such things? For Job, who lived before grace and before the Law, and who enjoyed no instruction, exercised such great forethought for his children that he trembled even over uncertain sins. Who, then, will excuse us who live in grace, who have received such great teachers, who possess such great examples and such exhortations, when not only do we not fear when sins are uncertain, but we even think little of those that are certain—and not only think little of them, but even drive away those who wish to correct them? Abraham, as I said above, along with his other virtuous deeds also accomplished this splendid action.

21. Since, then, we have such great examples, let us prepare trustworthy servants and ministers for God. For if the person who nourishes athletes for cities or who trains soldiers for kings receives great honor, how great a reward ought we to receive when we nourish noble and great men, or rather angels, for God? Therefore, let us do everything in order to leave them the wealth of piety as an inheritance, a wealth which lasts and accompanies them when they die, which can provide the greatest benefits not only in this life, but also in the next. For worldly wealth will not travel with you when you depart, and even in this life it perishes before its possessors, and often it causes its possessors to perish. But this other wealth will be safe both in this life and in the next; with great security it will preserve those who possess it.

This is how matters stand. The person who prefers earthly goods to spiritual ones will be deprived of them both. But the person who longs for heavenly goods by all means also will receive earthly ones. This is not my own word, but the word of the Lord who provides these things. *Seek*, he says, *the kingdom of heaven and all these things will be added to you.*[96] What could be equal to this honor? Take care, he says, for spiritual things, but give to me all that is your own. God acts just like a loving father who takes upon himself the care of his household and

---

[95] Job 1:5.
[96] Matthew 6:33.

charge over the servants and everything else, but who urges his son to devote himself solely to philosophy.

Let us obey, therefore, and let us seek the kingdom of God, and thus we will see our children approved everywhere, and we ourselves will be famous with them; we will enjoy present goods, if only we love the future and heavenly ones. If you obey these words, you will see a great reward; but if you contradict and refuse to obey them, you will see a most bitter punishment. For there can be no recourse to excuses, nor can anyone say that he had no one to teach him these things. Even before our speeches, there was no room for such an excuse, since nature has an accurate ability to judge what is good and what is not good, since this philosophy is present everywhere, and since the evils in this life are sufficient to lead to the desert even those who are greatly enamored of this life. Even if we had been silent, as I said, there would have been no room for excuses; but this is much more the case now after these long speeches and after such an exhortation, both from the facts at hand and even more clearly from the sacred scriptures.

Even if it were possible that those who remain at home ultimately might not perish, but could obtain the lowest rank of salvation, we would certainly not escape punishment if we prevented those who are hastening to enter upon a more diligent way of life, and if we detained in worldly affairs those who are hastening to fly into heaven. But since this is impossible, since destruction is absolutely inevitable, and since the danger concerns the ultimate things, what pardon will we have, what excuse, when we have taken upon ourselves the most severe chastisements, not only for our own sins, but also for the sins later committed by our children? For I do not think that they will be punished for their own failures, after they have been dragged down into this flood, as much as you who brought them into this necessity. For if it is fitting that he who scandalized one person be thrown into the sea with a millstone, what punishment and torture will be enough for those who display this cruelty and harshness towards their own children?

Therefore, I exhort you to put away contentiousness and to be fathers of children who are philosophers. You must not give the excuse which so many people give. What is that? "We have prevented them," they say, "because we knew that they could not attain the goal." Even if your foreknowledge were certain and not a mere conjecture—for many who were expected to fall have stood firm—even if you were quite sure in your foreknowledge, it would not be necessary to lead them out. For if we take those who are likely to fall and throw them to the ground, this certainly does not excuse us; on the contrary, it is this especially which condemns us. Why did you not allow your son's fall to happen as a result of his own laziness, instead of anticipating and siezing the sin beforehand and casting the whole thing upon your own head? Rather, you should not have allowed it. Why did you not do everything to ensure that your son would not fall? Therefore, it is precisely because you knew that he would fall that you are especially worthy of punishment. For the person who has this foreknowledge is required not to strike him down, but to lend a hand and to show greater zeal so that the one who is about to fall might stand firm nobly, whether he ultimately stands firm or not. For we must fulfill all that is in our power, even if others take no profit from us. "To what end," you say, "and for what reason?" So that God will call them, and not us, to account. God himself also said this when he accused the person who had done nothing with his talent. *You ought to have invested my money with the bankers,* he said, *and at my coming I should have received it back with interest.*[97]

So, then, let us obey the one who gives us this advice so that we might escape the punishment. For we cannot deceive God as we do men, for he scrutinizes hearts and brings everything out into the open and holds us responsible in every way for the salvation of the children. For if the man who did not invest the money was punished so severely, what will happen to the one who prevents those who wish to make the investment? Even if the children are not cast down into the midst of worldly affairs by our counsel, but rather nobly resist the assault and take to the mountains once again, those who wished to impede them will receive the same punishment. For just as the person who leads them to philosophy receives a complete reward, whether or not they fall (for he has done everything in his power), so, too, the person who wishes to destroy them, whether or not he succeeds, will receive the same punishment (for he likewise did everything in his power). And so, even if you are unable to upset and destroy the noble purposes of the children, nonetheless merely for attempting this you will pay as great a penalty as those who succeeded in destroying them.

Therefore, keeping all this in mind, and putting aside all excuses, let us strive to be fathers of noble children, builders of Christ-bearing temples, trainers of heavenly athletes, preparing them for combat, guiding them aright, working for their benefit in every way, so that

---

[97] Matthew 25:27.

we might share their crowns in the next life. But if you remain obstinate, the children, should they be noble, will enter this philosophy against your will and they will enjoy all good things; but you yourselves will suffer countless punishments, and then you will praise what we have said, when it is too late for this praise to help you.

BIBLIOGRAPHY

Works of John Chrysostom

Ad Theodorum lapsum, 1-2. Edited by J. Dumortier. Sources Chrétiennes, 117. Paris, 1966.

Adversus oppugnatores vitae monasticae. PG 47.319-86. Text also
edited in F. Dübner, *Sancti Joannis Chrysostomi opera selecta.* Paris:
Didot, 1861. pp. 1-75.

Comparatio regis et monachi. PG 47.387-92.

Ad Demetrium de compunctione, 1. PG 47.393-410.

Ad Stelechium de compunctione, 2. PG 47.411-22.

Ad Stagirium a daemone vexatum, 1-3. PG 47.423-94.

De sancto Babyla, contra Julianum et Gentiles. PG 50.533-572. Also
edited by M. Schatkin. Ph.D. Dissertation: Fordham University,
1967. English translation by M. Schatkin, *St. John Chrysostom.
Apologist.* Fathers of the Church, 73. Washington, DC: Catholic
University of America Press, 1985.

Demonstratio contra gentiles, quod Christus sit Deus. PG 48.813-38. Also
edited by N. McKendrick. Ph.D. Dissertation: Fordham University,
1966. English translation by P. Harkins, *St. John Chrysostom.
Apologist.* Fathers of the Church, 73. Washington, DC: Catholic
University of America Press, 1985.

Contra eos qui subintroductas habent. Edited by J.Dumortier. Paris,
1955. English translation by E.A. Clark, *Jerome, Chrysostom and
Friends. Essays and Translations.* New York: Edwin Mellen Press,
1979.

De virginitate. Edited by H. Musurillo. Sources Chrétiennes, 125. Paris,
1966. English translation by S. Shore, *John Chrysostom. On
Virginity. Against Remarriage.* New York and Toronto: Edwin
Mellen Press, 1983.

Ad viduam juniorem. Edited by B. Grillet and G. Ettlinger. Sources
Chrétiennes, 138. Paris, 1968.

De non iterando coniugio. Edited by B. Grillet and G. Ettlinger. Sources
Chrétiennes, 138. Paris, 1968. English translation by S. Shore, *John
Chrysostom. On Virginity. Against Remarriage.* New York and
Toronto: Edwin Mellen Press, 1983.

De sacerdotio. Edited by A.M. Malingrey. Sources Chrétiennes, 272.
Paris, 1980. English translation by G. Neville, *St. John Chrysostom.
Six Books on the Priesthood.* London: SPCK, 1964; reprinted
Crestwood, NY: St. Vladimir's Seminary Press, 1984.

Sermo cum presbyter fuit ordinatus. PG 48.693-700.

De incomprehensibili Dei natura. PG 48.701-812. English translation by
P. Harkins. *St. John Chrysostom. On the Incomprehensible Nature of
God.* Fathers of the Church, 72. Washington, DC: Catholic
University of America Press, 1982.

De inani gloria et de educandis a parentibus liberis. Edited by A.M.
Malingrey. Sources Chrétiennes, 188. Paris, 1972. English
translation by M.L.W. Laistner. *Christianity and Pagan Culture in
the Later Roman Empire.* Ithaca: Cornell University Press, 1951.

Laus Diodori episcopi. PG 50.761-66.

Homiliae 21 de statuis ad populum Antiochenum. PG 49.15-222. English
translation in *A Select Library of Nicene and Post-Nicene Fathers.*
vol. 9. pp. 317-489.

Panegyricum in Juventinum et Maximinum martyres. PG 50.571-78.

De Lazaro conciones 1-7. PG 48.963-1054.

In quadriduanum Lazarum. PG 48.779-84.

Homiliae 90 in Matthaeum. PG 57.21-472; PG 58.21-794. English
   translation in *A Select Library of Nicene and Post-Nicene Fathers.*
   vol. 10.

Homiliae 32 in epistulam ad Romanos. PG 60.391-682. English
   translation in *A Select Library of Nicene and Post-Nicene Fathers.*
   vol. 11. pp. 334-564.

Homiliae 44 in epistulam primam ad Corinthios. PG 61. 9-382. English
   translation in *A Select Library of Nicene and Post-Nicene Fathers.*
   vol. 12. pp. 3-269.

Homiliae 24 in epistulam ad Ephesios. PG 62.9-176. English translation
   in *A Select Library of Nicene and Post-Nicene Fathers.* vol. 13. pp.
   50-172.

Homiliae 18 in epistulam primam ad Timotheum. PG 62.501-600.
   English translation in *A Select Library of Nicene and Post-Nicene
   Fathers.* vol. 13. pp. 408-73.

Other Primary and Secondary Literature

Aldama, J.A. *Repertorium Pseudochrysostomicum.* Paris: Éditions du
   Centre National de la Recherche Scientifique, 1965.

Ameringer, T.E. *The Stylistic Influence of the Second Sophistic on the
   Panegyrical Sermons of St. John Chrysostom.* Washington, DC:
   Catholic University of America Press, 1920.

Ammianus Marcellinus. *History of the Roman Empire.* Edited and
   translated by J.C. Rolfe. 3 vols. Loeb Classical Library. Cambridge,
   MA: Harvard University Press, 1935-39.

Arnim, I. von. *Stoicorum veterum fragmenta.* 3 vols. Stuttgart: Teubner,
   1903.

Athanasius, *Life of Antony.* Translated by R.T. Meyer. Ancient Christian Writers, 10. Westminster, MD: The Newman Press, 1950.

Athanassiadi-Fowden, P. *Julian and Hellenism. An Intellectual
   Biography.* Oxford: Clarendon Press, 1981.

Aristotle. *Nichomachean Ethics.* Translated by M. Ostwald.
Indianapolis: Bobbs-Merrill, 1962.

Aubineau, M. *Grégoire de Nysse. Traité de la virginité.* Sources
Chrétiennes, 119. Paris, 1966.

Bartelink, G.J.M. "'Philosophie' et 'philosophe' dans quelques oeuvres
de Jean Chrysostome," *Revue d'ascétique et de mystique* 36 (1960)
486-92.

Basil of Caesarea. *Address to Young Men on Reading Greek Literature.*
Edited and translated by R.J. Deferrari and M. McGuire. Loeb
Classical Library. Cambridge, MA: Harvard University Press, 1961.

Baur, C. "Das Ideal der christliche Vollkommenheit nach dem heiligen
Johannes Chrysostomus," *Theologie und Glaube* 6 (1914) 564-74.

_____. *John Chrysostom and his Time.* Translated by M. Gonzaga.
2 vols. Westminster: Newman Press, 1959.

Baynes, N.H. "The Thought World of East Rome," in his *Byzantine
Studies and Other Essays.* London, 1955. pp. 24-46.

_____. "The Hellenistic Culture and East Rome," in *Byzantine
Studies and Other Essays.* pp. 1-23.

Bernardi, J. "La formule ποῦ εἰσιν: saint Jean Chrysostome a-t- il imité
saint Grégoire de Nazianze?" *Studia Patristica* 1 (TU 63; 1957) 177-
181.

Bonner, G. "The Extinction of Paganism and the Church Historian,"
Journal of Ecclesiastical History 35 (1984) 339-57.

Boswell, J. *Christianity, Social Tolerance, and Homosexuality.* Chicago
and London: University of Chicago Press, 1980.

Bowersock, G.W. *Julian the Apostate.* Cambridge, MA: Harvard
University Press, 1978.

Brock, S. "Early Syrian Asceticism," *Numen* 20 (1973) 1-19.

Brown, P. "The Rise and Function of the Holy Man in Late Antiquity," *Journal of Roman Studies* 60 (1971) 80-101. Reprinted in his *Society and the Holy in Late Antiquity*. Berkeley: University of California Press, 1982. pp. 103-52.

_____. "Town, Village and Holy Man: The Case of Syria," in *Society and the Holy in Late Antiquity*. pp. 153-65.

_____. *The Making of Late Antiquity*. Cambridge, MA: Harvard University Press, 1978.

Browning, R. "The Riot of A.D. 387 in Antioch. The Role of the Theatrical Claques in the Later Roman Empire," *Journal of Roman Studies* 42 (1952) 13-20.

_____. *The Emperor Julian*. Berkeley and Los Angeles: University of California Press, 1976.

Buckler, G. "Byzantine Education," in *Byzantium. An Introduction to East Roman Civilization*. Edited by N.H. Baynes and H. Moss. Oxford: Clarendon Press, 1962. pp. 200-220.

Bueno, D.R. *Obras de San Juan Crisóstomo. Tratados asceticos*. Madrid: Biblioteca de autores cristianos, 1958.

Burger, D.C. *A Complete Bibliography of the Scholarship on the Life and Works of Saint John Chrysostom*. Evanston, 1964.

Burns, M.A. *St. John Chrysostom's Homilies on the Statues. A Study of their Rhetorical Qualities and Forms*. Washington, DC: Catholic University of America Press, 1930.

Calder, W.M. and Crosby, M. "On the Silence of Socrates. A First Translation and Interpretation," *Greek, Roman and Byzantine Studies* 3 (1960) 185-202.

Canivet, P. *Histoire d'une entreprise apologétique au Ve siècle*. Paris: Bloud and Gay, 1957.

_____. *Théodoret de Cyr. Thérapeutique des malades helléniques*. Sources Chrétiennes, 57. Paris, 1958.

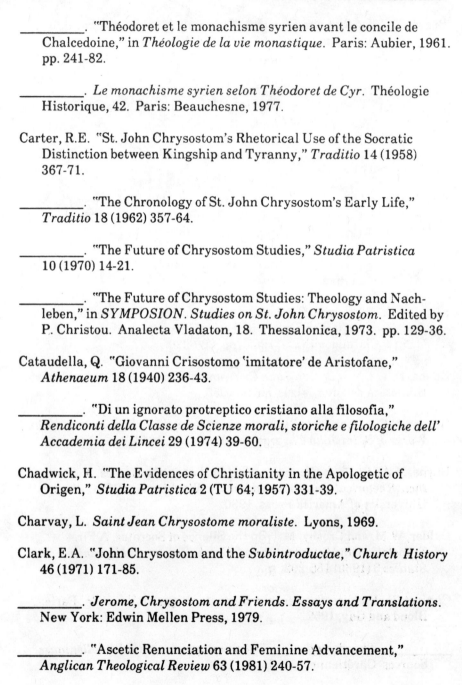

_____. "Théodoret et le monachisme syrien avant le concile de Chalcedoine," in *Théologie de la vie monastique*. Paris: Aubier, 1961. pp. 241-82.

_____. *Le monachisme syrien selon Théodoret de Cyr*. Théologie Historique, 42. Paris: Beauchesne, 1977.

Carter, R.E. "St. John Chrysostom's Rhetorical Use of the Socratic Distinction between Kingship and Tyranny," *Traditio* 14 (1958) 367-71.

_____. "The Chronology of St. John Chrysostom's Early Life," *Traditio* 18 (1962) 357-64.

_____. "The Future of Chrysostom Studies," *Studia Patristica* 10 (1970) 14-21.

_____. "The Future of Chrysostom Studies: Theology and Nachleben," in *SYMPOSION. Studies on St. John Chrysostom*. Edited by P. Christou. Analecta Vladaton, 18. Thessalonica, 1973. pp. 129-36.

Cataudella, Q. "Giovanni Crisostomo 'imitatore' de Aristofane," *Athenaeum* 18 (1940) 236-43.

_____. "Di un ignorato protreptico cristiano alla filosofia," *Rendiconti della Classe de Scienze morali, storiche e filologiche dell' Accademia dei Lincei* 29 (1974) 39-60.

Chadwick, H. "The Evidences of Christianity in the Apologetic of Origen," *Studia Patristica* 2 (TU 64; 1957) 331-39.

Charvay, L. *Saint Jean Chrysostome moraliste*. Lyons, 1969.

Clark, E.A. "John Chrysostom and the *Subintroductae*," *Church History* 46 (1971) 171-85.

_____. *Jerome, Chrysostom and Friends. Essays and Translations*. New York: Edwin Mellen Press, 1979.

_____. "Ascetic Renunciation and Feminine Advancement," *Anglican Theological Review* 63 (1981) 240-57.

_____. "Introduction," to the volume *John Chrysostom. On Virginity. Against Remarriage.* Translated by S. Shore. New York and Toronto: Edwin Mellen Press, 1983.

Cochrane, C.N. *Christianity and Classical Culture.* Oxford University Press, 1940.

Coleman-Norton, P.R. "St. John Chrysostom and the Greek Philosophers," *Classical Philology* 25 (1930) 305-17.

_____. "St. John Chrysostom's Use of Josephus," *Classical Philology* 26 (1931) 85-89.

_____. "St. John Chrysostom's Use of the Greek Poets," *Classical Philology* 28 (1932) 213-21.

_____. *Roman State and Christian Church.* 3 vols. London: SPCK, 1966.

Crosby, M. and Calder, W.M. "On the Silence of Socrates. A First Translation and Interpretation," *Greek, Roman and Byzantine Studies* 3 (1960) 185-202.

Dihle, A. "Ethik," *Reallexikon für Antike und Christentum* 6 (1966) 646-796.

Dio Chrysostom. *Discourses.* Edited and translated by J.W. Cohoon. 5 vols. Loeb Classical Library. Cambridge, MA: Harvard University Press, 1932-51.

Diogene Laertius. *Lives of Eminent Philosophers.* Edited and translated by R.D. Hicks. 2 vols. Loeb Classical Library. Cambridge, MA: Harvard University Press, 1925.

Downey, G. "*Philanthropia* in Religion and Statecraft in the Fourth Century after Christ," *Historia* 4 (1955) 199-208.

_____. "Ancient Education," *Classical Journal* 52 (1956-57) 337-45.

_____. "Themistius and the Defense of Hellenism in the Fourth Century," *Harvard Theological Review* 50 (1957) 259-74.

_____. "The Emperor Julian and the Schools," *Classical Journal* 53 (1957-58) 97-103.

_____. "Libanius' Oration in Praise of Antioch (or. XI)," *Proceedings of the American Philosophical Society* 103 (1959) 652-86.

_____. *A History of Antioch in Syria from Seleucus to the Arab Conquest*. Princeton University Press, 1961.

Dübner, F. *Sancti Johannis Chrysostomi opera selecta*. Paris: Didot, 1861.

Dumortier, J. "La valeur historique du Dialogue de Palladius et la chronologie de saint Jean Chrysostome," *Mélanges de science religieuse* 8 (1951) 51-56.

_____. "La culture profane de saint Jean Chrysostome," *Mélanges de science religieuse* 10 (1953) 53-62.

_____. "Les idées morales de saint Jean Chrysostome," *Mélanges de science religieuse* 12 (1955) 27-36.

_____. "L'auteur présumé du *Corpus asceticum* de saint Jean Chrysostome," *Journal of Theological Studies*, new series, (1955) 99-102.

_____. *Saint Jean Chrysostome. Les Cohabitations suspectes; Comment observer la virginité*. Paris: Les Belles Lettres, 1955.

_____. *Jean Chrysostome. À Theodore*. Sources Chrétiennes, 117. Paris, 1966.

Epictetus. *Enchiridion*. Translated by T.W. Higginson. The Library of the Liberal Arts. Indianapolis: Bobbs-Merrill, 1948.

Eunapius. *Lives of the Philosophers and Sophists*. Edited and translated by W.C. Wright. Loeb Classical Library. Cambridge, MA: Harvard University Press, 1968.

Fabricius, C. "Vier Libaniusstellen bei Johannes Chrysostomos," *Symbolae Osloenses* 33 (1957) 135-36.

_____. *Zu den Jugendschriften des Johannes Chrysostomos.*
Untersuchungen zum Klassizismus des vierten Jahrhunderts. Lund:
Gleerup, 1962.

Festugière, A.J. *Personal Religion Among the Greeks.* Berkeley and Los
Angeles: University of California Press, 1954.

_____. *Antioche païenne et chrétienne. Libanius, Chrysostome et les
moines de Syrie.* Paris: Éditions du Boccard, 1959.

_____. *Culture ou sainteté. Introduction au monachisme orientale.*
Vol. 1 in his *Les moines de orient.* Paris, 1961.

Fevier, P. "La ville et le 'désert' (à propos de la vie religieuse au IVe et
Ve siècles," in *Les mystiques du desert dans l'Islam, le Judaisme, et le
Christianisme.* Association des Amis de Sénanque, 1974. pp. 39-62.

Field, G.C. *Plato and his Contemporaries. A Study in Fourth Century Life
and Thought.* 3rd edition. London: Methuen, 1967.

Fluck, J. *Die ascetischen Schriften des heiligen Johannes Chrysostomus.*
Freiburg-im-Breisgau: Herder, 1864.

Fordyce, C.J. "Declamatio," *Oxford Classical Dictionary.* 2nd. edition.
Oxford, 1970. pp. 316-17.

Gast, M. "Expérience du desert et formation morale," in *Les mystiques
du desert dans l'Islam, le Judaisme, et le Christianisme.* Association
des Amis de Sénanque, 1974. pp. 17-24.

Gauthier, A. *Magnanimité. L'idéal de la grandeur dans la philosophie
païenne et dans la théologie chrétienne.* Paris, 1951.

Geerard, M. *Clavis Patrum Graecorum.* vol. 2. Turnhout: Brepols, 1974.

Geffcken, J. *The Last Days of Greco-Roman Paganism.* Translated by S.
MacCormack. Amsterdam, New York and Oxford: North Holland
Publishing Company, 1978.

Göbel, R. *De Ioanni Chrysostomi et Libanii orationibus quae sunt de
seditione Antiochensium.* Göttingen, 1910.

Gorge, D. "Mariage et perfection chrétienne d'après Jean Chrysostome,"
    Revue des études carmelitaines 21 (1936) 245-84.

Gregg, R. *Consolation Philosophy.* Patristic Monograph Series.
    Philadelphia, 1975.

Gregory Nazianzus. Orations 4 and 5. Edited by J. Bernardi, *Grégoire de
    Nazianze. Discours 4-5. Contre Julien.* Sources Chrétiennes, 309.
    Paris, 1983. English translation by C.W. King in *Julian the
    Emperor.* Bohn Classical Library. London, 1888.

Gribomont, J. "Le monachisme au sein de l'Eglise en Syrie et
    Cappadocia," *Studia Monastica* 7 (1965) 7-24.

Hadas, M. and Smith, M. *Heroes and Gods. Spiritual Biographies in
    Antiquity.* London and New York: Harper and Row, 1965.

Haddad, G. *Aspects of Social Life in Antioch in the Hellenistic-Roman
    Period.* New York, 1949.

Hare, B.W. "St. John Chrysostom on Education," *Prudentia* 6 (1974)
    99-104.

Harkins, P. "Chrysostom the Apologist on the Divinity of Christ," in
    KYRIAKON. Festschrift Johannes Quasten. Vol. 1. Münster:
    Aschendorff, 1970. pp. 440-51.

_____. *St. John Chrysostom. Apologist.* Fathers of the Church, 73.
    Washington, DC: Catholic University of America Press, 1985.

Hubbell, H.M. "Chrysostom and Rhetoric," *Classical Philology* 19 (1924)
    261-76.

Hunter, D.G. "Resistance to the Virginal Ideal in Late-Fourth-Century
    Rome: The Case of Jovinian," *Theological Studies* 48 (1987) 45-64.

_____. "Borrowings from Libanius in the *Comparatio regis et
    monachi* of St. John Chrysostom," *Journal of Theological Studies*,
    new series, 39 (1988) 525-31.

_____. "Libanius and John Chrysostom: New Thoughts on an Old
    Problem," *Studia Patristica* 22 (1989) forthcoming.

Jaeger, W. Paideia: *The Ideals of Greek Culture.* 3 vols. Oxford and New York: Oxford University Press, 1939-44.

_____. *Early Christianity and Greek Paideia.* Cambridge, MA: The Belknap Press of Harvard University, 1961.

Jones, A.H.M. "St. John Chrysostom's Parentage and Education," *Harvard Theological Review* 46 (1953) 171-73.

_____. "The Social Background to the Struggle between Paganism and Christianity," in *The Conflict between Paganism and Christianity in the Fourth Century.* Edited by A. Momigliano. Oxford, 1963. pp. 17-37.

_____. *The Later Roman Empire 284-602. A Social Economic and Administrative Survey.* 2 vols. Norman: University of Oklahoma Press, 1964.

Judge, E.A. "The Earliest Use of *monachos* for 'monk' and the Origins of Monasticism," *Jahrbuch für Antike und Christentum* 20 (1977) 72-89.

Julian. *The Works of the Emperor Julian.* Edited and translated by W.C. Wright. 3 vols. Loeb Classical Library. Cambridge: Harvard University Press, 1949-54.

Kennedy, G. *The Art of Persuasion in Greece.* Princeton: Princeton University Press, 1963.

_____. *Greek Rhetoric under Christian Emperors.* Princeton: Princeton University Press, 1983.

King, C.W. *Julian the Emperor.* Bohn's Classical Library. London, 1888.

Kopecek, T. "Curial Displacements and Flights in Later Fourth Century Cappadocia," *Historia* 23 (1974) 319-42.

Labriolle, P. de. *La réaction païenne. Étude sur la polémique anti-chrétienne du Ier au VIe siècle.* Paris: L'Artisan du Livre, 1934.

Laistner, M.L.W. *Christianity and Pagan Culture in the Later Roman Empire.* Ithaca: Cornell University Press, 1951.

Lampe, G.W.H. *A Patristic Greek Lexicon.* Oxford: Clarendon Press, 1961.

Lassus, J. *Sanctuaires chrétiens de Syrie.* Paris: Geuthner, 1947.

Leduc, F. "La thème de la vaine gloire chez saint Jean Chrysostome," Proche-orient chrétien 29 (1969) 3-32.

_____. "L'eschatologie, une préoccupation centrale de saint Jean Chrysostome," *Proche-orient chrétien* 29 (1969) 109-37.

Legrand, P.E. *Saint Jean Chrysostome. Contra les détracteurs de la vie monastique. Introduction et traduction.* Paris: Gabalda, 1933.

Leroux, J.M. "Monachisme et communauté chrétienne d'après saint Jean Chrysostome," in *Théologie de la vie monastique.* Paris: Aubier, 1961. pp. 143-90.

_____. "Saint Jean Chrysostome et le monachisme," in *Jean Chrysostome et Augustin.* Edited by C. Kannengiesser. Paris: Beauchesne, 1975. pp. 125-44.

Levi, D. *Antioch Mosaic Pavements.* 2 vols. Rome, 1971. This is a reprint of the 1947 edition by arrangement with Princeton University Press.

Libanius. *Opera.* Edited by R. Förster. 8 vols. Leipzig: Teubner, 1903-27.

_____. *Libanius' Autobiography (Oration I): The Greek Text.* Edited and translated by A.F. Norman. Oxford, 1965.

_____. *Selected Works.* Edited and translated by A.F. Norman. 2 vols. Loeb Classical Library. Cambridge, MA: Harvard University Press, 1969 and 1977.

_____. *Discours moraux.* Edited and translated by B. Schouler. Paris, 1973.

Liebeschuetz, J.H.W.G. *Antioch. City and Imperial Administration in the Later Roman Empire.* Oxford: Clarendon Press, 1972.

_____. *Continuity and Change in Roman Religion.* Oxford: Clarendon Press, 1979.

Lloyd, A.C. "The Later Neoplatonists," in *The Cambridge History of Later Greek and Early Medieval Philosophy.* Edited by A.H. Armstrong. Cambridge, 1967.

Maat, W.A. A *Rhetorical Study of St. John Chrysostom's de sacerdotio.* Washington, DC: Catholic University of America Press, 1944.

MacIntyre, A. *After Virtue. A Study in Moral Theory.* University of Notre Dame Press, 1981.

MacMullen, R. "Social Mobility and the Theodosian Code," *Journal of Roman Studies* 54 (1964) 49-53.

_____. *Enemies of the Roman Order.* London, 1967.

_____. *Paganism in the Roman Empire.* New Haven: Yale University Press, 1981.

_____. *Christianizing the Roman Empire (A.D. 100-400).* New Haven: Yale University Press, 1984.

Malherbe, A. *The Cynic Epistles.* Missoula, Montana: Scholars Press, 1977.

Malingrey, A.M. *"Philosophia": Étude d'un groupe de mots dans la littérature grecque, des Présocratiques au IVe siècle après J.C.* Paris: Klincksieck, 1961.

_____. "Le personnage de Socrate chez quelques auteurs chrétiens du IVe siècle," in *Forma futuri. Studi in onore di M. Pellegrino.* Turin, 1975. pp. 159-78.

Malley, W.J. *Hellenism and Christianity,* Rome: Università Gregoriana Editrice, 1978.

Markowski, H. *De Libanio Socratis defensore.* Breslau, 1910; reprinted New York and Hildesheim: G. Olms Verlag, 1970.

Marrou, H. *A History of Education in Antiquity.* London, 1956.

_____. "Diatribe," *Reallexikon für Antike und Christentum* 3 (1957) coll. 998-99.

_____. *Saint Augustin et la fin de la culture antique.* Paris: Boccard, 1958.

_____. "Synesius of Cyrene and Alexandrian Neoplatonism," in *The Conflict between Paganism and Christianity in the Fourth Century.* Edited by A. Momigliano. Oxford, 1963. pp. 128-50.

_____. "Antioche et l'Hellenisme chrétien. À propos d'un livre recent," *Revue des études grecques* 76 (1963) 430-36.

Maur, I. auf der. *Mönchtum und Glaubensverkündigung in den Schriften des heiligen Johannes Chrysostomos.* Paradosis, 14. Freiburg, 1959.

Mendieta, A. de. "L'amplification d'un thème socratique et stoïcien dans l'avant-dernier traité de Jean Chrysostome," *Byzantion* 36 (1966) 353-81.

Meredith, A. "Asceticism, Christian and Greek," *Journal of Theological Studies,* new series, 27 (1976) 313-32.

Meyer, L. *Saint Jean Chrysostome. Maître de perfection chrétienne.* Paris: Beauchesne, 1933.

Misson, J. "Libanios et Christianisme," *Musée Belge* 24 (1920) 72-89.

_____. *Recherches sur le paganisme de Libanios.* Louvain, 1914.

Moulard, A. *Saint Jean Chrysostome. Le défenseur du mariage et l'apôtre de la virginité.* Paris, 1923.

Murphy, F.X. "The Moral Doctrine of St. John Chrysostom," *Studia Patristica* 11 (1972) 52-57.

Nägele, A. "Johannes Chrysostomos und seine Verhaltnis zum Hellenismus," *Byzantinische Zeitschrift* 13 (1904) 73-113.

_____. "Chrysostomos und Libanios," in *XPYCOCTOMIKA. Studi e richerche intorno A.S. Giovanni Crisostomo*. Rome: Pustet, 1908. pp. 81-142.

Natali, A. "Christianisme et citè à Antioche à la fin du IVe siècle d'après J. Chrysostome," in *Jean Chrysostome et Augustin*. Edited by C. Kannengiesser. Paris: Beauchesne, 1975. pp. 41-59.

Neville, G. *Saint John Chrysostom. Six Books on the Priesthood*. London: SPCK, 1964; reprinted Crestwood, NY: St. Vladimir's Seminary Press, 1984.

Nock, A.D. *Conversion. The Old and the New in Religion from Alexander the Great to Augustine of Hippo*. Oxford, 1933.

_____. "The Praises of Antioch," *Journal of Egyptian Archaeology* 40 (1954) 76-82.

Norman, A.F. "The Library of Libanius," *Rheinisches Museum für Philologie* 107 (1964) 158-75.

Nowak, E. *Le chrétien devant la souffrance. Étude sur la pensée de Jean Chrysostome*. Paris: Beauchesne, 1972.

O'Donnell, J.J. "The Demise of Paganism," *Traditio* 35 (1979) 45-88.

Origen. *Contra Celsum*. Translated by H. Chadwick. Cambridge, 1965.

Pack, R. *Studies in Libanius and Antiochene Society under Theodosius*. Ann Arbor: University of Michigan, 1935.

Palladius. *Dialogue on the Life of St. John Chrysostom*. Translated by R.T. Meyer. Ancient Christian Writers, 45. New York: Newman Press, 1985.

Pasquato, O. *Gli spettacoli in S. Giovanni Crisostomo. Paganesimo e Cristianesimo ad Antiochia e Costantinopoli nel IV secolo*. Orientalia Christiana Analecta, 201. Rome, 1976.

Petit, P. *Libanius et la vie municipale à Antioche au IVe siècle apres J.C.*
Paris, 1955.

_____. "Recherches sur la publication et la diffusion des discours de
Libanius," *Historia* 5 (1956) 479-509.

_____. *Les étudiants de Libanius.* Paris, 1956.

Pharr, P.C. *The Theodosian Code and Novels and the Sirmondian
Constitutions.* Princeton: Princeton University Press, 1952.

Plato. *The Collected Dialogues of Plato.* Edited by E. Hamilton and
H. Cairns. Princeton: Princeton University Press, 1961.

Plutarch. *De liberis educandis.* In *Plutarch. Moralia.* vol. 1. Edited and
translated by F.C. Babbitt. Loeb Classical Library. Cambridge, MA:
Harvard University Press, 1927.

_____. *An virtus doceri possit.* In *Plutarch. Moralia.* vol. 6. Edited
and translated by W.C. Helmbold. Loeb Classical Library.
Cambridge, MA: Harvard University Press, 1939.

_____. *De cupiditate divitiarum.* In *Plutarch. Moralia.* vol. 7.
Edited and translated by P. de Lacy and B. Einarson. Loeb Classical
Library. Cambridge, MA: Harvard University Press, 1959.

Puech, A. *Un réformateur de la société chrétienne au IVe siècle. Saint
Jean Chrysostome et les moeurs de son temps.* Paris: Librairie
Hachette, 1891.

Quasten, J. *Patrology.* 3 vols. Westminister, MD: Newman Press,
1950-60.

Ritter, A.M. *Charisma im Verständnis des Johannes Chrysostomos und
seiner Zeit.* Göttingen, 1972.

Rougé, J. "Néro à la fin du IVe et au début du Ve siècles," *Latomus* 37
(1978) 73-84.

Rousseau, P. *Ascetics, Authority and the Church in the Age of Jerome
and Cassian.* Oxford University Press, 1978.

Ruether, R. *Gregory of Nazianzus. Rhetor and Philosopher.* Oxford: Clarendon Press, 1969.

Russell, D.A. "Rhetoric, Greek," *Oxford Classical Dictionary.* 2nd edition. Oxford, 1970. pp. 920-21.

Sawhill, O.A. *The Use of Athletic Metaphors in the Biblical Homilies of John Chrysostom.* Princeton, 1928.

Schatkin, M.A. *Critical Edition of, and Introduction to St. John Chrysostom's De sancto Babyla, contra Julianum et Gentiles.* Ph.D. Dissertation: Fordham University, 1967.

_____. "The Authenticity of St. John Chrysostom's De sancto Babyla, contra Julianum et Gentiles," in *KYRIAKON. Festschrift Johannes Quasten.* vol. 1. Münster: Aschendorff, 1970. pp.474-89.

_____. *St. John Chrysostom. Apologist.* Fathers of the Church, 73. Washington, DC: Catholic University of America Press, 1985.

Schouler, B. *Libanios. Discours moraux.* Paris, 1973.

_____. "Dépasser le père," *Revue des études grecques* 93 (1980) 1-24.

_____. *La tradition hellénique chez Libanios.* Paris: Les Belles Lettres, 1984.

Sherry, P. *Spirit, Saints and Immortality.* Albany: State University of New York Press, 1984.

Shore, S. *John Chrysostom. On Virginity. Against Remarriage.* New York and Toronto: Edwin Mellen Press, 1983.

Sieben, H.J. "Jean Chrysostome (pseudo-)," *Dictionnaire de spiritualité* 8 (1974) 355-62.

Smith, M. and Hadas, M. *Heroes and Gods. Spiritual Biographies in Antiquity.* London and New York: Harper and Row, 1965.

Socrates Scholasticus. *Ecclesiastical History.* PG 67.29-872. English translation in *A Select Library of Nicene and Post-Nicene Fathers.* Second Series. vol. 2. pp. 1-178.

Sozomen. *Ecclesiastical History*. PG 67.844-1630. English translation in
  A Select Library of Nicene and Post-Nicene Fathers. Second Series.
  vol. 2. pp. 236-427.

Soffray, M. "Saint Jean Chrysostome et la littérature païenne," *Phoenix*
  2 (1947) 82-85.

Synesius of Cyrene. *Dio*. In *Dio Chrysostom*. Vol. 5. Edited and translated by H.L. Crosby. Loeb Classical Library. Cambridge, MA:
  Harvard University Press, 1951.

Tchalenko, G. *Villages antiques de la Syrie du Nord*. 3 vols. Paris:
  Geuthner, 1953-58.

Theodoret of Cyrus. *Thérapeutique des malades helléniques*. Edited and
  translated by P. Canivet. Sources Chrétienes, 57. Paris, 1958.

_____. *Histoire des moines de Syrie*. Edited and translated by P.
  Canivet and A. Leroy-Molinghen. Sources Chrétiennes, 234 and
  257. Paris, 1977 and 1979. English translation by R.M. Price, *A
  History of the Monks of Syria*. Kalamazoo, MI: Cistercian
  Publications, 1985.

_____. *Ecclesiastical History*. PG 82.882-1280. English translation
  in *A Select Library of Nicene and Post-Nicene Fathers*. Second Series.
  vol. 3. pp. 1-348.

Thompson, E.A. *The Historical Work of Ammianus Marcellinus*.
  Cambridge, MA: Cambridge University Press, 1947.

Ubaldi, P. "Di due citazioni di Platone in Giovanni Crisostomo," *Revista
  di Filologia e Istruzione Classica* 28 (1900) 69-75.

Uleyn, A. "La doctrine morale de saint Jean Chrysostome dans le
  Commentaire sur saint Mattheieu et ses affinités avec la diatribe,"
  Revue de l'Université d'Ottawa 27 (1957), section spéciale, 5-25,
  99-140.

Vance, J.M. *Beiträge zur byzantinischen Kulturgeschichte am Ausgänge
  de IV Jahrhunderts aus den Schriften des Johannes Chrysostomos*.
  Jena, 1907.

Vööbus, A. *A History of Asceticism in the Syrian Orient.* 2 vols. Louvain, 1958.

Wenger, A. "Jean Chrysostome (saint)," *Dictionnaire de spiritualité* 8 (1974) 331-55.

Weyer, J. *De homiliis quae Joanni Chrysostomi falso attribuuntur.* Dissertation: Bonn, 1952.

Whittaker, J. "Christianity and Morality in the Roman Empire," *Vigiliae Christianae* 33 (1979) 209-25.

Wilken, R.L. "Towards a Social Interpretation of Early Christian Apologetics," *Church History* 39 (1970) 437-58.

_____. "Pagan Criticism of Christianity: Greek Religion and Christian Faith," in *Early Christian Literature and the Classical Intellectual Tradition.* Edited by W.R. Schoedel and R.L. Wilken. Théologie Historique, 53. Paris: Beauchesne, 1979. pp. 117-34.

_____. "The Jews and Christian Apologetics after Theodosius I's Cunctos Populos," *Harvard Theological Review* 73 (1980) 451-71.

_____. *John Chrysostom and the Jews. Rhetoric and Reality in the Late Fourth Century.* Berkeley: The University of California Press, 1983.

_____. *The Christians as the Romans Saw Them.* New Haven and London: Yale University Press, 1984.

Wolf, P. *Vom Schulwesen der Spätantike. Studien zu Libanius.* Baden-Baden: Verlag für Kunst und Wissenschaft, 1952.

_____. "Libanius und sein Kampf um die hellenische Bildung," *Museum Helveticum* 11 (1954) 231-42.

Zitnik, M. "Θεὸς φιλάνθρωπος bei Johannes Chrysostomos," *Orientalia Christiana Periodica* 41 (1975) 76-118.

INDEX